DIGITAL MEDIA & SOCIETY

Sara Miller McCune founded SAGE Publishing in 1965 to support the dissemination of usable knowledge and educate a global community. SAGE publishes more than 1000 journals and over 800 new books each year, spanning a wide range of subject areas. Our growing selection of library products includes archives, data, case studies and video. SAGE remains majority owned by our founder and after her lifetime will become owned by a charitable trust that secures the company's continued independence.

Los Angeles | London | New Delhi | Singapore | Washington DC | Melbourne

2ND EDITION

DIGITAL MEDIA & SOCIETY

SIMON LINDGREN

Los Angeles | London | New Delhi
Singapore | Washington DC | Melbourne

Los Angeles | London | New Delhi
Singapore | Washington DC | Melbourne

SAGE Publications Ltd
1 Oliver's Yard
55 City Road
London EC1Y 1SP

SAGE Publications Inc.
2455 Teller Road
Thousand Oaks, California 91320

SAGE Publications India Pvt Ltd
B 1/I 1 Mohan Cooperative Industrial Area
Mathura Road
New Delhi 110 044

SAGE Publications Asia-Pacific Pte Ltd
3 Church Street
#10-04 Samsung Hub
Singapore 049483

Editor: Michael Ainsley
Assistant editor: Ozlem Merakli
Production editor: Rachel Burrows
Copyeditor: Sarah Bury
Proofreader: Bryan Campbell
Indexer: Cathryn Pritchard
Marketing manager: Lucia Sweet
Cover design: Lisa Harper-Wells
Typeset by: C&M Digitals (P) Ltd, Chennai, India
Printed in the UK

Library of Congress Control Number available

British Library Cataloguing in Publication data

A catalogue record for this book is available from the British Library

ISBN 978-1-5297-2250-5
ISBN 978-1-5297-2249-9 (pbk)

At SAGE we take sustainability seriously. Most of our products are printed in the UK using responsibly sourced papers and boards. When we print overseas we ensure sustainable papers are used as measured by the PREPS grading system. We undertake an annual audit to monitor our sustainability.

PRAISE FOR THE FIRST EDITION

'An impressive accomplishment. The book will reward both students and advanced scholars with its comprehensive overview, deft and accessible style, and an array of significant insights contributing to our developing understanding of social media and, most broadly, a coming post-digital society.' – Charles M. Ess, University of Oslo

'A brilliantly written, essential text for understanding how digital media are changing society and how we can theorize and empirically study digital transformations.' – Christian Fuchs, University of Westminster

'*Digital Media and Society* is a remarkably clear and engaging guide to understanding the complex interactions between technology and the everyday. The compelling current examples beautifully illustrate concepts and theories, making learning a pleasant ride.' – Stefania Milan, University of Amsterdam and University of Oslo

CONTENTS

ABOUT THE AUTHOR

Simon Lindgren is Professor of Sociology at Umeå University. He is also the director of DIGSUM, an interdisciplinary research centre studying the social dimensions of digital technology, and the editor-in-chief of the *Journal of Digital Social Research*. His research is about the relationship between digital technologies and society. Lindgren studies the transformative role of digital communication technologies (internet and social media), and the consequences of datafication and algorithms, with a particular focus on politics and power relations. He uses combinations of methods from computational social science and network science, and analytical frameworks from interpretive sociology and critical theory. Lindgren's books, as well as this one, include *Data Theory* (2020) and *New Noise* (2013). More information can be found at www.simonlindgren.com

1

DIGITAL SOCIETY

Key Questions

- What is digital society?

- What is the relationship between technology and social change?

- What does it mean, from a social perspective, that things are digital?

- In what social and historical context was the internet created, and how has it evolved?

- What is the relationship between digital media and society?

- How does 'the digital' impact on what it means to live in, and to do research on, our present-day social world?

Key Concepts

Digital society * digital media * the internet * social change * post-industrial society * information society * media ecology * deep mediatisation

Today we have the internet. We have smartphones, smart homes, digital doctors, and online courses. We have apps, social media, and wearable digital devices tagged onto our bodies. One stunning statistic after another tells us about the extreme amounts of data flowing through the silicon, copper, optical fibre, and wireless infrastructures in the skies, under the ground, and in our laps and pockets. In many respects, historical science fiction visions of a future where the boundaries between humans and machines are blurred have become reality. Even if not in the exact same forms that may have been predicted. There is no doubt, however, that digital forms of communication are today more than ever putting their mark on social – cultural, political, and economic – life in our world. Instead of digital things in society, we increasingly have a truly digital society.

It wasn't always like this, however. Like the wheel, the printing press, the steam engine, the telephone, and television before it, digital media have put their mark on society of today. At the same time, people in society continuously contribute to shaping the new media through the ways in which they use, adapt, or resist them. In general, this process of society transforming and being transformed by media happens along the lines of what historian of technology Melvin Kranzberg (1986: 545–546) has called Kranzberg's first law. It goes like this:

> Technology is neither good nor bad; nor is it neutral. […] Technology's interaction with the social ecology is such that technical developments frequently have environmental, social, and human consequences that go far beyond the immediate purposes of the technical devices and practices themselves, and the same technology can have quite different results when introduced into different contexts or under different circumstances.

This book is about digital media and society, and I have chosen to use the concept of 'digital society' throughout the book to refer to the result of the equation of digital media + society. As you will soon become aware, there are many other potential suggestions, both for what is the best equation for describing society today, and as regards to how it is best resolved. This is because social scientists love to name things. We like to develop sets of concepts – theories – that we imagine will grasp some of the key features of some slice of reality. Among the things we love the most is to give names to phases and periods in the history of society. The early sociologists battled each other to put labels on the emerging industrialised society and early modernity, and on social patterns and phenomena within those frameworks. Now, since about half a century back, the race is on to characterise our present age of multitude, fragmentation, computerisation, and global connectivity. As you will see in the first few chapters of this book, there is definitely no lack of suggestions, but there is, however, a lack of consensus over which concepts are the best. For the time being, then, let's call our present society *digital society*. I mean, then, society as affected by digitally networked communication tools and platforms, such as the internet and social media.

In this first chapter, I discuss what the *digital* is, and how it can affect the *social*. I give a historical background to the internet, a set of technologies at the centre of a relatively new form of society – the one that I call digital society, remember? Depending on which social theorist you ask, this same society might also be called by a number of fancy names, such as a post-industrial society, an information society, a network society.

2

I also introduce in this chapter what *media* are, from a perspective where they are seen as *environments* for social interaction, rather than simply as channels for the transmission of information. Today's media environments are increasingly complex and entangled, as new tools and technologies are introduced so frequently.

Internet or internet?

The word for the globally interconnected network of computers is sometimes written with a capital 'I', and sometimes not. I have chosen to go with the non-capitalised version of the word in this book. I will talk about the internet rather than the Internet. Early in its history, in the 1970s, the name of this new fantastic network was most commonly written as 'the Internet', and this is still a very common form today. In fact, the internet is still quite fantastic. Actually, in some documents up until the early 1990s, the internet was even called the INTERNET, with all capitals (Post 2013). While views differ, and there might indeed be some good arguments for retaining the capital 'I', one must decide on one of the options when writing a book like this. I think a good way of seeing it is that, today, the internet is incorporated into the lives of people in a way similar to radio (not Radio) and television (not Television). I have used the same logic in writing about the web rather than the Web.

MEDIA AND SOCIAL CHANGE

Throughout history, different media, such as cave paintings, television, or the internet and mobile phones, have all played a specific role in how we relate to the world, and how we understand how society has transformed, and is continuously transforming. Media are tools, channels, platforms, and strategies which we can use to obtain, produce, and share knowledge about the world around us, through communication and interaction. Media are at the centre of how we, as groups and individuals, relate both to society at large – as a structure – and the many social activities that happen within it – as a setting for our lives together. In general, people are making sense of their lives, their sociality, and their place in history through their relationships with media. And as media today are largely digital – smartphones, laptops, smart watches, the internet, Facebook, Instagram, YouTube, and TikTok – it is quite expected that these platforms are embedded in how we are doing social things.

Media don't just enable us to say, think, and do things. They involve possibilities as well as limitations for how we can act and interact. This is what we mean when we say that they are structures. If we regard media as just television, radio, the internet, and so on, there is, of course life beyond media, where people can think, create, and do stuff. But a wider definition of media includes our very languages – both written and spoken – and the more abstract cultural and symbolic 'mythologies' and ways of thinking. Media enable and limit actions in the same way that languages do. Just as a 1990s television producer could not transmit either smell or touch to the audience, and bloggers in the early 2000s could not embed, and express themselves with, video as easily as is the case in the age of YouTube, Instagram, Snapchat, and TikTok, languages also 'decide' what can be said and done, or not. Depending on the media – broadly defined – that we are using, some things are more likely to be created, thought, done, or achieved than others. This is why a science of the social must deal with the media of its time. Beyond the specialisms of media studies, where things like film genres or journalistic conventions are analysed, there is also a need for social scientists more generally to examine the role of media. No matter if one adheres to Marxism; to the theories of sociological classics like Weber, Durkheim, or Simmel; to traditions in social theory such as symbolic interactionism, structuralism, or post-structuralism; there is always an interest in the tools and structures used in the creation and maintenance of social reality, and thus in media – even if broadly defined.

DISCUSSION

Different tools and platforms that we use to get or spread information, and communicate, enable and limit what we can do in their own specific ways. The medium used will alter our ways of seeing, speaking, and acting. Think about the difference between learning about current events from the website of a big media corporation and from friends on Facebook or Twitter. In what ways are your uses of television and YouTube similar, and how do they differ? How do you act in a phone call as compared to in text messaging with the same person? Try to think of other examples of how different media lead to different ways of thinking and behaving.

Throughout history, key shifts in technological ability and practice have changed how people relate to the social sphere and the world around them. The invention of writing by the Sumerians around 3,000 years BCE enabled the transition from reliance on spoken word and memory to the preservation of laws, stories, and other items through the creation of written text. Media theorist Marshall McLuhan wrote, back in the 1960s, that one of the most crucial transformations of people's ways of being social following the transition from oral to written cultures was the separation of thought and action. McLuhan claimed that this was because the process of externalising spoken sounds into media, such as letters, changed people's 'mental processes'. With the subsequent historical emergence of other technological developments – the introduction of the printing press, radio, telephones, television, computers – McLuhan (1962: 32) identified a development towards an 'externalization of our senses' that creates:

> a technological brain for the world. Instead of tending towards a vast Alexandrian library the world has become a computer, an electronic brain, exactly as in an infantile piece of science fiction. And as our senses have gone outside us, Big Brother goes inside. So, unless aware of this dynamic, we shall at once move into a phase of panic terrors, exactly befitting a small world of tribal drums, total interdependence, and super-imposed co-existence.

Even if he was quite pessimistic about what life would be like inside the 'electronic brain' of society, McLuhan made the vital point that it is impossible to analyse or theorise about social and cultural change without focusing on how people and their communication and interactions are affected by the media that they use. Much like, as he put it (1962: 64), 'the alphabet is an aggressive and militant absorber and transformer of cultures', and that 'a nomadic society cannot experience enclosed space', any digital media application – Twitter, YouTube, Snapchat, or any other – will affect and shape sociality, and influence what we can say, do, or experience, or not. At the same time, people's uses of the applications will also contribute in turn to shaping them.

Social science needs to concern itself with the roles of the prevailing media formats in the development of the social and how this evolves and transforms. This is especially important for the new media of any era, as they might be harder to approach critically during the time that we familiarise ourselves with these technologies and integrate them into our everyday existence. As scholars we must, as McLuhan (1962: 40) wrote, try to capture the new 'translation of culture' which happens alongside the introduction of new media technology. One particular challenge of this is that:

> Every technology contrived [...] by man has the power to numb human awareness during the period of its first interiorization. (1962: 153)

Today, we live in a digital society in the sense that we are in an era where our lives, our relationships, our culture, and our sociality are digitalised, datafied, and affected throughout by digital processes. When we repeatedly speak of 'the digital' in this way, we use it as an encompassing notion for our current experience of social life. But what is 'the digital', really? Is it a purely technological phenomenon? How does it relate to humankind? To communication and interaction? Are there measurable qualities to what it is to be 'digital' or has it rather to do with subtler or gradual processes? What does it mean that society 'becomes digital'? What changes have digital technologies and digital media introduced to the forms and methods through which we relate to each other and the world around us, and how can such transformations be analysed?

WHAT IS THE DIGITAL?

From the outset, the digital has to do with mathematics. Being digital, then, means simply using numbers – digits – rather than analogous objects to convey information. When some form of input is numerically encoded, it can be subjected to mathematical processes such as addition, subtraction, multiplication, or division, through algorithms – procedures by which computers carry out stuff – that are defined in software programs. In computing, input values are converted to binary numbers, 0 and 1, instead of using all numbers ranging from zero to nine. The binary system was invented by philosopher and mathematician Gottfried Leibniz in the 1600s. He used this system for coding, computing, and controlling information when experimenting with ideas for machines that could do calculations by using things such as marbles – being in place, or not – and punched cards – having holes, or not. This is how the computers that we have today, in anything from smartphones and laptops to refrigerators and drones, work too, but with refined microelectronics instead of marbles or holes.

The usefulness of binary numbers for building computers, robots, and other gadgets has to do with the electronic aspects, as in e(lectronic)-mail or e(lectronic)-democracy. In digital electronics, the number '0' means that the electricity is off, while '1' means that it is on, and different computerised things communicate – transfer instructions and information – with the help of electronic pulses of these ones and zeroes. The power of binary is that it works with the smallest and most efficient computer programs, or circuits, which are created through series of 1/0 switches. Technologically speaking, this binary system forms the basis for everything we do that is digital.

Experiments similar to those of Leibniz were developed by scientist Charles Babbage in the 1800s, through his work to first construct a 'Difference Engine' (difference as in the 0/1 idea of binary), and later, a more complex 'Analytical Engine'. Ada Lovelace, who worked on creating instructions for the Analytical Engine, is considered to be the world's first computer programmer. While neither the computer nor the code was ever finished or tested, these early attempts paved the way for the subsequent development of computers and software throughout late modern history. Lovelace, who wrote in her notes about possibilities for computing that included many other uses than just calculating numbers, was a visionary. She made the important distinction between the numbers, the operations to be performed, and the results to be achieved. She wrote in one of her notes that the Analytical Engine:

> might act upon other things besides number, were objects found whose mutual fundamental relations could be expressed by those of the abstract science of operations, and which should be also susceptible of adaptations to the action of the operating notation and mechanism of the engine. [...] Supposing, for instance, that the fundamental relations of pitched sounds in the science of harmony and of musical composition were susceptible of such expression and adaptations, the engine might compose elaborate and scientific pieces of music of any degree of complexity or extent. (Toole 1992: 178–179)

At their core, then, computers have been invented and developed to solve mathematical problems, but their actual capabilities, obviously, stretch far beyond mathematics. During the latter parts of the 20th century, digitisation had advanced beyond purely scientific applications, as text, sound, graphics, and images became digitally encodable. Today, computers can store and transmit data, which changes how we deal with anything from our family photos and recipes to government documents or business plans. We have also learnt that computers can manage communication networks, and this has transformed how we form friendships, and how we connect and stay in touch with people, sometimes across large geographical distances. Furthermore, computers can process text, images, and sound, which has changed the ways in which writers write, musicians play, and painters paint. Spaceships and airplanes are flown by computers, and digital devices are increasingly entangled in our everyday lives, in the form of laptops, tablets, smartphones, and things like robot vacuum cleaners and other smart home technologies. Digitalisation of ourselves and sociality continually moves ever closer with wearable devices and smart scales, showers, and toilets. Still, at the heart of every computer lie circuits that contribute to all of these social and cultural transformations, through the breaking down of operations into mathematical equations. As Paul Ceruzzi (2003: 1), a computer historian, puts it:

> Deep inside a computer are circuits that do those things by transforming them into a mathematical language. But most of us never see the equations, and few of us would understand them if we did. [...] As far as the public face is concerned, 'computing' is the least important thing that computers do.

When we speak of today's society as being digital, we don't very often mean to say that it just draws upon binary numerical operations. What we do tend to mean is that it has been transformed in a number of quite drastic ways, following the development of the early 'computing' machines into smart devices which have increasingly enabled large-scale networked connections, coordination, and communication in both automated and human-driven ways.

THE RISE OF INFORMATION SOCIETY

The binary numerical system, and the advances in computing that were enabled by it, made digital information, communication, and solutions into crucial tools, dimensions, and forces of social life. This social transformation happened gradually during the 20th century, and is still constantly evolving today. In the early 1970s, sociologist Daniel Bell had already described the emergence of a future society where handling and relating to information would be at the very centre of daily life, even though today's social media, tablets, smartphones, and wearable devices might not have been exactly what he envisioned.

Bell (1973) used the term *post-industrial society* – which he later came to partly replace with the notion of an *information society* – to refer to entirely new forms of production and community that he claimed had replaced the previously prevailing industrial society. He said that this happened because of a powerful convergence between telecommunications and computer technologies. Bell talked about how different forms of work had been predominant during different historical eras, and argued that this had defined various types of society in different periods. Pre-industrial agricultural societies were dominated by the 'extractive work' of farmers, while the defining form of work in the subsequent industrial society had been the labour of fabrication, carried out by factory workers. The coming of the post-industrial society in the Western world, during the latter parts of the 20th century, was characterised by service employment and 'information activities'. Bell's idea was that as the form of work that was predominant in a certain era became rationalised to a certain level, a shift happened to the next form: when farming became highly automated, people turned to cities for work; as factories were increasingly robotised, people had to turn somewhere else.

Bell argued that what was emerging during the second half of the 20th century was an information society that met new needs that were arising among a post-industrial workforce. For Bell, the most important things that were then produced were services, and he felt that services were always 'games between people'. He said that information had become the material of work for a majority of people. Banks do transactions, therapists are engaged in dialogues, teachers convey and stimulate knowledge, software developers write code, and advertisers and journalists compose and transmit images and symbols. All of these jobs are about delivering services, and the service work that is done is also largely information work. As a result of this, Bell said that 'information professionals' represented the most prominent category of jobs on the new labour market. This did not mean that everyone was now a journalist or a marketer, but that nearly everyone dealt with information in some form as a key part of their work. While Bell talked optimistically about this, in terms of 'the rise of knowledge experts', the same development has more recently come under debate as critical researchers have seen both the information work of professionals and consumers in digital society as a sort of *digital labour* – a concept that I will return to in Chapter 8. What the likes of Bell saw in terms of opportunity, democratisation, personal development, learning, and enjoyment can, from another perspective, be seen as just another form of mass value production for the benefit of capitalists.

DISCUSSION

Think about the notion of information work and information professionals. Is it still true today that the majority of people work with information in various ways? Envision a pre-digital society (agricultural or industrial) and try to think of jobs in that society which you think were *not* information work. Try to think of ways that those jobs might still be defined as being dependent on various forms of information. Think of some jobs today that are clearly about dealing with information. Now try to think of ways to argue that these jobs are also about material aspects of social reality. Do you agree that we now live in an information society? What has happened with industrial capitalism? Has it been replaced?

Another proponent of the post-industrial perspective, futurist Alvin Toffler (1970, 1980), claimed – like Bell – that mediated information was now to become de-massified. Instead of the standardised messages that were transmitted, broadcast as it were, through traditional *mass media* channels from a few select senders to the uniform masses of the many, we were now to get something that he called 'narrowcasting'. This idea is quite similar to what writer and entrepreneur Chris Anderson argued some decades later in his book *The Long Tail* (2006). Anderson said that things with small niche audiences will survive, and are important, in the digital world, in ways that they could not possibly be in a situation where one had to focus on a small number of things with huge audiences. In the early 1980s, Toffler imagined that digital media would work very much like they do now in the 2020s. Writing about what he called the 'bedlam of blip culture', he predicted, as many writers and researchers have more recently discussed, that the myriad small pieces of content offered through electronic media over time will make people more active in navigating and piecing things together by themselves:

[People today become] more at ease in the midst of this bombardment of blips – the ninety-second news-clip intercut with a thirty-second commercial, a fragment of song and lyric, a headline, a cartoon, a collage, a newsletter item, a computer printout. […] Rather than trying to stuff the new modular data into the standard […] categories or frameworks, they learn to make their own, to form their own 'strings' out of the blipped material shot at them. (Toffler 1980: 166)

This, it could be argued, is what we do now as we piece together our own individualised everyday media flows by stringing together bits such as tweets, news service notifications, Instagram live broadcasts, Netflix episodes, and so on. Some of these we choose ourselves, while others are offered or even pushed to us by automated recommendation systems.

Another often emphasised feature of digital society is that it compresses time and space and makes both of them less important. For example, when we send texts, direct messages, or emails to each other, there is – quite obviously – no need for us to be in the same place to be able to communicate. The exchange need not be instantaneous either, as we can respond to digital messages whenever it suits us. In Chapter 4, I will discuss such transformations in more depth. But for the time being, let's just ask ourselves whether these characteristics of computer-mediated communication really are that revolutionary? Haven't we already since ancient times – since the first symbolic language, actually – been able to get past limitations of space and time through various forms of mediated communication, ranging from rock carvings and pen and paper to the printing press and the telephone? This is a question of whether the coming of information society rather marks a *gradual difference*, or if it signals the transition into a *completely new form* of society.

Bell argued that the changed conditions for everyday micro-interaction brought on by digital technology contributed to profound social transformations. The power and influence of territorially based bureaucratic and political authorities would lessen, as would that of history and tradition. The punch clocks, schedules, and timetables that so strongly grounded and confined industrialism in space and time were to be replaced by other notions of time and space that were more fluid and dynamic – and that made physical presence less important.

Bell and Toffler generally thought that this development was steeped in opportunities, and they were both very optimistic about what was supposed to happen in the future. There would be no more manual work; people would become more intellectual and friendly; there would be an end to 'radical politics' (which they thought was a good development). Even though the high volumes of information floating about could sometimes be frustrating, and in spite of the stressful pace of blip culture, they both hoped – in Toffler's (1980: 2–3) words – for 'the death of industrialism and the rise of a new civilization'. Society was to become 'more sane, sensible, and sustainable, more decent and more democratic than any we have ever known'. People would no longer be reduced to numbers, or analysed only in terms of how much income they could generate (this is interesting in relation to debates today about people being reduced to data more than ever). Their vision of the electronic future was utopian: we would all live in a communal society where the environment, care, and education were the priorities, at the cost of individualism, capitalism, and competition (Bell 1973: 220, 283). There would be a sort of consensus democracy where no dictator could survive. Such utopian hopes, tied to the development of digital technology, alongside their counterpart in the shape of utopian fears, will be addressed further in Chapter 3.

The history of technology in general is marked by a series of disagreements over what impact new technologies will have on the society, and on the economy and culture. But aside from the debate over whether digital society is good or bad, there is also a debate about whether digital society ('the information society', 'post-industrial society') has happened at all. On the one hand, there is no denying that much of the assertions of theorists such as Bell and Toffler have become reality. We need only look to our own daily lives to find plenty of proof that digital tools, platforms, and information are now immensely important, even if in varying ways, to most of us. Digital technology and digital media are an integrated and important part of a huge number – if not the majority – of common social activities. Banking and payments, travel and communications, culture and entertainment, cooking and cleaning, business and commerce. One can think of nearly any sector or activity, and quite easily realise how an ongoing digitalisation is a rather vital part of what goes on there. We buy our train tickets in mobile applications, we stay up to date with global news on tablets, our cars and tumble dryers are connected to the internet, environmental activists mobilise with the help of social media platforms, and so on. In short, it is very easy to make the case that we live in a highly digitised world which is abundant with information flows.

This is so obvious that even those who might be critical of the theories about the information society still agree that digital information plays a very important role today, and might do so even more tomorrow. For example, there are some Marxist theorists who were quite in opposition to Bell's ideas about post-industrialism. Some of them suggested that we instead speak of 'post-Fordism' (Lipietz 1987), referring to a transition from an era marked by mass production to an era of 'flexible specialisation' (Piore & Sabel 1984). While such writers argued that capitalism, like in the industrial society, was to remain the dominating force, they identified a number of changes similar to those discussed by Bell and Toffler. They said that information processing had become more important, and that an increasing share of workers were now doing things with information, such as analysing and manipulating symbols, managing ideas, and constantly retraining themselves to deal with the increased flexibility and globalised character of social reality. Similarly, theorists who have described the late 20th-century social transformations in terms of 'post-modernity' also argue that the new age is marked by increased symbolic complexity and intensified flows of information (Lyotard 1984).

EVOLUTION, REVOLUTION AND CRISES

But even if most seem to agree that we now live in a society where 'information', in its broadest sense, is crucial, does this automatically mean that the social and cultural changes which have followed from the technological innovations have been enough to allow us to say that we have a *new* society? Are the changes comparable to the all-encompassing societal transformation that happened during the industrial revolution? While some writers obviously argue that this is the case, quite a few others remain sceptical. Critics, such as, for example, the Marxists mentioned above, have said that digital information technologies might have changed many things, but not the fundamental continuity of capitalist industrialism. After having convincingly argued in several ways that we indeed live in a society where flows of information are at the very centre, sociologist Manuel Castells (1996: 520) wrote:

> However, this evolution towards networking forms of management and production does not imply the demise of capitalism. The network society, in its various institutional expressions, is, for the time being, a capitalist society. Furthermore, for the first time in history, the capitalist mode of production shapes social relationships over the entire planet.

In making this point, Castells spoke of a network society rather than an information society. While these two notions are largely overlapping, I will deal in more detail with the idea of a network society in Chapter 5. In either case, information society theorists like Bell and Toffler have been criticised by some for being historically short-sighted. Those who have denounced the 'information revolution' have argued instead that the developments during the latter half of the 20th century did not cause any dramatic shift, but were rather the culmination of trends in communication which stretch way back into the past. For example, sociologist and historian James Beniger (1986: 435) has suggested that we are dealing with a 'control revolution' that had started already in the mid-1800s:

> The Information Society has not resulted from recent changes [...] but rather from increases in the speed of material processing and of flows through the material economy that began more than a century ago. Similarly, microprocessing and computing technology, contrary to currently fashionable opinion, do not represent a new force only recently unleashed on an unprepared society but merely the most recent installment in the continuing development of the Control Revolution.

Beniger's argument is that 'control crises' followed from the acceleration of society's entire processing system in the wake of the industrial revolution. In these crises, information-processing and communication technologies had a hard time keeping up with the speed of society. Thus followed the control revolution – a series of rapid technological changes in the arrangements used for collecting, storing, processing, and communicating information. These tendencies are in fact rather similar to what has been discussed in more recent years in terms of *big data* (see Chapter 10). So what may appear to be the advent of a new informational society, Beniger argues, is rather a digital intensification of industrialism.

Throughout the chapters of this book, I will deal with a number of research areas where studies have been made that, at least in some respects, can shed light upon whether the 1970s and 1980s prophecies and prognoses were right or wrong about what the emerging information society would entail in terms of social and cultural consequences. In most cases, we will see that the answer is neither a clear yes nor a definite no. As the digital society plays out in practice, things turn out to be quite a bit more complicated than those futurologists expected. In the end, it is not that important really whether one should label our present-day society 'post-industrial', 'post-Fordist', 'post-modern', or as an 'information society', 'network society' or a 'control society'. Such debates might be interesting for theorists who want to lay claim to having 'discovered' and named a certain era. In the end, however, one must be careful with such labels. Sociologist Krishan Kumar (2009: 29) writes:

> Labels, like rumours, can take on a life of their own. The labels of intellectual discourse are no exception. Once sufficiently established, they can govern reality [...], at least scholarly reality. They inspire conferences, books, television programmes. They can create a whole climate of critical inquiry which, especially in these days of academic entrepreneurship and the multinational scholarly enterprise, feeds on itself. 'The lonely crowd', 'the affluent society', 'the technological society', 'the hidden persuaders', 'the power elite': these are all well-known examples of labels which in recent decades have generated much activity of this sort.

Indeed, there might also be ideological reasons for choosing certain concepts for describing things. 'The information society', and some of its related notions, actually fit quite well with Western neoliberal thinking. The idea that innovation and technology lead to a richer and hence better world maintains a faith, similar to that of the enlightenment, in progress and rationality. It is of course no secret today – with debates about surveillance, digital labour, consumer profiling, targeted advertising, and computational propaganda – that the information society idea is related in complex ways to big business and large-scale politics.

In this book, I use the notion of digital society to refer roughly to all of these developments. The concept is just as awkward as any alternative, but I think it is important not to be blinded or constrained by concepts that carry a lot of historical baggage. I try to use 'digital society' in a pragmatic way, as a fairly neutral label, when dealing with the social and cultural uses and consequences of digital media and digital technologies.

A GLOBAL NETWORK OF COMPUTERS

Before moving on to a more specific discussion of what digital *media* might mean, we must focus first on one of the key inventions of digital society – namely, the internet. This global network of computers, which enables and structures an unmeasurable amount of social activity around the world, feels today as if it was always there. But in fact, it only became widely available in the mid-1990s, through the invention of a protocol for something called the World Wide Web. In reality, the history of the internet goes quite a bit further back than the 1990s, and it is important to keep in mind that its emergence was shaped by a number of specific circumstances. The web did not just materialise, it was the product of certain efforts and projects.

In 1959, at the height of the Cold War, Paul Baran, a computer scientist at the RAND Corporation, a US military think tank, was given the task of creating a communications system able to withstand a nuclear attack. At least that's how the story goes. The strategy was to establish a computer network that did not rely on centralised command, and thus was not vulnerable to attacks targeting central hubs (Galloway 2004). Baran's network was based on the technology of packet-switching, through which messages are distributed in small fragments to be reassembled at the receiving end. The system was finally realised at the end of the 1960s through funding from the Advanced Research Projects Agency (ARPA), President Eisenhower's response to the Soviet Sputnik launch. The agency's ARPANET, the first computer network based on packet-switching, was used by the military and by academics to transfer and exchange information. Castells (2002: 24–25) describes how the Network Working Group, which was doing most ARPANET design in the late 1960s, consisted mainly of graduate students who had studied in the same secondary school in Southern California, later to become students of Leonard Kleinrock at UCLA. The so-called RFCs introduced in 1969 by one member of this group – Steve Crocker – became important for the subsequent development of the internet as a space for open communication: RFCs (Request for Comments) were memos about work in progress, and their 'intelligent, friendly, co-operative, consensual attitude [...] set the tone for the way the Net developed' (Naughton 1999: 135). The young ARPANET developers, and the student culture of which they were part – as well as the wider context of late 1960s counterculture – is often said to have had a crucial impact on how the global internet came to emerge. Castells (2002) writes that the birth of the internet happened at the rather unlikely intersection of science, military interests, and libertarian culture. It is a common misinterpretation that the internet was created solely as a military command-and-control mechanism, when it was in fact co-opted already from the start by academics (and others).

'E-mail', which was initially called network mail, was introduced in 1972, and the term internet itself appeared in 1974 as an abbreviation for 'internetworking'. Control of the network was transferred from the Department of Defense to the National Science Foundation by the end of the 1980s, and then to commercial telecommunications interests in 1995. The fact that a global telecommunications network was already in place increased the efficiency by which the network could be distributed globally. The previously mentioned user interface called the World Wide Web was developed in 1991 by programmer Tim Berners-Lee, at the European Organisation for Nuclear Research (CERN), which had adopted connections to so-called IP addresses internally in 1985 and externally in 1989. The first graphical web browser, Mosaic, was released in 1993, and by 1998, all countries worldwide were part of the network. Since then, tools using the internet infrastructure – such as the web, social media, mobile apps, and smart devices – have become a crucial part of how people today obtain information, communicate, and interact, but also of how people are mapped and registered.

Like many other new media in their time, the internet was surrounded by an aura of magic during the first period of its expansion. In some respects, it has yet to wear off. In the 1990s, tales about what the net was, and what it would become, told stories about large-scale social change. The internet was claimed by many to be set to revolutionise most areas of social life as we knew it. The digitally networked social reality instigated by the internet would lead to a new economic system where everyone could take part. It offered new and efficient ways of putting suppliers, producers, and consumers in contact with each other. Innovation would be democratised and disruptive, while the playing field between big corporations and small startups would be levelled. The internet was also said to be destined to embody a new form of global democracy, based on mutual understanding and respect between people, no matter where they were from. Such predictions resonated with McLuhan's (1962: 8) vision that '[t]he new electronic interdependence recreates the world in the image of a global village' where the 'entire human family' is sealed 'into a single global tribe'. This would, the internet optimists thought, make people more knowledgeable about, and therefore more tolerant towards, one another.

As media researcher James Curran (2012a: 3) puts it: 'the internet would be an unstoppable force: like the invention of print and gunpowder, it would change society permanently and irrevocably'. But today, many people, including some of those who were previously more optimistic, have become increasingly sceptical and pessimistic about the effects of the internet on society. Some of the utopian predictions have been realised, at least in part, but they have also come at the price of 'dotcom bubbles', economic crises, increased surveillance, and censorship. Large corporations and already powerful political and other social actors are dominating and controlling most parts of the net.

One reason for the initial strong optimism is that as the net became part of mainstream culture and society, it brought with it some baggage from its subcultural days. Notably, it carried dreams of a utopian existence in the science fiction of 'cyberspace'. Because of this, stories about the rise of the internet are often 'celebratory chronicles' or narratives about heroism (Curran 2012b: 35). In addition to the military-scientific influences that led to the internet infrastructure being flexible and modular, as well as based on exchange of information, it was also shaped by the ideals of 'hippy' values among countercultural groups who were early adopters of the network during the 1980s and 1990s. Berners-Lee (1996), the creator of the World Wide Web, was also driven by ideals of public service, since he wanted to make a 'shared information space'.

Furthermore, when the public internet began to be commercialised from 1991 onwards, its technical aspects were simplified and made increasingly user-friendly. So around the year 2000, everything about digital society seemed to be fantastic and transformative. The dynamic mix of academic, countercultural, and public service influences had given rise to a seemingly open, decentralised, and diverse public space. However, porn and gambling, rather than 'creative works of minority artists' (Curran, 2012b: 42), seemed to be the easiest things to sell on the internet. And when more intense and developed forms of online commerce took off, many were forced to realise that this came at the price of ever more intrusive forms of advertising and spamming. At the same time, wealth was concentrated in the hands of huge corporations like Apple, Microsoft, Google, and, later, Facebook. The internet was progressively commercialised as big media companies with fast-growing fortunes established websites which looked and functioned better than anything non-commercial actors could yet create, and as search engine companies started to harvest data for advertising purposes, they also ushered new forms of commercial surveillance technologies into the mix. Around the same time, legislation strengthening intellectual property rights on the internet was passed in several countries. More recently, as progressive and democratic hopes as well as fears of disinformation and computational propaganda have been connected to the internet, its political role has become more debated. We shall return to this dualism (Chapter 3), as well as the political role of digital media more broadly (Chapter 9).

DISCUSSION

You have read about the history of the internet as a military/academic project started in the 1960s. Since the mid-1990s, the internet has become increasingly commercialised and widespread. Today, it is ever-present to the point where it is nearly transparent to its users. It tends to feel like part of our lives to the extent that we don't think about when we are 'on the internet' or not. Try to think of situations when the internet, as a technology, becomes visible to you. What types of situations are these? What do you think about them? How do you deal with them? What about when you hear of how the data traces that you leave behind can be exploited by others? What about when you are in situations when you can't access the internet for some reason? Try to think of other examples of when the net comes into view.

MEDIA ECOLOGY

From the perspective of *media ecology*, the internet – as an intrinsic part of digital society – is a medium because it is an environment. And conversely, it is an environment because it is a medium. Media ecologists such as McLuhan (1964) and media theorist Neil Postman (1970) have maintained that media must be defined as something more wide-ranging than the traditional informational devices, such as radio, television, newspaper, movies, sound records, computers, and so on. Instead, they argued, a medium is any symbolic structure, or social environment, that in some way, and under certain circumstances, defines human interaction and the production of culture. From this perspective, a newspaper is a medium because it provides us with a certain way of relating to the world – through print text, still images, and certain journalistic genres and conventions. It also establishes limits, as a conventional printed news*paper* does not allow for things like moving images, sounds, and online reader comments. In a similar way, from a media ecology perspective, coffee-houses, bowling alleys, and classrooms are also media, for the same reasons: they offer certain ways of relating to the world, while at the same time establishing boundaries for what can be said, done, expressed, learnt, or achieved. Sociologically speaking, this means that media, like the internet, are social structures.

Social structures offer resources – symbolic and others – that people can draw upon while doing things in society (Giddens 1984). This is also similar to what social psychologist Erving Goffman (1959) argued with his 'dramaturgical' perspective on interaction. People in society enter different roles and stages, while performing socially with a degree of agency, but always in relation to certain limitations or expectations.

The environment of the interaction thus affects what we do, and how we do it. From the perspective of media ecology, media – such as the internet and its various incarnations and platforms – are such environments: symbolic structures within which we are situated and through which we engage.

This situatedness and embeddedness happens on two levels. First, there is the sensorial level, where things like a Facebook page, a Twitter profile, a TikTok video, or an Instagram feed each employ our senses in different ways, much like reading is visual, radio is auditory, and video games are visual and auditory, as well as tactile. In a way, the reality we sense is constructed or reconstructed through the medium at hand. Famously, McLuhan (1964: 35) defined media as 'extensions' of our senses that decide how people experience and become aware of the world around them. This also relates to what McLuhan meant when he, even more famously, declared that 'the medium is the message'. Switching from one medium to another reconfigures our senses and alters the ways in which we comprehend and reconstruct the world around us.

Second, there is the symbolic level, at which every medium is constituted by a certain systematic set of rules and codes in the form of vocabulary, grammar, and other conventions. While a director creating a film has to master and relate to certain cinematic vocabularies, posting an Instagram photo might similarly require knowledge of conventions such as using hashtags and applying filters. And this is not mainly about knowing *how* to apply the filter or type the hashtag, but about mastering the social rules for *when* to use them and how to make them *mean* certain things. As we learn these skills or attitudes, we are at the same time socialised and acculturated into the symbolic environment of the medium. In this sense, a medium is quite similar to a language or a culture that is used to make sense of the world.

Media ecologists talk of some major changes throughout history and how these introduced crucial social transformations. The shift from a culture of talking to a culture of writing meant that the elders' role as experts and unique sources of knowledge diminished. The introduction of the printing press meant a further democratisation of information, and the arrival of electronic media contributed even more to balancing the temporal, spatial, and symbolic constraints for who could speak, where and when, and to whom. Today, we live in a world with a growing number of co-existing media, which means that we relate not to one, but to a combination of several environments. It is not sensible to conceive the internet as part writing, part still image, part moving image, part sound, part computer, part telephone, part television, and so on. Rather, it must be approached as a whole, and then as a whole that might be more than the sum of its parts.

While the content of radio, television, or the internet might be a football game or a political debate, the *message* – in McLuhan's terms – of each of these media is not that. The message is instead equal to the social changes that a medium generates. McLuhan (1964: 20) wrote that 'the "message" of any medium or technology is the change of scale or pace or pattern that it introduces into human affairs'. He also argued that the content of a medium is always another medium: the content of television might be the medium of a theatrical play, the medium of football, and so on. He wanted to make the point that by just studying the content, we risk becoming entangled in this spiral of media within media within media. It was therefore better, he thought, to instead focus on understanding media in terms of the ways in which they transform the social.

The user

The word 'user' might have a negative ring to it. And this is not only in those cases when it is related to drugs and addictions. In computing, there is the concept of the 'end user' who stands in contrast to the expert developers, programmers, or hackers who command the system, product, or service to be used. The end user is assumed to be less competent than the experts. In discussions of 'media use', the notion of usage tends to evoke an image of audience behaviours where something is served up for people to use, in order for them to get various forms of gratifications. The user, then, appears not only to be less knowledge-able, but also less resourceful and creative. In media studies during the last few decades, however, there has been increased talk about users being active participants. They have been shown in many contexts to be just as competent as the creators of content. Their expertise is sometimes of a different kind, and comes into expression in how they make use of media content in smart and unexpected ways. But more and more often they also create entirely new things by and for themselves. Because of this, words like *prosumer*, or *produser*, or *participant* have become more popular than 'user' in some contexts. In this book, I have still opted for the word 'user' in many cases. I do this from a pragmatic perspective as I think it is a neat word which is easy to use (!) and understand, and because using things may indeed also mean using them to produce or create something other or new. I defi-nitely agree that users of digital tools and platforms may indeed draw on these tools and platforms in their own production and circulation of things (tweets, blog posts, video clips, remixes, manifestoes, etc.). They may use them to participate, and they may use them in ways that alter their intended or current meanings and functions.

TOWARDS DEEP MEDIATISATION

This leads us further onto a set of interrelated theories about remediation, media logics, and mediatisation – theories which all deal with different and overlapping aspects of the increased complexities of how media affect, and are affected by, our everyday lives.

Writing about *remediation* – how digital media continuously absorb and repurpose other forms of media – media scholars Jay David Bolter and Richard Grusin (1999) felt that McLuhan's notion of media nested within other media might not be refined enough to describe the direction that this process has taken in digital society. On the one hand, they show how this nestedness or layering can contribute to a sense of immediacy. A computer user might be so familiar with a particular interface that, when using it, it becomes transparent to them. Likewise, a gamer might be so immersed in a particular world or story that they forget about the mediated aspects of how the story is told. Thus, the content of digital media might be experienced in very immediate ways. On the other hand, Bolter and Grusin write about 'hypermediacy' which is, in a way, the opposite. This is what occurs when the interface is instead very obvious and visible, allowing the user to interact with it, as, for example, on a website where different views can be selected or toggled, or with any platform where profile photos and info are added, where templates are customisable, and so on.

Media researchers David Altheide and Robert Snow (1979) presented the theory of *media logic* as a critique of the one-sided focus in mass communication research on the effects of media content on audiences. Instead of looking at the media as 'variables of impact', they argued that one must comprehend the contextualised role of media. How does a medium function as a form of communication, and how do they change our ways of seeing, speaking, and acting? This is similar to what McLuhan said.

To describe what media logic is, Altheide and Snow referred to classic sociologist Georg Simmel, who was interested in what he called social forms. Social forms, such as domination, conflict, or exchange, could be studied, Simmel (1971) said, separately from the actual content of specific occurrences of such forms. In other words, the interesting thing for a sociologist is the 'form' of, for example, conflict as it might occur and re-occur throughout times and places, rather than the specific content of any one conflict, and so on. Altheide and Snow (1979: 15) defined media logic as a 'processual framework through which social action occurs'. This means that the media researcher looking at such logics is interested not in specific content, but in how media operate as forms for organisation, presentation, and communication. Studies of, for example, sports events, protests, or politics, using data from digital media communication, can be carried out within fields like sports studies, social movement studies, and political science, without necessarily being interested in the digital aspects. Digital social research, relatively independent of the particular topic of communication, is interested in the (media) logic by which digital media alter social circumstances around, and for, sociality, communication, and interaction. Media scholar Stig Hjarvard (2013: 17) provides a clear definition:

The term 'media logic' is used to recognize that the media have particular modus operandi and characteristics ('specificities of media') that come to influence other institutions and culture and society in general, as they become dependent on the resources that the media both control and make available to them. [...] The logic of the media influences the social forms of interaction and communication, such as how political communication is performed in the media [...] and media logic also influences the nature and function of social relations, as well as the relationships between sender, content, and recipient of communication.

From this perspective, the analysis of a blog would not have to be mainly about the actual topic of the blog – what it is specifically saying about fashion, racism, heteronormativity, or gaming. It *could* be about that, but in order to qualify as digital social research it would definitely also have to be about how the medium of the internet, and/or the web, and/or user-generated self-publishing, and/or blogs as platforms affect how social relations are constituted, and how they function. It would also have to ask questions about what this particular medium does to the relationships between what is said, by whom, to whom, as compared to how those things work in other media or environments – following other 'logics'.

So as you can see, thinking in terms of media logic does not have to mean that all media follow one, unified rationality. This might be the case in some studies of media logic, where focus has largely been on the meaning production of mainstream news (preferably on television). More generally, however, the notion refers to a variety of ways of working ('modus operandi' as Hjarvard has it) that different media might have. Different media distribute resources differently, and adhere to different formal and informal rules, opportunities, and limitations. For example, while politics in the 1980s mainly had to adjust its ways of speaking to get the maximum impact in newspapers and on television, politics in digital society can meet a wider range of different media logics: that of mainstream corporate media, that of citizen media, that of hashtag activism, and so on.

At the most general level, digital media affect the social through processes of mediatisation. Mediatisation describes how media have become an increasingly entangled part of our realities, a process that is accentuated by digital technology. This is not only in terms of how the mere quantity of media platforms and communication tools have increased. It is just as much about qualitative changes in how media communication is dispersed in new ways – temporally, spatially, and socially in digital society. Technologically mediated communication is now accessible all the time, at any place, so that more and more social settings are affected and shaped by communication through media.

As digital technology becomes more and more embedded in society and culture, it is likely to become increasingly transparent – so omnipresent that we don't think of it as a separate phenomenon. Some have written about a movement towards a *postdigital* state – an era where the digital is no longer new and exciting but something that is commonplace and assumed to the degree that it becomes invisible. The concept of the postdigital 'looks forward not to its end but to its ubiquity – to when it ceases to be interesting' (Tinworth 2012: n.p.). We are in a phase which, digital journalist Adam Tinworth (2012: n.p.) says,

> marks the transition from the era where we're excited by the shiny new digital toys that we have, and start to become excited by the changes that these shiny not-so-new toys are making in the way we live.

As argued by Nick Couldry and Andreas Hepp (2017), we live today in an age of *deep mediatisation*, where media can no longer be seen as specific channels of centralised content. Rather, media are now better understood as ever-present platforms for enacting social life itself (van Dijck, Poell, & de Waal, 2018). This is symptomatic of a transition from a mass media system to a social media ecology. Following ongoing processes of digitalisation (e.g. internet and social media), and datafication (e.g. algorithms and automation), our social world is suffused with technological media of communication that bring about a refiguring of the world in, and on, which we act. The point here is that social life of today is so entangled with the complex system of digital media platforms that more or less everything we do is mediatised in one way or another. We can imagine earlier historical eras when people were sometimes listening to the radio, and at other times not. Sometimes they were in front of their televisions, and sometimes not. Today, however, many of us are virtually 'always on', through digital means of interaction and information. People still today watch movies in actual theatres, and visit physical bank offices, voting stations or therapists, but these, like most other social and societal activities, have become more or less mediatised in the sense that they may happen completely, or at least partly, in relation to digital devices, apps, and platforms. Couldry and Hepp (2017) illustrate how social relations today are actualised through a system of variously connected digital platforms, that bring about a much more intense embedding of media in social processes than was ever the case before. More and more aspects of society, and of our social lives, are saturated with digital communication media, in ways that transform our social domains in quite drastic ways.

ABOUT THIS BOOK

Digital media are seated at the centre of an ongoing process of social transformation. This process is not only about zeroes, ones, and technology, but about the societal changes that result from, enter into, and work through the software and hardware. These changes include new textual experiences in terms of genre and form, new ways of representing the world, new relationships between people (producers and consumers, teachers and students, politicians and citizens, and so on), new conceptions of the relationship between the body, nature, and technology, as well as new patterns of organisation and production.

This book is about digital society – our present-day society, which is deeply affected by and entangled with digital media. I discuss what has been thought and said about it, what it is and what it could be, and how it can be understood from a social perspective. The first three chapters of the book offer a broad theoretical and conceptual framework. While this chapter has provided the basis for approaching digital society, I deal with social media platforms in Chapter 2, and with the issue of optimistic versus pessimistic perspectives on digital media's effect on society in Chapter 3. The subsequent chapters (4–11) deal with a number of topical areas within the field of digital media and society. Chapter 4, *Interaction and identity*, provides a framework for understanding how digital media have contributed to altering the parameters for how people interact and for how society is held together. In general, while analogue things tend to be fixed in time, space, and materiality, the digital tends towards a state of flux. It can move instantly across space and place; it can be edited, re-edited, and re-mixed. The digital also offers novel, low-threshold tools for the creation and circulation of content. It potentially enables new or transformed social roles and relationships, and such developments are addressed in Chapter 5 (on *Communities and networks*) and Chapter 6 (about *Visuality and visibility*). I also discuss how the internet and social media offer new ways of seeing and feeling – or being seen and felt (Chapters 6, *Visuality and visibility*, and Chapter 7, *Emotions and affect*). I also discuss how digitally networked media can contribute to challenging, altering, or potentially giving rise to new forms of participation, power, and politics (Chapter 8, *Power and exploitation*, and Chapter 9, *Activism and mobilisation*). In Chapter 10, *Datafication and algorithms*, I deal with issues of data surveillance, algorithmic power, and data justice, while Chapter 11, *Software and devices*, addresses how the softwarisation of society, as it plays out on a range on internet-connected things and gadgets, demands new research perspectives. The main body of the book concludes with a Chapter (12, *Researching digital society*), which introduces how to carry out empirical research on digital media and society. I discuss the importance of mixed-methods approaches when analysing emerging and rapidly-changing phenomena such as those at the intersection of digital media, society, and culture. Attention is also devoted to some of the specific challenges – ethical and others – that are introduced when working with data from the internet and social media. I outline a framework for digital social research that rests firmly on an ethnographic foundation, but which also branches out into computational techniques for mapping and mining digital society. In the epilogue to the book (Chapter 13), I broaden the discussion about the relationship between digital media and social change, and briefly draw out some pointers towards the future.

CHAPTER SUMMARY

In this first chapter of the book, we have looked at what it means to live in a digital society. Over the last half-century, computers, the internet, and social media have contributed to important transformations of our social world. At the same time, society has shaped the digital technologies. We have looked at different ways of describing the world we live in, focusing, for example, on previous writings about a post-industrial society or an information society. I have suggested that 'digital society' is a general term that can be used to encompass all such definitions, especially if one wants to focus on the digital aspects of this transformation, which also has other dimensions. We have also seen how media can be fruitfully approached from a so-called ecological perspective, where media (digital and other) are seen as social environments that enable certain forms of social action. Finally, we have looked at literature around deep mediatisation, which underlines that digital media must be seen as deeply embedded in social practices. In the next chapter, we will look more closely at one of the key phenomena in digital society, namely social media platforms.

FURTHER READING

Altheide, David (1995). *An Ecology of Communication*. New York: Aldine de Gruyter.
In this book, Altheide, one of the originators of the notion of 'media logic', discusses how changes in communication media alter social processes, relationships, and activities. He underlines the importance of not just analysing the content of media, but also the different social environments created through different media.

Webster, Frank (2006). *Theories of the Information Society*. London: Routledge.
Webster provides an introduction to several of the different theoretical perspectives on the information society, but also argues in favour of looking beyond ideas of a dramatic historical shift and instead looking at how social patterns that are long-established persist but become 'informatised'.

Couldry, Nick & Hepp, Andreas (2017). *The Mediated Construction of Reality*. Cambridge, UK: Polity Press.
This text provides a comprehensive introduction to what its authors define as 'deep mediatisation'. It describes and discusses how society is reshaped through digital media and their related infrastructures. Deep mediatisation means a drastic transformation of social reality and its impacts on institutions, organisations, communities, and individuals.

McLuhan, Marshall (1962). *The Gutenberg Galaxy*. London: Routledge.

Meyrowitz, Joshua (1985). *No Sense of Place*. Oxford: Oxford University Press.

Castells, Manuel (1996). *The Rise of the Network Society*. Malden, MA: Blackwell.

These books by McLuhan, Meyrowitz, and Castells are examples – from the 1960s, the 1980s, and the 1990s, respectively – of scholarly writing about new media and social change.

Ceruzzi, Paul (2012). *Computing: A Concise History*. Cambridge, MA: The MIT Press.

This book offers a broad account of the history of computing from its very early days up to today's smartphones, and also gives a background to the internet, the web, and social media.

2

SOCIAL MEDIA PLATFORMS

Key Questions

- What are *social media platforms* and how have they developed throughout the history of the internet?
- What are the key characteristics of social media platforms?
- What is user-created content? What is virality? What are memes?
- How can classic sociological theories help us understand the *social* in social media?
- What are *networked publics*? Why are they important and how do they relate to social change?

Key Concepts

Social media * virality * memes * platforms * user-created content * web 1.0 * web 2.0 *social facts * social actions * social cooperation * self-presentation * networked publics

In this chapter, I discuss how the internet and its uses and applications have developed in an increasingly social direction, especially over the last fifteen years. Key to this development is the emergence of a number of social media platforms. I discuss a number of characteristics of these platforms – such as user-created content, virality, and memes – before going back to a set of classic sociological theories that can shed light on how we can conceive the *social* dimension of what is popularly known today as *social media*. Society is held together by structures in relation to which we perform social actions – cooperate, form our individuality, and interact with others in innumerable ways. The internet and social media help us do these things in partially new ways. While classic theories might explain some of the things that are going on online, the transformations in the media ecosystem also introduce changes that demand new perspectives to make sense of people's social strategies and relations. One such theoretical concept is that of networked publics, which describes how the changes brought on by digitally networked media have connected and mobilised people in new ways across social spheres, cultures, and nations, globally (Ito 2008). The world now functions according to a logic that internet researchers Lee Rainie and Barry Wellman (2012) call networked individualism (see Chapter 5): people relate to each other through individually centred networks that are looser, more open, and more diverse than those of previous historical periods.

SOCIAL MEDIA PLATFORMS: DEFINITION AND HISTORY

While all media have a social aspect to them, we are concerned here not with all media that are social, but with the narrower concept of *social media*. It refers to those digitally networked platforms for communication and interaction that now dominate people's social uses of the internet: Facebook, Twitter, YouTube, Instagram, Snapchat, TikTok,[1] alongside a hybrid ecosystem of websites, blogs, and forums. In this sense, 'social media' are not simply any media through which people get to know things about the social world around them, such as a print newspaper. Nor are 'social media' any media by which people can communicate socially with each other, such as an analogue telephone. Nor are they any media by which people can build a sense of community. Rather, they are large-scale, internet-based, environments for making connections and sharing content, either by linking or self-creation, as well as responding to that content. Social media provide a framework for participation on platforms that are content-agnostic (meaning that they don't explicitly tell you what to post), and offer features for community building (Gauntlett 2018).

In our everyday lives, it is more common that we refer to various social media as 'apps' or maybe 'services', but in the academic setting they are commonly labelled

---

[1] Obviously, it is quite risky to namedrop platforms like this in a printed book, as the landscape of platforms, as well as their relative popularity, changes quickly. Some platforms have more longevity than others.

as *platforms*. A platform, according to media researchers van Dijck, Poell and de Waal (2018: 9) can be defined as 'a programmable architecture designed to organize interactions between users'. The concept takes into account, on the one hand, that platforms are technological tools with which people do things online – sharing, commenting, buying, watching, listening, booking. But it also, on the other hand, accounts for the fact that platforms have a strong impact on how society is organised and, by extension, on how we live our lives. This is in line with the discussion in the previous chapter about 'media' serving as 'environments' or structures that enable and limit our scope of action. According to van Dijck and Poell (2013), social media platforms contribute to shaping social life through several different logics, such as:

- *Connectivity*. Platforms enable users to connect and share content, which is sometimes user-generated. Users can connect actively with a wide range of people, groups or content, but can also be automatically connected to some people, groups or content through recommendation systems or other algorithmic mechanisms of the platform.
- *Programmability*. The underlying software code of the platform, its algorithms, can steer the user in certain directions, while the user can also to some degree contribute to shaping the platform, and/or resist its programming.
- *Popularity*. Platforms have various mechanisms for boosting the popularity of some users and some content, through a process which is both algorithmically and socio-economically shaped. The platform will promote some content over other, but users may also succeed in gaining huge popularity for their messages or causes.

Something that is common for all these principles is that they are double-edged. On the one hand, they empower users to make connections, use the platforms to their advantage, and to gain popularity. On the other hand, they empower the platforms to control all of these processes, and to do so in quite invisible ways. Social media is about power and control, both for the users and for the platforms.

The coming of social media has meant a gradual realisation of the interactive and collaborative potentials of the early internet, and most new platforms that have been introduced over the years can be seen as evolutions of the previous ones. This is in the sense that new platforms, or new versions of already existing platforms, draw on the earlier ones, but often introduce some new function that may pull the patterns of use in a certain direction.

Connecting to the discussion of the birth of the internet in the previous chapter, we can locate the pre-history of today's social media platforms with BBSs and Usenet. BBSs, bulletin board systems, were a form of independent computer servers that functioned as meeting places where users could download files or games as well as post text messages to one another. BBSs, popular from the late 1970s to the mid-1990s, were accessed with modems over the telephone line, and were mostly run by hobbyists and often with a focus on technology-related interests. Other precursors to the social internet as we know it were USA's CompuServe (1969–2009) and France's Minitel (1978–2012), both being pre-web online services that, among other things, included chats or functionality similar to that of web discussion forums. Usenet, popular around the same time as BBSs, is a similar system, but without a central server, where users can post entries in a wide variety of categories (newsgroups). In the United States, the paid online service AOL (America Online) also offered, in the 1990s, member-created communities with searchable member profiles.

Those of us who remember starting to use the web in the 1990s will recall the experience of quite static forms of content, and of a relative lack of two-way communication. A few years into the 2000s, however, there was increasing talk of a transition from an early form of the web – web 1.0 – to something that was called web 2.0. The latter is a concept with several dimensions. First, it was a buzzword used in business lingo when gurus made promises that where people uploaded videos to YouTube, 'liked' stuff on Facebook, and blogged about their favourite brands there was also unthinkable amounts of money to be made. Second, it referred to certain technological solutions and innovations – blogging platforms, RSS feeds, wikis, social network sites – that encouraged participation, networking, and creativity among peers. Third – and most importantly from a sociological perspective – it related to a certain frame of mind and action which is about different forms of making and connecting (Gauntlett 2018).

The epitome of the 1.0 era was the traditional web 'page', which allowed for very little interaction, maybe just a clickable link to send an email to the creator of the page. Popular sites that emerged in the 2.0 era are Wikipedia, YouTube, Facebook, and Twitter, and these differ largely from the old web as they are designed to allow for new levels of user interactions, and to fill very different functions altogether. They also introduce a whole new sociological dimension to digital media through notions such as those of friends, groups, likes, and so on. As the idea of a web 2.0 was popularised, especially through the talks and writings of tech entrepreneur Tim O'Reilly (2007), the essential difference between the old and new web came to be defined in terms of the latter being focused on any participant being a potential creator of content. So while web 1.0 technologies and services assumed and promoted that the vast majority of users just consumed content passively, web 2.0 included lots of tools to maximise the potentials for *user-created content*. People could do stuff by themselves, and enhance them together. Computer scientists Graham Cormode and Balachander Krishnamurthy (2008: n.p.) describe how democratisation, creativity, remix, interaction, and complex networking are central aspects of web 2.0:

The democratic nature of Web 2.0 is exemplified by creations of large numbers of niche groups (collections of friends) who can exchange content of any kind (text, audio, video) and tag, comment, and link to both intra-group and extra-group 'pages.' A popular innovation in Web 2.0 is 'mashups,' which combine or render content in novel forms.

In other words, web 2.0 technology enabled and encouraged a number of social activities that were not as prominent with web 1.0. The web 2.0 was developed in order to realise the interactive and collaborative potentials of the internet in better ways than web 1.0. With innovations like blogs, social-networking sites, wikis, tagging, and sharing, 2.0 emphasises social interaction, creativity, and the production of knowledge among peers. It also enables the co-creation and constant editing by multiple users of multimodal content, that is, content which mixes several modalities (written text, photographic images, videos, sounds, etc.). When we speak of online platforms for such types of interaction, networking, and creativity today – Twitter, Facebook, Wikipedia, YouTube, Instagram, etc. – we tend to call them social media. But this does not mean that people didn't socialise, create, and share things through media before. Web 2.0 should be seen rather as an extension than a transformation of social phenomena that existed a long time before it – much like social networks among friends who liked each other existed long before social networks on the internet among 'friends' who 'like' each other, in the Facebook sense (Baym 2011: 386).

PEOPLE DO WEIRD THINGS ON THE INTERNET

Virality is a word for the process where content – images, ideas, slogans, jokes, manners of speaking, videos – run rampant through the sometimes turbulent and ambivalent networks of social media. It is about things that catch on, and that spread through social networks in a 'contagious' manner. Digital media researcher Tony D. Sampson (2012: 20) draws a parallel between virality and late-19th-century sociologist Gabriel Tarde's writings about 'imitative repetitions' in relation to a wide range of areas, such as education, language, legal codes, crime, fashion, economy, and governance. Tarde assumed a nearly chemical perspective on how society comes into being through the agglomeration of myriad micro-interactions among individuals. With its key concepts of innovation, imitation, adaptation, and opposition, Tarde's writings on the laws of imitation provide a sociological antecedent to what we today call viral phenomena. He wrote, more than 110 years ago, about how:

the incessant struggle between minor linguistic inventions which always ends in the imitation of one of them, and in the abortion of the others, finally comes to transform a language in such a way as to adapt it, more or less rapidly and completely, according to the spirit of the community, to external realities and to the social purposes of language. (Tarde 1903: 143)

Alongside the democratised access to the tools of communication, the potential virality – the possibility that ideas and behaviours spread rapidly, widely, and exponentially through networks of people – is one of the most crucial characteristics of how the internet works in the 21st century. Let us look at an example.

In 2016, the British Natural Environment Research Council (NERC) launched an online contest to name its new polar research vessel. The 129-metre-long ship was scheduled to be completed and ready to depart in 2019 to carry out research missions as part of the British Antarctic Survey. Shortly after the launch of the online poll, large numbers of visitors were raiding the website and started suggesting unconventional and goofy names for the ship. Most notably, on that very same day, the name of RSS Boaty McBoatface was jokingly submitted by former BBC Radio presenter James Hand. Following this, the NERC's #NameOurShip campaign soon went viral on Twitter and other social media platforms.

Already in the first 24 hours of the poll, RSS Boaty McBoatface had seized the lead with a sizable margin. The suggestion further inspired other quirky entries such as RSS It's Bloody Cold Here, RSS Boatimus Prime, RSS Usain Boat, and RSS Ice Ice Baby. People seemed to enjoy taking part in this playfulness, as the NERC website experienced several outages because of traffic overload. When the poll closed, RSS Boaty McBoatface came out as the runaway winner. Boaty, alongside the full range of silly name suggestions was officially welcomed by the NERC, but still in the end, the name of RSS Sir David Attenborough was used for the boat instead. The reason for this was that it was felt that a boat that was to be used to do serious stuff must have a serious name (Friedman 2016). In the face of public pressure, as a concession, the NERC instead decided to use the name Boaty McBoatface for the uncrewed submarine that was to be brought along aboard the RSS Sir David Attenborough.

The official naming of the ship was met with a series of mixed online reactions. For example, a petition on the site change.org was started with the aim of Sir David Attenborough, the person, changing his legal name to Boaty McBoatface. A few days after #NameOurShip went viral, a railway worker on the service between Portsmouth and London's Waterloo station temporarily renamed the train Trainy McTrainface. About a year and a half later, this same name came out winning in a Swedish competition held by the transport company MTR Express to name a set of new express trains on the Stockholm–Gothenburg line. Calming those worrying that the choice of the masses would again be snubbed, MTR's chief of marketing told a journalist that 'I can guarantee with my life that the train will be called Trainy McTrainface' (Roden 2017). Other spin-offs across the world included suggestions to name a Texas school Schoolie McSchoolface, a US B-21 bomber aircraft Bomby McBombface, and the actual namings of an Australian racehorse Horsey McHorseface and a Sydney ferry Ferry McFerryface. Boaty was now since long a *meme* – an imitable, spreadable, customisable social form which was passed along as it evolved into a phenomenon shared by a large number of people.

Coined by evolutionary biologist Richard Dawkins in his 1976 book *The Selfish Gene*, 'meme' is a shortened form of the Greek word mimeme ('imitated thing'), and it refers to a unit of cultural transmission:

> Examples of memes are tunes, ideas, catch-phrases, clothes fashions, ways of making pots or of building arches. Just as genes propagate themselves in the gene pool by leaping from body to body via sperms or eggs, so memes propagate themselves in the meme pool by leaping from brain to brain via a process which, in the broad sense, can be called imitation. (Dawkins 2006: 193)

While the term has existed since before today's internet culture, it has risen in popularity as a word to refer to products of a certain type of online user creativity. Internet memes are images, videos, pictures, concepts, formats, or catch-phrases that are passed along to the point where they evolve bit by bit into becoming shared and recognisable social phenomena (Shifman 2014). Social media platforms offer express paths by which memes can be diffused. Internet memes also tend to reproduce as people often repackage them by mimicking or remixing them in various ways.

Memes are, however, not simply fun and games. In fact, in some contexts, they can become appropriated and taken over by various political interests. Let us look at one such example.

Also in 2016, a couple of months after the Boaty meme took off, there was an incident at the Cincinnati Zoo in the United States, where a three-year-old boy crawled past a railing and fell fifteen feet into the gorilla enclosure. One of the gorillas, a 17-year-old Western lowland silverback named Harambe, started interacting with the boy. As Harambe became increasingly stressed and agitated, he started dragging the boy around, eventually carrying him up a ladder. Zoo officials feared for the boy's life and made the difficult decision to shoot and kill Harambe. A bystander captured parts of the dramatic incident on video and uploaded it to YouTube where it quickly went viral to gain attention and sparked controversy around the world, as observers disagreed over whether Harambe had been likely to harm the child or not. In a wave of affect and outrage, many people on social media blamed the boy's parents for, through their neglect, having caused the untimely and unnecessary death of the gorilla.

Amid these emerging controversies over animal keeping and parenting, things took another turn. A kind of ironic mocking – maybe of the social media spectacle rather than of the incident itself – started to take over. A petition called 'Justice for Harambe' was created and got several hundred thousand signatures on the change.org website. It called for the authorities to hold the boy's parents responsible for Harambe's death. At the same time, hashtags such as #RIPHarambe and #JusticeForHarambe went crazy on Twitter and Facebook. And then off it went: parodies of songs, with Harambe inserted into lyrics, were created, while Harambe was photoshopped into meme images and ironic portraits alongside beloved celebrities such as David Bowie and Prince, who had died in 2016. At the Republican National Convention in Cleveland in July of 2016, someone managed to get a 'Bush Did Harambe'-sign into the frame of a news broadcast. This was, in turn, a meta-reference to the 'Bush Did 9/11'-meme, which has often been used satirically to mock conspiracy theorists. The Harambe meme reached a bizarre and controversial peak with the coining and popularisation of the phrase 'dicks out for Harambe' (Hsieh 2016). It was around this time that the meme also became co-opted by groups on the political right to spin jokes based on the 'funny African name', and to make racist comparisons between gorillas and black people. As argued by Lovink and Tuters (2018), 'efforts to turn the gorilla into an avatar for animal rights failed'; instead, the meme came to play a surprisingly crucial role in the rise of the alt-right in the United States during 2016:

> On Twitter Harambe was used to parody a particularly American form of political correctness, a target of critics on both the left and on [the] right (though mostly on the right these days). While provocateurs initially used this totemic image in the name of parody, the jokes got darker and darker with the 'the maze of irony' around the meme allowing cover for sinister reactionary political formations. The Harambe incident anticipated an explosion of racism in America that would accompany Donald Trump's insurgent rise whereby racism would be justified with the rejoinder that they were just jokes and examples of trolling. Over the course of 2016, incentive structures seemed to pull trolls and their audiences further and further to identify with the newly insurgent alt right. (Lovink & Tuters 2018: n.p.)

The examples above refer to processes in society that could not have played out in the same way without the existence of the internet, and particularly not without social media. They illustrate the often complex and contradictory consequences of the particular type of culture and communication that social media give rise to. And while the examples of Boaty and Harambe paint a picture of mere playfulness in one case, and of playfulness being channelled into politics of hate in the other, we have also come to know social media, and especially a number of large-scale hashtag campaigns, as tools for progressive politics and calls for justice. There have been a number of compelling examples of this throughout the last two decades. The United States elected its first black president in 2008, following a social media-fuelled campaign that famously generated large-scale popular engagement and a record turnout. There were the largely digitally organised and communicated mass protests in Iran in 2009 at election results that were allegedly rigged, the Arab Spring and the Indignados movement in 2011, and the Umbrella revolution in Hong Kong in 2014. Overall, social media mobilisations have been strongly connected, especially in the way that things have been popularly and academically highlighted, to progressive and emancipatory politics in the fields of race (as in #BlackLivesMatter), class (as in #Occupy), and gender (as in #MeToo).

It becomes clear, then, that social media, while providing a social environment with certain possibilities for action, do not by definition get any universally predictable consequences. In brief: they can be used both for good and for bad. We shall return to that issue in the next chapter, but first we must devote some time to defining what social media are, and how they have developed.

User-created content

Since the mid-2000s, there is increasing talk of 'user-generated' or 'user-created' content. This refers to the transformation of the media landscape by which ordinary people increasingly put in an effort to create stuff – text, photos, videos – which is posted online. In the age of newspapers, radio, and television, media audiences had very little direct power by which to shape media content or to take the stage. Content was produced by professionals, and record companies, publishing houses, and big media corporations were regulating who was seen and heard. The digital environment leads to an expansion of the reach and the scope of what users can create and publish. Blogs and tweets challenge traditional news reporting, television channels are struggling while 'regular' kids achieve world-wide celebrity on YouTube, and so on. The rise of user-created content signals a possible democratisation of media and thereby the public sphere. I discuss this more in Chapter 9. At the same time, the increased commercialisation of most social media platforms comes with a risk that large companies start making money off the back of the 'free work' put in by the users. Internet researcher Nancy Baym (2011) aptly points out that the early internet was indeed highly user-created, but that the new thing since web 2.0 and social media is that for-profit businesses run most of the platforms.

The first social media site that was similar to the things that we call social media today was Six Degrees (1997–2001). Named after the theory of 'six degrees of separation' (see Chapter 12), it was based on users creating profiles and 'friending' each other. This was similar to what American users had been able to do with former classmates on the Classmates.com site since 1995. After this, the social internet was dominated for a few years by blogging. Blogs (short for 'weblogs') emerged in 1998–99 with platforms such as Open Diary, LiveJournal, and Blogger. Blogs are social media in the sense that the blogging platforms connect blogs socially through links and comments into a 'blogosphere'. Aside from blogs, instant messaging – with clients like ICQ, AOL Instant Messenger, and MSN Messenger – was also popular in the late 1990s and early 2000s.

The first surge in what we know now as social media came with the launch of Friendster in 2002, and more massively with MySpace (launched 2003). These were both social network sites as we know the format today. LinkedIn, a networking site for businesspeople, was also launched in 2003. The following year, Mark Zuckerberg famously started Facebook – first as TheFacebook.com, and then only for Harvard students – from his dorm room. Facebook now has around 1.6 billion monthly active users world-wide, and is seen by many people as synonymous with 'social media'. Twitter, sometimes labelled a 'microblog' service, was created in 2006, allowing users to post 'tweets' that can be responded to and recirculated ('retweeted'). Twitter now has more than 300 million active users.

The key characteristics of social media platforms, in this sense, is that they are based on users having accounts or profiles through which they can 'friend' or follow each other, and that content can be liked/favourited, commented, and shared. After Facebook and Twitter, the social media logic has been applied in a growing and evolving number of services, such as Instagram (for social photo sharing), YouTube (for social video sharing), and variations like Snapchat and TikTok. Today, 'social media' is best seen as a name for the complex ecosystem of many different social media platforms that serve similar purposes, but in different ways and with different flavours. Each user will use their own combination of tools to connect and interact.

Platforms

In digital media research, social media such as Facebook, WhatsApp, Snapchat, or Twitter, are increasingly referred to not as sites, services, or apps, but rather as platforms. As defined by digital media scholars van Dijck, Poell and de Waal (2018: 9), platforms are programmable architectures that are designed to organise interactions between users. The important idea here is that the platforms are not mere tools in the hands of its users. They are not just things that we use to make our lives easier, more fun, efficient, and so on. Rather, we now live in 'a connective world where platforms have penetrated the heart of societies' (van Dijck et al. 2018: 9). The platforms affect our economy, our institutions, as well as our social and cultural behaviours and relationships. So, just as I argued in the previous chapter, platforms are a form of social structures that allow people to do certain things, but which also contribute to shaping and organising the society in which they live.

Platforms are embedded in a technological and economic system, expressed through how they are designed – which actions they allow, which data they collect on users, which algorithms decide what content flows where, and so on. While the minds and actions of users are not entirely controlled by platforms, the dynamics of platforms – and the way in which platforms also connect to one another in the techno-economical system – always 'stage' user interactions in ways that will encourage some behaviours and connections while discouraging others. In a deeply mediatised society (cf. Chapter 1), social media platforms are inextricably entangled with society.

As discussed in the previous chapter, media are tools for making sense of the world around us, and it would thus be fair to say that all media are social. On the other hand, no media are social in themselves, unless people use them in social ways. The things that we call social media are both preceded and surrounded by many other tools that enable online sociality, engagement, and community-building. In spite of hailing from the days of web 1.0, things like online forums, email, and instant messaging are also still used widely. But social media platforms like Facebook, Instagram, YouTube, and TikTok have definitely contributed to a major transformation of the information and communication ecosystem. We have acquired new infrastructures for social exchange, and these infrastructures are becoming more and more sophisticated.

An important aspect is that users of social media platforms are identifiable and present through some sort of 'profile', which allows for a certain amount of experimental work with who we want to be and how we want to present ourselves to others. The actual visibility of the profile will vary, as Facebook makes it possible to elaborate our persona rather extensively while Snapchat or TikTok only hint at who the user is, thereby demanding that people have some extra knowledge about who they are interacting with. Apart from the profiles, there are also often functions for reacting to, or interacting with, content by liking it, disliking it, sharing it, commenting on it, responding to it, and sometimes editing or remixing it. In this case as well, the availability and design of functions will differ between platforms.

Most social media platforms also include some sort of messaging or chat function, by which users can communicate one-on-one or in groups aside from the more public flow of communication.

Media and creativity researcher David Gauntlett (2018) appropriately concludes that social media are seldom easily defined as tools, but rather as broad platforms. For Gauntlett, YouTube is a prime example of a digital creative platform because of three things:

- It is a *framework for participation*. The wide range of types of video that are uploaded by people ranging from poets and skateboarders to medics and engineers illustrates that this is 'just' a platform. There is nothing about it which prescribes what types of things should be performed on its stage. The technological features might promote certain behaviours (such as liking, responding, etc.), and rules like the ones prohibiting pornography and piracy definitely set some limitations. But generally, the platform is open to a very wide range and variety of content.
- The platform is *content-agnostic*, which means that it neither knows nor cares about all of the uploads, experimentations, and innovations that its users might be doing. YouTube does not care whether a big news corporation registers an account to post its professionally produced features, or if an 'ordinary person' goes on the site to share gaming walkthrough videos.
- The platform has *community features* by which users can communicate and connect to promote their own videos, to share knowledge and skills, to entertain or support each other.

Social media platforms – whether they are forums, blogs, social network sites, or other social apps – are about sociality. In a sociological sense, they are about what Georg Simmel (1950: 10) called 'sociation', that is, they enable processes of mediation by which individuals become 'connected by interaction' to form groups and, by extension, build society. Sociation and society, however, can mean many different things. Therefore, let us turn to some of the classic sociological theories about social action, interaction, community, and cooperation for some help with delineating and untangling things.

SOCIAL FACTS

Social media researcher Christian Fuchs (2017: 39–46) turns to Émile Durkheim, Max Weber, Ferdinand Tönnies, and Karl Marx. While all of their perspectives help us interpret the social characteristics and impact of digital media, I would also like to add Georg Simmel and Erving Goffman to the mix. This is because their perspectives focus on some of the processes that I see as key to the ways in which people interact in digital society, namely the fragmentation of our social beings (which Simmel talks about) and the corresponding symbolic management of our selves and identities (which Goffman talks about).

Classic sociologist Durkheim discussed the social in terms of *social facts*. In his book on *The Rules of Sociological Method* (1895/1982), he explained this notion by giving a series of examples of how society – the social – imposes itself upon us. When we do things, it is not always because we want to do these things ourselves, but rather that we somehow know that we ought to do these things. Durkheim (1895/1982: 50) writes:

> When I perform my duties as a brother, a husband or a citizen and carry out the commitments I have entered into, I fulfil obligations which are defined in law and custom and which are external to myself and my actions. Even when they conform to my own sentiments and when I feel their reality within me, that reality does not cease to be objective, for it is not I who have prescribed these duties; I have received them through education. [...] Similarly the believer has discovered from birth, ready fashioned, the beliefs and practices of his religious life; if they existed before he did, it follows that they exist outside him.

In other words, society is not only the sum of what individuals do, but rather something more or larger than that. Something which is super-individual – that exists above and beyond the different individuals that are the building blocks of society. Society has got properties of its own in the shape of collective systems of meaning and communication that we draw upon to function together as an organism. Today, the internet and social media are no doubt part of this super-individual realm. When reading social media from a Durkheimian perspective, Fuchs notes – as I discussed earlier – that media can be seen as social to the extent that they are products of social processes between people. Social structures are built into and expressed through them. So when someone posts a picture of their lunch onto an online photo-sharing service, or when a person sets up the design for their blog, or composes their profile for an online dating site, he or she does this in relation to the social structures that exist – independent of individuals – in and through social media. Already back in 1895, Durkheim (1895/1982: 51) made a similar point:

> The system of signs that I employ to express my thoughts, the monetary system I use to pay my debts, the credit instruments I utilise in my commercial relationships, the practices I follow in my profession, etc., all function independently of the use I make of them. [...] Thus there are ways of acting, thinking and feeling which possess the remarkable property of existing outside the consciousness of the individual. Not only are these types of behaviour and thinking external to the individual, but they are endued with a compelling and coercive power by virtue of which, whether he wishes it or not, they impose themselves upon him.

As discussed in the previous chapter, theorists like Giddens and Goffman remade the point that the social consists of systems of rules and resources that are constantly produced and reproduced by people. So, when we see the internet and social media in McLuhan's terms as extensions of ourselves, this can be seen, from a Durkheimian point of view, as the individual using these tools for extending into the realm of the social.

DISCUSSION

If you are regularly using more than one social media platform, for example, Facebook and Twitter, or Twitter and Instagram, etc., think about how your social behaviour differs because of the platform. Are you showing or expressing different parts of yourself depending on the possibilities of the platform? What are the differences between platforms as regards what behaviour they encourage? To what extent can you act freely with the platform as a tool, and to what extent do you feel restrained by the platform, or even forced to act in certain ways?

SOCIAL ACTIONS

If we turn to Weber, one of his key concepts was *social action*. He said that social relations are constituted by a certain form of actions (i.e. social ones) that are meaningful interactions between people. An action is social when the person acting does something which 'is oriented to the past, present, or expected future behavior of others' (Weber 1922/1978: 22). In other words, much of the things we do on social media, such as sharing, messaging, liking, subscribing, inviting, and so on, are indeed very likely to be social actions. Weber makes clear, however, that all things that crowds do – and the internet is definitely full of crowds, as in participants, publics, followers, commentators – are not social. He writes:

> Social action is not identical [...] with the similar actions of many persons or with every action influenced by other persons. Thus, if at the beginning of a shower a number of people on the street put up their umbrellas at the same time, this would not ordinarily be a case of action mutually oriented to that of each other, but rather of all reacting, in the same way to the [...] need of protection from the rain. (Weber 1922/1978: 23)

In other words, much of the discussions of whether the internet should be seen as a social force for empowering people, making the world a better place, and bringing about a new public sphere, relate to the tension between social actions – in Weber's terms – and other types of (crowd) actions. Some have suggested that digital social media mostly promote *clicktivism*, that is, quite mindless crowd behaviours, rather than actions with a genuine social foundation and impact (Morozov 2013). Others have argued that even though clicktivism does not follow the traditional pattern of socially impactful action, it might still be of great importance to society (Halupka 2014). It is important to think about whether interaction through social media gives rise to entirely new types of action, which we must interpret according to other criteria than those we are used to. These things are dealt with in more detail in Chapter 4.

SOCIAL COOPERATION

Tönnies, with his notion of *Gemeinschaft*, and Marx, speaking of 'co-operation' as fundamental for human existence, contribute to an understanding of the social in terms of collaboration. For Tönnies, *Gemeinschaft* is what holds society ('*Gesellschaft*') together. Society is merely people co-existing, but community ('*Gemeinschaft*') is the language, the ways, the mores, and the beliefs that bring about social coherence and unity. This state can be described in terms of kinship, intimacy, and togetherness:

> (1) Relatives and married couples love each other or easily adjust themselves to each other. They speak together and think along similar lines. Likewise do neighbours and other friends. (2) Between people who love each other there is understanding. (3) Those who love and understand each other remain and dwell together and organize their common life. (Tönnies 1887/1974: 55)

Returning to Durkheim, one might say that what makes society into more than the sum of its parts is the same magical ingredient which *Gemeinschaft* adds to *Gesellschaft*. According to Marx and Friedrich Engels, writing about cooperation, something becomes 'social' when it entails several individuals working together to produce something:

> The production of life, both of one's own in labour and of fresh life in procreation, now appears as a twofold relation: on the one hand as a natural, on the other as a social relation – social in the sense that it denotes the co-operation of several individuals, no matter under what conditions, in what manner and to what end. It follows from this that a certain mode of production, or industrial stage, is always combined with a certain mode of co-operation, or social stage, and this mode of co-operation is itself a 'productive force'. (Marx & Engels 1932/1998: 48–49)

So, while Tönnies was more focused on intimacy and emotions, and Marx and Engels rather on material production, both of their perspectives on the social are unified by their emphasis on the importance of people doing creative things together. These questions about connections and community among people are dealt with further in Chapter 5.

SOCIAL PRESENCE

Georg Simmel, another one of the classic sociologists, saw sociality in terms of the movement of individuals towards communal forms of thinking, talking, and acting. He argued, however, that society is not the result of people giving up their individuality completely, nor can individuals exist in isolation outside society. Rather, we are 'composed out of reciprocal relationships to others', while existing neither as purely 'natural objects', nor as mere 'societary beings' (Simmel 1910: 385–386). One aspect of this interplay between individual and society is that the full complexity of a person can never be fully represented within the realm of society. There is always something more, or something else, to the individual than what he or she displays in relation to others. This means that our social presence is different from, but often overlapping with, our individual persona. When we interact socially, we are always understood by ourselves and others in ways that are altered, sliced, or distorted by the 'mask' that we are wearing in the presence of others. Therefore, Simmel (1910: 379–380) claims, all social beings are fragments:

> We are all fragments, not only of the universal man, but also of ourselves. We are onsets not merely of the type human being in general, not merely of the type good, bad, etc., but we are onsets of that not further in principle nameable individuality and singularity of our own selves which surrounds our perceptible actuality as though drawn with ideal lines. The vision of our neighbor, however, enlarges this fragment to that which we never are completely and wholly. He cannot see the fragments merely side by side as they are actually given, but as we offset the blind spot in our eye so that we are not conscious of it, in like manner we make of these fragmentary data the completeness of an individuality.

With this, Simmel points to an irreducible difference between the essence of an individual on the one hand, and his or her expression in society on the other. Social media communication relies to a large extent on small bits of communication – tweets, status updates, Instagram images, snapchats – and in Simmel's terms we can see these bits and pieces as fragments of individuality that make up increasingly important parts of the social selves of many people in the world. His perspective can be read in hindsight as a criticism of the structural inability of society – or social media – to fully represent individuals. Even though the tools and platforms that we have at hand to express and represent ourselves may be powerful in many ways, Simmel also warned about a form of alienation following from the fact that a human being's move towards society can never be complete.

DISCUSSION

It is impossible to give a complete image of ourselves through social media. Like social interaction more generally, the digital platforms we use allow for only some aspects of our personality to be expressed. The things we express may differ from platform to platform, and depending on who we are interacting with. Think about any discrepancies that are evident between what you feel to be your 'real self' and your 'online self'? Are these selves multiple and, if so, how do their variations relate to the different platforms you use? Is there a tendency to portray our 'ideal selves', in order to demonstrate what we think is expected in a given setting? Can social media be an esteem booster, or is it the other way around? Is there a risk that social media gives people a false or inflated sense of self?

Writing about 'the tragedy of culture', Simmel concluded that every social setting or culture bears something tragic; namely, that the very same tools and means that allow people to develop their individuality further are at the same time limited in ways that make it impossible to ever really, fully, represent oneself. There might be a risk with social media and web 2.0 technologies, which rely so heavily on certain templates and styles, that 'the abstract person' mediated through our profiles and the content we create and circulate obscures 'the real person' (Lanier 2010: 70). There is a complexity 'outside' society (or media) that can never be fully or entirely or universally expressed 'inside' it. As Goffman (1959: 1–2) puts it:

Many crucial facts lie beyond the time and place of interaction or lie concealed within it. For example, the 'true' or 'real' attitudes, beliefs, and emotions of the individual can be ascertained only indirectly, through his avowals or through what appears to be involuntary expressive behaviour. Similarly, if the individual offers the others a product or service, they will often find that during the interaction there will be no time and place immediately available for eating the pudding that the proof can be found in. They will be forced to accept some events as conventional or natural signs of something not directly available to the senses.

This idea about the social resting on a number of tacit and sometimes even random and floating presuppositions is similar to the ideas later popularised within the post-structuralist theoretical tradition about the impossibility of fixing definite meanings of things. Reality has an infinite number of possible meanings. But some of these meanings – which are always in some sense temporary compromises, or the effect of some form of symbolic violence where some meanings are imposed at the cost of others – become dominant and held to be 'true' in certain times, places, or cultures.

SELF-PRESENTATION

This irreducibility of the outside gives rise to a number of social strategies and tactics. Goffman (1959) described how such strategies for *self-presentation* in social interaction develop. He did this by famously drawing on a set of dramaturgical metaphors. In our social lives we enter into various roles on different stages, acting in relation to different scripts. People around us in society are like an audience that reacts to our performance. Similar to the above notion of an inside and an outside of society, Goffman thinks in terms of the stage as a 'front region' in relation to which there is also a 'back region' – a backstage dimension where we can get rid of our assumed or ascribed roles or identities.

On a digital and social photo-sharing platform like Instagram, for example, users prepare their performance (snapping the photo, deleting it, snapping a new one, cropping it, filtering it, captioning it, tagging it, etc.) in a back region which is not visible to the audience. Once edited and composed, the performance that is the Instagram photo is presented in the front region. But access to the front region is also controlled as regards who is supposed to take part of the performance as all performances do not address all thinkable people in society. In the case of Instagram, these things will be decided by things like whether the user has a public or private account, who is a follower, who has been blocked, whether users follow a hashtag that has been used as part of the performance, and so on. Goffman (1959: 152) writes that 'access to these regions is controlled in order to prevent the audience from seeing backstage and to prevent outsiders from coming into a performance that is not addressed to them'.

This process will look different depending on the social setting as different settings will offer different tools for interaction. This has been conceptualised in terms of 'affordances'. This concept was introduced in research on digital media to balance between, on the one hand, seeing technology as causing certain social actions and, on the other hand, seeing technology as completely shaped by social actions (Juris 2012). The theory of affordances, as formulated by psychologist James Gibson (1977), sees technologies in terms of the 'action possibilities' that are latent – and can be realised depending on the abilities of the individual – in a given environment, tool, or platform. A chair allows for sitting, a touchscreen for manipulating content by touch, a video camera for capturing moving images and sound, and so on.

Similar to how people in society must relate to social conventions, expectations, cultural norms, rules, and laws, when carrying out their actions, anyone who uses a medium has to relate to the functional and relational aspects of that very medium. Goffman's idea that we draw on different sorts of 'expressive equipment' to perform our personal front goes well with this. He calls the work we do with this 'impression management' (1959: 49). In different social contexts – a book club, the workers in a factory, a thread in a discussion forum, followers, and users of a certain hashtag – people work together to define and make sense of this particular social situation or setting. This entails agreeing – even if tacitly – on certain rules of interaction. Which assumptions is the interaction resting on? Which things are important and which are not? What is seen as good and bad behaviour? This idea of Goffman's is in fact very similar to what sociologist Pierre Bourdieu (1990) later described as the 'logic of practice' in different social 'fields'. Among certain social groupings, there will exist varying degrees of familiarity and solidarity in relation to such agreements. Also, in different fields, or different settings, the agreements between participants over how one should act will vary. There is, however, a tendency among participants 'to accept the definitional claims made by the others present' (Goffman 1959: 4). People are social beings who communicate, interact, and care about what others think and do.

In other words, we 'make' the social together. As we have learned from the classic theories that were discussed above, the social is also more than the sum of the individuals who come together socially. This is because people create communities and negotiate rules and come to formal or informal agreements. People cooperate and work reflexively on their identities by mirroring themselves in those around them. The result of such activities is social structures, the systems of formal and informal rules and agreements that define the various social settings that we enter into. When we add media technologies to this, the structures are still social but at the same time technological, where different technologies – much like social settings – have different possibilities for action. Thus, settings and media – the town square, the football match, Instagram, Twitter, the phone call, the first date, the touchscreen, and so on – all enable a field of possible social action. Our next question, then, is what specific field of social possibility we enter when it comes to digital media.

THE RISE OF NETWORKED PUBLICS

Today, as our online connections with old and new friends and strangers merge together through networked technologies, the social landscape is restructured. This leads to the emergence of what cultural anthropologist Mimi Ito (2008) calls *networked publics*. She discusses how, during the 1990s and early 2000s, the dominant metaphors that had been used previously to describe the digitisation of the media landscape and the internet changed from being about things like artificial intelligence, virtual reality, and cyber-space, to being about networking and communication between real and actual people.

In line with what I have discussed thus far in this book, she sees a connection between the technological changes and a number of important shifts in society and culture. Networked publics, therefore, is a term that refers to a set of social, cultural, and technological transformations that have followed from the transition to a soci-ety where digitally networked media are central to communication. Ito notes that the media, as well as patterns of media use and consumption, have not changed com-pletely. There are still lots of quite passive – non-creative – ways of taking in media, and the mass media communication model where one, or a few, speak to many is still predominant in many areas of social and cultural life. What surely has changed, how-ever, is the way in which people today are 'networked and mobilized with and through media' (Ito 2008: 2).

By using the word 'public', rather than 'audience' or 'consumers', Ito wants to put the more engaged stance of people interacting with media in digital society in the fore-ground. In talking about the publics as 'networked', she emphasises how we – in the age of social network apps and portable gadgets connected to the internet – communicate increasingly through large and elaborate networks that may go in any thinkable direction, such as bottom-up, top-down, or side-to-side. Furthermore, participants – Ito prefers this label ahead of users, consumers, or audience members – are actively (re-)making and (re-)distributing content in emerging systems of many-to-many communication and interaction. These systems co-exist with, and often route around, the conventionally commercial forms of media distribution, such as television, film, and professional news reporting. This is not to say, however, that new digital media can never be com-mercial. A key component of the networked media ecology is *personal media* (Lüders 2008). While it is hard to maintain a strict division between mass media on the one hand and personal media on the other, an important difference is that the latter – such as email, discussion forums, and social network sites – are more symmetrical. In con-trast to news, TV series, or films, personal media don't only enable but in fact require that participants, at least to some degree, are active as both receivers and producers of the content in question.

This shifting of roles, where the reader is also the writer, the student is also the teacher, the citizen is also the politician, and the novice is also the expert, is maybe the most fundamental point made by those who believe that digitally networked media have made – and will continue to make – the world a better place. This point has been repeated many times and in many forms. McLuhan and Barrington Nevitt (1972: 27) wrote that 'we live in an age of simultaneity rather than of sequence. We start with the effects before the product. The consumer becomes producer.' As mentioned in Chapter 1, Toffler (1980: 266) wrote about 'what might be called "prosumers"', peo-ple who are 'neither producers nor consumers in the usual sense', and about 'the rapid spread of the market or exchange network – that maze of channels through which goods or services, produced by you, reach me and vice versa'. Similarly, digital media researcher Axel Bruns (2008) has used the concept of 'produsage' when writing about the social and cultural move towards collaboratively driven forms of user-created content, where information is never static but always changing and evolving.

Ito argues that these, increasingly symmetric and participatory, media ecologies are becoming more prominent in our daily lives, even though we are still obviously in a moment of change and transition. Also, it is important to remember, always, that old and new ways of communicating and getting information and knowledge tend to co-exist rather than replace each other completely. The networked publics are groups and constellations of people who may be located in different physical places but who are connected to each other. They can also be seen as examples of what theorist Benedict Anderson (1983) called *imagined communities*. He was talking about the social construction of nations, and argued that they were imagined as communities because most people who consider themselves as part of a nation never hear about, meet, or get to know the majority of the other members. But, as he poetically put it, 'yet in the minds of each lives the image of their communion' (Anderson 1983: 6). These connections and feelings of community in networked publics are built with the help of social media, and other emerging technologies, both as platforms and tools. The best way to conceive networked publics is to see them as spaces. They are spaces where people using digital social platforms express, perform, manage, or create identities (see Chapter 4), and connect (see Chapter 5).

Throughout the rest of this book, I will deal with topics that relate to a number of questions about this alleged and debated transition towards a society organised around networked publics. Rainie and Wellman (2012) have described a triple revolution towards what they call networked individualism (see Chapter 5), which is an idea quite similar to that of networked publics as it emphasises the move away from longstanding hierarchical, bureaucratic, and tightly-knit social arrangements in favour of looser, more fragmented and diverse, but increasingly networked ways of connecting, communicating, and exchanging information. This system is not necessarily more egocentric in the sense that people become more narcissistic (even though that might sometimes be the case) or selfish (even though that too can of course happen), but it is a system based on individualism because each individual is at the centre of her or his own network. As internet researchers Nicole Ellison and danah boyd (2007) argue, the proliferation of digital social platforms shifts the focus of the social matrix away from communities and interests towards people and connections. I will discuss this transformation at some length in Chapter 5. The key point for the time being is that the social world is now made out of networks rather than groups.

That insight has certainly opened up new avenues and areas for research that considers questions about the characteristics and modes of functioning of digital society.

What is special about it? What are the similarities or differences between online and offline behaviours and phenomena? How are activities and relationships changed when they are moved into, mediated by, or otherwise intersecting with digital media? Much of the early internet research in the 1990s dealt with questions like these in a rather straightforward fashion, assuming that there was an online 'virtual reality' or 'cyberspace' on the one hand and a 'real' and material offline sphere on the other. Since then, digital media have become increasingly entangled in our everyday lives with ubiquitous wireless connectivity, portable gadgets (laptops, smartphones, tablets, wristbands, watches), and an ever more complex ecosystem of platforms. Therefore, focus has shifted towards seeing the online and the offline as overlapping, inseparable, or even indistinguishable. Digital media definitely play a role in many of our 'offline' activities, while at the same time many purely 'online' activities, such as anonymous forums, viral tidbits, and snippets of information – like memes – or multi-user role-playing games are both influenced by and influencing the 'offline' activities.

This is why there has been increasing talk in digital social research and media studies about how the dimensions that we previously talked about as online and offline, digital and material, are coming together in hybrid forms (Lindgren 2014). It is important to remember that this is not to say that people's realities become less real or that nothing means anything. Basically, it just states that we now use digital media in ways that make it more and more difficult to see that use as a clearly delineated activity which can be analysed in isolation from 'non-digital' things and activities. This very entanglement is at the centre of a social transformation where digital social platforms connect people, through their interaction, giving way to the emergence of networked publics that challenge the entire 'social operating system' (Rainie & Wellman 2012). This transformation is not new, but has been happening gradually throughout the last fifty-or-something years with the concurrent development towards a world marked by increasing individualisation where new forms of social relationships take shape in an increasingly networked and global system of communication.

CHAPTER SUMMARY

While the previous chapter provided a broad introduction to digital media and social change, we have zoomed in – in this chapter – on social media. We have focused on understanding the history of social media, and on how social media today can be seen as a set of interrelated platforms through which significant parts of our lives play out. I have introduced some key characteristics of social media and have put particular emphasis on their reliance on user-created content, and on their potential for spreading content virally, sometimes in the form of what we call memes. Furthermore, the chapter has introduced how some classic, and quite generic, social theories can help shed light on what is 'social' about social media, and how to focus on different forms of sociality when analysing them. One of the most important effects of social media platforms, from a social science perspective, is their enablement of the emergence of so-called networked publics. The platforms' architecture and interconnection allow for people to organise at large scale, but often with fairly low thresholds for participation while at the same time achieving powerful results.

FURTHER READING

van Dijck, J., Poell, T. and de Waal, M. (2018). *The Platform Society: Public Values in a Connective World*. Oxford: Oxford University Press.

This book by van Dijck and colleagues provides an analysis of the role played by interconnected platforms in an increasingly connective world. The authors make a critical analysis of how platforms affect and disrupt markets, labour relations, institutions, as well as democratic processes.

Gauntlett, David (2018). *Making is Connecting: The Social Power of Creativity, from Craft and Knitting to Digital Everything* (2nd ed.). Cambridge, UK: Polity Press.

Gauntlett's book is about creativity and making, and the role of the internet for those things. Drawing on a variety of cases and theories, he discusses the ethos and approach of web 2.0 as a social platform for creativity. Importantly, Gauntlett broadens the perspective to see if the idea of web 2.0 and user-created content also works with bigger issues that span both offline and online activities.

Ito, Mizuko (2008). Introduction. In Kazys Varnelis (Ed.), *Networked Publics*. Cambridge, MA: The MIT Press.

Ito's introductory chapter to the edited volume *Networked Publics* offers a great overview of several key issues and concepts related to social media, social change, and new 'user' behaviours.

Fuchs, Christian (2017). *Social Media: A Critical Introduction* (2nd ed.). London: Sage.

This book by Christian Fuchs is an introduction to what social media is, and how it can be analysed from the perspective of critical theory. It is a good example of how 'old' theories can be fruitfully applied to 'new' media. The book emphasises going beyond the hype surrounding much of social media, instead being critical and focusing on the power structures inherent in them.

(Continued)

Goffman, Erving (1959). *The Presentation of Self in Everyday Life.* New York: Doubleday.
Goffman's classic from 1959 is about how people use 'impression management' and other strategies to navigate how they are perceived by others as they craft their social 'performances' in everyday life. It is interesting to read the book while trying to translate the points made by Goffman to digital society.

3

BEYOND OPTIMISM AND PESSIMISM

Key Questions

- What is technological determinism, and how is it affecting both the optimistic and the pessimistic perspectives on digital media and social transformation?

- What are the main arguments of those optimists who think that the internet and social media will make the world better? What are the counter-arguments of the sceptics and pessimists?

- How can one find a middle-ground perspective that manages to balance between optimism and pessimism?

Key Concepts

Technological determinism * internet centrism * technological solutionism * communicative capitalism * collective intelligence * peer production

In this chapter, I will introduce the debate and relevant literature on how the internet has been thought to transform society. There are two main perspectives: one optimistic, one pessimistic. Different aspects of these tend to be mobilised at different points with various aims in a range of contexts. But digital technology does not have uniquely positive or negative effects on society. As I have argued elsewhere (Lindgren 2013), the most sensible approach to the division between these optimistic and pessimistic perspectives is a pragmatic position in between. This is because both the optimistic and the pessimistic views draw on technological determinism, which means that they don't take the socio-technical complexity of the digital society into account. By seeing and analysing how things actually work socially on the internet, we can tell that sometimes the potential of something good happening is realised, and sometimes those who expect the worst are correct. Most of the time, it's a little bit of both.

TECHNOLOGICAL DETERMINISM

Technological determinism is the view that technology, such as the railroad, electricity, or digital media, is the crucial driver of history and of social change. With such a perspective, things that happen in the social, cultural, economic, and political worlds are seen as being caused by technological change. Technological determinism sees the innovation, development, and implementation of new technologies as the motor that drives society. While it has been defined in somewhat different ways, it is generally based on the view that technological development determines social change. And while history has told us a quite clear story about how this perspective is sometimes completely wrong, and most of the time an extreme oversimplification, the view still seems to 'lurk in the shadows of many explanations of the role of technology in human history' (Bimber 1994: 80). In its actual use, the term is often seen as meaning somewhat different things.

In the harder forms of technological determinism, technology is seen as an abstract, near magical, force governing history. Technologies, without any human mediation, have a causal effect in themselves as if through a law of nature (Cohen 1978: 147). Once a given type of technological development is underway, society must simply adapt its thinking, politics, and forms of social life to it. Any introduced technology will mean that we have to adapt to it, and to do so in universal ways. Given a specific technological state, society will have to develop in ways dictated by the technology. In other words, 'technological developments occur according to some naturally given logic, which is not culturally or socially determined' (Bimber 1994: 84).

In the softer forms of technological determinism, the relationship between technology and society is conceived in ways that are less law-based. Such perspectives instead focus on the unintended consequences that technologies may have (Winner 1978). This view emphasises that the introduction and implementation of any given technology – such as a social media platform aimed at increasing democratic dialogue – can acquire dramatically different, and sometimes unexpected, outcomes – for example, if that social media platform instead proves to foster hate speech or in other ways bring people further apart. This view, while not seeing technology as a universal and predictable driving force of social change, is still technologically determinist in the sense that is sees technology as shaping society in ways that are beyond human control.

The most common interpretation of technological determinism lies between these two forms and can be summarised as seeing technology as a relatively autonomous force that will to a large degree shape society in its mould. Advocates of this view, such as, for example, critical sociologist Jürgen Habermas (1971), worry that political and ethical considerations will be set aside as considerations about the mere efficiency or productivity of the technologies will become the dominating focus. So, for example, the common predictions in the 1990s that the internet would make the world better, more fun, more informed, and more democratic were based on the wrongful assumption that technological changes and shifts in human relationships to these technologies were bound to generate certain forms of progressive social, cultural, and political change. This form of thinking is a clear example of technological determinism, and it fits well with a Western history of thought, which emphasises development, enlightenment, and scientific rationality. But, as argued by writer and researcher Evgeny Morozov (2011: 291):

> Throughout history, new technologies have almost always empowered and disempowered particular political and social groups, sometimes simultaneously – a fact that is easy to forget under the sway of technological determinism. Needless to say, such ethical amnesia is rarely in the interests of the disempowered.

Countering technological determinism, one must realise that technologies are merely tools rather than agents, and that tools can always be used for both 'good' and 'bad' purposes. For example, it is just as possible that the internet works to promote ignorance as it does to promote knowledge. As argued by computer philosopher Jaron Lanier (2010: 49), technology is dependent on what is put into it:

> Some of my colleagues think a million, or perhaps a billion, fragmentary insults will eventually yield wisdom that surpasses that of any well-thought-out essay, so long as sophisticated secret statistical algorithms recombine the fragments. I disagree. A trope from the early days of computer science comes to mind: garbage in, garbage out.

Similarly, social psychologists Katelyn McKenna and John Bargh (2000) use the example of television to once again make the point that the context and motivations of users – rather than technology in itself – decide what social effects the internet will have. They write:

> Television can link a world together and help bring down the Berlin wall, but it is also fertile ground for the cultivation of couch potatoes. The Internet can bring people of like interests and minds together in ways heretofore unseen, but those

similarities can range from a past history of sexual abuse among people in great need of anonymous social support, to virulent hatred of other racial groups. (McKenna & Bargh 2000: 6)

The 1990s prophecies also assumed that the technological properties of the internet specifically – its global reach, its interactivity, and its relative uncontrollability – would be of particular importance. This line of reasoning is known as *internet centrism*, and it forgets about the more gradual historical development of several other media technologies, such as the telephone, television, the VCR, or the fax machine. These technologies may also have contributed to lowering barriers to obtaining knowledge and the establishment of social connections. Morozov (2011) underlines the importance of letting go of internet centrism in order to save the internet from 'authoritarianism'. The two factors of technological determinism and internet centrism were important reasons why the prophecies of an internet-based 'brave new world' were never fully realised. In spite of the complexities and changing character of the relationship between the internet and society, there is strong evidence which points to the firm conclusion that society in general shapes the internet more than the other way around (Curran 2012a). This explains why most predictions about society based on technological changes are not fulfilled: they are based on inference from the digital technology, rather than from evidence about what people actually do with technology, and vice versa.

FROM OPTIMISM TO PESSIMISM

In the late 1990s, when optimism over the potentials of the internet was running high, shares in the emerging IT companies were predicted to guarantee everyone's wealth and prosperity in the future, and became incredibly popular investments. Starting around 1998, stock markets in the industrialised nations of the Western world saw the nominal value of the NASDAQ index soar to extreme levels, and there was much talk of a 'dot-com bubble'. This bubble burst, as the stock market collapsed in the late winter of 2000, and the value of equities reached their low point in 2003. Some tech companies died, while a lucky few survived. Since then, of course, many new IT companies have entered the market, and it is no secret that from time to time there is still quite some optimism over digital business opportunities. In 2020, Apple, Microsoft, Facebook, Google, and Amazon are among the world's most profitable companies, but at the same time their image – in the shadow of debates over data integrity and ownership concentration – is not necessarily rosy. While there had still been hype surrounding social media during large parts of the 2000s, the turn of the decade around 2010 saw a sea change in discourse about the internet and social media. Discussions became much more conflict-ridden in the wake of surveillance scandals, targeted advertising, increased commercialisation, and debates over net neutrality.

Around that time, internet scholar Geert Lovink (2011) argued that yet another bubble had now burst. He referred to the overblown idea of the internet as a completely open, unregulated, and exceptional sphere. Lovink pointed to other critical theorists, such as Jodi Dean, who had also argued that social media might not actually be the new frontier of free speech. Where many had expected to see these technologies establish new forms of direct democracy, increased participation and creativity, and the destabilisation of old hierarchies of power, there were instead areas where a proliferation of social control and commercialisation emerged, as users found themselves inside the 'echo chambers' of *communicative capitalism*. Communicative capitalism, says Dean (2010), is a social system where lots of content is indeed produced by people freely and openly, yet this lacks any substantial potency to transform society and drive it in a better direction. Lovink (2011: 1) proclaimed that 'the forgettable Web 2.0 saga has run its course'.

As you can see, the pendulum of optimism and pessimism swings back and forth. We have witnessed this throughout history at every point during which a new technology has been introduced within wider society. It encourages polarisation – there are those people who see all its advantages, as well as people who see nothing but problems and risks. This cycle has repeated itself many times: when assembly-line production replaced mechanised agriculture, when new means of transportation by water, rail, road, or air have been introduced, when steam power was challenged by electric power, and then nuclear power. Similar attitudes have been seen with new advances within medicine (such as vaccination, surgery, and cloning), as well as communications technologies, from the earliest use of the telegraph and the telephone, through radio and television, and on to the digital. Technology and media researcher Adam Thierer (2010: 61) writes that:

The cycle goes something like this: A new technology appears. Those who fear the sweeping changes brought about by this technology see a sky that is about to fall. These 'techno-pessimists' predict the death of the old order (which, ironically, is often a previous generation's hotly-debated technology that others wanted slowed or stopped). [...] [The optimists], by contrast, look out at the unfolding landscape and see mostly rainbows in the air. Theirs is a rose-colored world in which the technological revolution du jour improves the general lot of mankind. If something must give, then the old ways be damned!

Indeed, the efforts by researchers, writers, and public intellectuals to make sense of the evolving digital society fall into two broad positions: one optimistic and celebratory, and one sceptical and pessimistic. I call these 'positions' as, although some people clearly belong firmly within one of these camps, some of them have spent time in both (McChesney 2013: 4). I also think that many scholars considering the impact of digital media on the social can switch between the different positions depending on the context under consideration. Such switches do not necessarily mean that the scholars are indecisive, but rather highlight the main point with going beyond a view based on technological determinism, namely that technologies – digital and others – will have different consequences for different people in different contexts. I shall return to the question of how to move beyond technological determinism at the end of this chapter after providing a historical overview of the pessimistic and optimistic arguments.

EARLY VIEWS ON THE INTERNET'S IMPACT ON SOCIETY

The clash between pessimism and optimism in the particular context of the internet and digital media can be traced back to two books published in the early to mid-1990s: *Technopoly* (1992) by Neil Postman and *Being Digital* (1995) by Nicholas Negroponte. Postman presented a very negative outlook on the emerging digital society and what would become of it. Reading his book presents the image that he did not like technology at all, and neither did he like those who glorified it. He certainly believed, however, that it plays an important role in society:

> New technologies alter the structure of our interests: the things we think about. They alter the character of our symbols: the things we think with. And they alter the nature of community: the arena in which thoughts develop. (Postman 1992: 20)

These attitudes towards technology are clearly in line with Postman's media ecological perspective (as discussed in Chapter 1). Like McLuhan, Postman saw media (technologies) as 'extensions of man' – as what we think through and with. But in his 1992 book he feared that this extension would take us over completely. When writing about 'technopoly', he defines it as 'the submission of all forms of cultural life to the sovereignty of technique and technology' (Postman 1992: 52). In his dystopian vision of what would happen if the technologisation of society was to advance unfettered, he painted a grim picture where technology commands culture, the defences that protect us from the masses of information 'generated by technology' have crumbled, and where we turn to technology itself to protect us from the monster.

This critique of the mindless embracing of digital solutions to systemic problems was later to be echoed in Evgeny Morozov's book *To Save Everything, Click Here* (2013), in which he warns of the dangers of *technological solutionism*. Back in 1992, Postman worried that people had started to believe that technological progress was the same thing as human progress. One of his main concerns was that technopoly would erase the moral centre of society and replace it with a one-sided focus on efficiency and economic advancement. He wrote (1992: 179) that it 'casts aside all traditional narratives and symbols that suggest stability and orderliness, and tells, instead, of a life of skills, technical expertise, and the ecstasy of consumption'.

In stark contrast to Postman's ideas of a technopoly, Negroponte's *Being Digital* (1995) stands as one of the early key texts of digital optimism. Programmatically, Negroponte formulated many of the positive and hopeful ideas about digital media that were floating around at the time. He stated (1995: 230) that when people are 'being digital', 'previously impossible solutions become viable'. From Negroponte's perspective, the aggregated power of the growth and advancement of technology would make the world a fantastic place where there will be no contradiction between work and play, love and duty, self-expression and group work. Decentralisation would become the organising principle and defining logic for all of society, and a participatory mindset would flood every corner of the world. Society was to become harmonised: there would be collaboration instead of competition, and everyone – so it seemed – was to become empowered. For Negroponte, there were three key components to this recipe for success: access, mobility, and the ability to effect change. He wrote that being digital was not simply about retrieving various types of information from online repositories. Instead, it was much more about the emergence of communities that would create 'a totally new, global social fabric' (1995: 183).

Like Postman, Negroponte was sure that computers and the internet – 'like a force of nature' (cf. technological determinism) – would bring about unprecedented social and cultural transformations, whether we like it or not. The difference between these authors is that Negroponte (1995: 227) did not see this as a bad thing, even though he concedes that 'every technology or gift of science has a dark side'. He writes about the 'ultimate triumph' of the digital age and envisions how:

> your right and left cuff links or earrings may communicate with each other by low orbiting satellites and have more computer power than your present PC. Mass media will be redefined by systems for transmitting and receiving personalized information and entertainment. Schools will change to become more like museums and playgrounds for children to assemble ideas and socialize with other children all over the world. (1995: 6)

Today we have witnessed the actual incarnations that Negroponte envisioned, in the form of wearable technology (smart watches, etc.), personalised information and entertainment (recommendation algorithms such as those of online streaming and shopping services), and kids going online to connect with others. As a parallel to all the positive sides of these things, we have now *also* (but not only) seen the dark side of these things in the form of the risks of extreme self-tracking (Lupton 2016: 115), targeted advertising, 'filter bubbles' (Pariser 2011), and political polarisation (Sunstein 2017), as well as new online opportunities for radicalisation (Lennings et al. 2010), grooming, and predators (Machimbarrena et al. 2018).

Negroponte (1995: 150) also envisaged that we would interact with human–computer interfaces that are like:

> a well-trained English butler. The 'agent' answers the phone, recognizes the callers, disturbs you when appropriate, and may even tell a white lie on your behalf. The same agent is well trained in timing, versed in finding the opportune moments, and respectful of idiosyncrasies. People who know the butler enjoy considerable advantage over a total stranger. That is just fine.

We also recognise this development today in the form of smart assistants, often controlled by voice commands, but we also know things about their downside in the form of integrity concerns. It has been debated, in relation to well-known services of this type (Siri, Alexa, Cortana), to what degree people are aware when devices may be passively listening, and to where the data may potentially be sent (Malkin et al. 2018).

CRITICAL ARGUMENTS

There is a clearly identifiable genre of literature following in the Postman technopoly tradition. The writers of these books generally conceive digital media as contributing to a number of negative things: an abundance of information will be generated as an end in itself, in volumes that people will not be able to process; the digital platforms will most likely be (mis)used for abusive purposes; society will become more fragmented and polarised. In his book *Digital Vertigo* (2012), Andrew Keen writes about how social media have not actually empowered people. Rather, they have contributed to weakening and dividing us. He argues that being connected through the often-superficial networks on social media platforms only makes us lonelier.

A similar view was expressed more than ten years earlier by Clifford Stoll in the book *High-Tech Heretic* (1999). Here, Stoll claims that the use of computers and the internet will make people isolated, addicted, unhappy, and generally dissatisfied with life. What connections we make online might merely be illusions of any real companionship. Technology researcher Sherry Turkle writes in *Alone Together* (2011) about how mobile phones and other gadgets make people focus on their devices instead of face-to-face interactions, even when they are in physical places 'together' with other people. She writes that digital communication used to be a substitute for other more direct forms – we could send an email instead of talking to someone directly if they happened to be unavailable at the time. Today, she argues, digital communication has become the mode of choice even for communication within families or among people who share the same office space.

DISCUSSION

In the early days of the internet, it might have been easier than today to claim that the odd nerds who were glued to their bulky computers risked becoming isolated from the real world. In the age of social media and smartphones, however, it has become increasingly difficult to legitimately claim that being online is an asocial activity. But more recently, researchers such as Turkle have argued that other aspects of always-on social media and gadgets disconnect people from true togetherness. Think about your own experiences of these things. In what ways is your social life extended and enriched through digital tools and platforms? To what extent do you risk missing out on important things in life because of social media and the internet? What ways are there to balance your use to make it as rewarding as possible?

The pessimistic perspective also assumes that the potential for bottom-up mobilisation through digitally networked media will be thwarted by the dominance of proprietary models of production. Keen has written about this in *The Internet is Not the Answer* (2015), and while he recognises that the internet and the web were consciously designed to be without a centre, he argues that money and power has made it possible for the 'alien overlords of our digital age' to make the digital future as hierarchical as the analogue past (Keen 2015: 301). Morozov (2011) also discusses how authoritarian strategies may thrive on the internet. He argues that while the internet's decentralised character might have made it much harder for governments to censor what people say, it may at the same time have made propaganda much more effective.

But Keen does not only warn about the internet giants. In a previous book, *The Cult of the Amateur* (2007), he also argues that the rising tide of user-created content and its rapid circulation will undermine the authority of experts and professionals, and thereby destroy both our economy and our societal values. When no one is filtering the information available online, and upholding certain moral and intellectual standards, we are in a situation where the 'monkeys are running the show' (2007: 9).

Being an amateur, as in non-professional, creator of content is not something that all people see as negative; neither does everyone think that undermining established expertise is always a bad thing. So saying that 'the monkeys are running the show' is of course a provocative statement. Lovink (2011: 7), for one, thinks that Keen 'comes off as a grumpy and jealous representative of the old media class'. Yet Keen seems quite convinced that web 2.0 is a negative force, as it challenges mainstream media with its relativism. Where the optimist perspective sees social media as a potential contributor to democratisation, participation, and the emergence of a new public sphere, Keen (2007: 68) feels that:

> The YouTubification of politics is a threat to civic culture. It infantilizes the political process, silencing public discourse and leaving the future of government up to thirty-second video clips shot by camcorder-wielding amateurs with political agendas.

While proponents of the optimist perspective would claim that 'amateurs with political agendas' will in fact revitalise and save, rather than threaten, civic culture, Keen is clearly of a different opinion.

Furthermore, the possibility of being anonymous, the liberating potential of which is celebrated within the optimist perspective, is seen from the pessimist perspective as contributing to a debasement of culture as it removes personal accountability. Some of these criticisms echo century-old worries over the proliferation of a superficial and consumerist 'mass culture' that will dumb down people and make them into nothing more than passive consumers. This is the topic of Nicholas Carr's book *The Shallows* (2010), in which he argues that our brains and minds are reshaped in a negative way by 'the crazy quilt of web content'. He writes that we will develop shorter attention spans, become more distracted, and therefore also less able to experience 'actual' things such as love, hate, compassion, and pleasure. Similar to Max Weber's dystopic imaginary of a future in the 'iron cage' of ice-cold rationality, Carr predicts that 'calculative thinking' will marginalise all other ways of thinking. The frenzied development of digital technologies – similar to that of other technologies preceding them in history – poses a risk that the very essence of humanity, in the form of empathy, contemplation, and reflection, is suffocated. He raises a warning that maybe we shouldn't welcome the digital 'frenziedness into our souls' (Carr 2010: 222).

In his book *You are Not a Gadget* (2010), Jaron Lanier is also concerned about the loss of humanity within the digital machinery. He fears that real people will be replaced by abstract automated functions, and that we will stop being individuals, and instead be dissolved into 'numb mobs' which will exist in 'the lifeless world of pure information'. Lanier (2010: ix) writes that the unfortunate fate of any digital content we produce today is that it will be:

> minced into atomized search-engine keywords within industrial cloud computing facilities located in remote, often secret locations around the world. They will be copied millions of times by algorithms designed to send an advertisement to some person somewhere who happens to resonate with some fragment of what I say. They will be scanned, rehashed, and misrepresented by crowds of quick and sloppy readers into wikis and automatically aggregated wireless text

message streams. Reactions will repeatedly degenerate into mindless chains of anonymous insults and inarticulate controversies. Algorithms will find correlations between those who read my words and their purchases, their romantic adventures, their debts, and, soon, their genes. Ultimately these words will contribute to the fortunes of those few who have been able to position themselves as lords of the computing clouds.

With this, Lanier sums up many of the main points of the pessimistic perspective: atomisation, information overload, detachment, commercialisation, speed and sloppiness, automation, aggregation, degeneration, mindlessness, anonymity, controversy, capitalism. There are different types of 'pessimism', however, and another way of wording it can sometimes be that such writers that we may label as being pessimistic, if one compares what they write about to the early optimistic views of the internet, are simply being critical, which is a more positive word for questioning the optimistic views. In recent years, interesting work of this kind has been published continuously, for example in the form of Fuchs' *Digital Demagogue* (2018), and Benkler, Faris and Roberts' *Network Propaganda* (2018). The digital society is ever changing, and while much of what has been discussed here relates to perspective on the internet as such, many of the debates over the impact of the digital on society and democracy is now taking place in the research areas that are particularly concerned with algorithms and datafication (see Chapter 10).

UTOPIAN HOPES

Just as the variety of literature discussed above has flourished, a variety of predominantly optimistic accounts have been published. The perspectives presented in these books are generally about how digital media are effective tools for liberation, empowerment, self-actualisation, and participation. The authors of these books often briefly acknowledge the 'dark side' of the internet and social media, but their main focus is on embracing amateur creativity, the openness and 'smartness' of digital networks, and the idea that everything will be better if we just let people connect with each other to get, as well as generate, knowledge. Those in opposition to this view often claim that it is 'uncritical' to simply assume that all of these fantastic things will magically happen as long as the tools are in place. Sometimes optimist writers are mockingly called 'evangelists', and their message is said to be bordering on, in the words of Morozov (2011: 276), 'quasi-religious discourse'.

Philosopher and media scholar Pierre Lévy (1997) is known for using the term *collective intelligence* to refer to the product of people pooling their resources, in the form of knowledge and agency, online. In *The Wisdom of Crowds* (2004), James Surowiecki drew further on Lévy's key idea and argued that collective thinking will always give better results than individual thinking. He argued that no matter how brilliant or skilled a person may be, insights, solutions, and decisions will always be better if we are thinking and acting collectively. People connect and share resources and creativity to generate what writer and consultant Clay Shirky (2010) calls a *cognitive surplus*.

Collective intelligence

When defining 'collective intelligence', Pierre Lévy (1997) starts from the idea that no one knows everything, but everyone knows something, and argues that this collective knowledge can be harnessed through digital media. When people are networked and share things, it results in a form of intelligence that, according to Lévy, is universally distributed, coordinated in real time, and constantly enhanced. This enables an effective mobilisation of people's skills for political as well as other creative purposes. Lévy's vision is similar to what actually seemed to become a reality some four years after the publication of his book, when Wikipedia was launched. The open and collectively editable online encyclopaedia is in several respects a prime example of his vision. Lévy wrote that digital media would make people members of a shared virtual universe of knowledge that they would foster together. The social tie was to become the most important currency in the society of the future. He argued that collective intelligence will disrupt the power of government and lead to a diversification of knowledge and motivations. The utopian result would be a form of real-time democracy, where knowledge is no longer 'padlocked like a treasure' but instead 'pervades everything, is distributed, mediatized, [and] spreads innovation wherever it is found' (1997: 212). This prophecy may or may not have become a reality in different settings in digital society throughout the last couple of decades.

Obviously, this view flies in the face of that of hardline pessimists such as Keen and the like. In Lévy's, Surowiecki's, and Shirky's view, having 'the monkeys running the show' seems to be the best outcome that could occur. Surowiecki's argument means that we must get past the focus on experts and professionals. When crowds make wise decisions, there is a tendency to give a few prominent or smart individuals of the group credit, although the power and wisdom actually comes from the crowd itself. So, this perspective turns the fear of 'amateurs' taking over on its head, and legal scholar Cass Sunstein's book *Infotopia* (2006) does the same with the dread of information overload. Sunstein predicts a revolution as information is aggregated and knowledge is accumulated online. He acknowledges that people's online strategies may indeed lead to problems – extremism, errors, complacency, withdrawal into 'information cocoons' (cf. the filter bubble), etc. – but he maintains that the internet has made it possible for diverse groups of people to participate in creative processes that will benefit everyone. For Sunstein, open source science is a central aspect of this, which programmer and scientist Michael Nielsen develops in *Reinventing Discovery* (2012). Here, Nielsen promotes the notion that we are entering an entirely new era with regards to how knowledge is generated. This decentralised networked logic will affect all of society.

All of these perspectives that I have outlined above are related to an increased focus in the debate on society being based on participation with the help of media, rather than on people's passive consumption of media. The power comes from the ways in which the digitally networked tools, and the participatory mindset that is assumed to come along with them, become embedded in our everyday lives.

Clay Shirky (2009) has said that the tools become socially interesting at the point when they become technologically boring. Shirky conceives the introduction of the internet and social media as one of the great communication revolutions in our history. It is the first medium that has far-reaching support for many-to-many communication, rather than one-to-one or one-to-many communication. In this ecology, the audience can become producers. We can note the connection here to previously discussed concepts such as Toffler's (1980) 'prosumer' and Bruns' (2008) 'produsage'. This is important for things such as creativity and cultural expression, but also for society in general. When events or disasters happen today, be it earthquakes or protests, governments often learn from citizens about these events through digital media, rather than the other way around. The digital communication tools enable swift, smart, and virtually unstoppable coordination among the networked users. As Don Tapscott and Anthony Williams, authors of *Wikinomics* (2006), write: 'Mass collaboration changes everything.'

Even though the internet might not change literally everything, at least it can bring about some important changes in how people can create, communicate, and network. David Gauntlett, in *Making is Connecting* (2018), discusses how web 2.0 tools have provided people with free or inexpensive easy-to-use platforms that enable them to share and circulate their creations online. The architecture and user-base of popular platforms, such as YouTube, WordPress, or Flickr, makes it easy for like-minded people to find each other. In addition, functions that allow for commenting, liking, responding, or subscribing, facilitates making connections and building relationships or collaborations. While Gauntlett's main focus is on 'makers' from an arts and crafts perspective, the logic is certainly valid for all connections made through digital media platforms. We see new forms of participatory patterns spreading throughout society.

During the last decade, this has obviously happened more than once, for example in those cases where ordinary citizens stage rapidly coordinated street protests (Shirky 2008: 310). It happens in any context where evolving digital communication technologies are used for agile real-time coordination. Technology writer Howard Rheingold calls these groups *smart mobs*. These groups use 'swarming' strategies, and he exemplifies this by referring to how anti-globalisation activists used mobile phones in the protests during the World Trade Organisation meeting in Seattle in 1999:

> Individual members of each group remained dispersed until mobile communications drew them to converge on a specific location from all directions simultaneously, in coordination with other groups. (Rheingold 2002: 162)

In summary, then, the optimistic perspective focuses on the good and beneficial things provided by the use of the internet and social media, such as affordances for helping people connect their different resources, skills, and knowledge in empowering ways. Networked publics are enabled to think and act collectively within a communication infrastructure that encourages participation, creativity, and sharing. The subjects and information that are circulated may also pose challenges to traditional ways of doing things. The division between experts and amateurs is challenged in all fields of society as a result of the positive impact of digital technologies. Connections, sharing, participation, peer production, coordination, creativity, mobilisation – these are some of the buzzwords crucial to the optimist view on how the internet and social media will change society for the better. As networks grow larger, as more people own smartphones, as the tweets keep coming, humanity will harmonise into a global community, where everyone is a creator and where everybody has a voice.

Peer production

In his book *The Wealth of Networks* (2006), legal scholar Yochai Benkler describes the changes in terms of a more general development towards a form of 'peer production'. He argues that this form of non-professional and non-market production has been enabled by the digitally networked environment. The internet and social media enable 'radically decentralized, collaborative, and non-proprietary' forms of production wherein individuals who are loosely connected with each other make things together, beyond things like 'market signals or managerial commands' (2006: 60). People have always been engaged in non-market production, but the significantly lowered thresholds for acquiring the tools to do so, as well as connecting with large numbers of other people, see a huge upscaling of this phenomenon. Networked publics can perform much more complex tasks than their analogue predecessors. People participate and contribute based on their own interests, as they are motivated not by money, but by social and psychological forces. They think that it's fun, exciting, or in other ways rewarding. Naturally, the motivations and rewards can differ widely from contributor to contributor. According to Benkler, the quintessential example of this form of production can be found in the free software and open source movements, but Wikipedia is also a good example. Today, the peer production model is expanding into every domain of the economy, society, and culture. Benkler predicts that peer production will change the dominant mode of market production.

Phenomena such as Wikipedia, the Occupy Movement ('we are the 99%'), #BlackLivesMatter, #MeToo, and the overthrowing of dictatorships through alleged Facebook and Twitter revolutions are often referred to as evidence – 'exhibits A and B through Z', communications researcher Robert McChesney (2013: 8) writes – that all of the optimistic predictions are true. In this light, those turning instead to the pessimist perspective are Luddites and technophobes. So again, we are stuck in the dead-end of technological determinism. Optimists will say that if we just add digital, we can rest assured that everything will be fine. Quite famously, Wael Ghonim, who was one of the most prominent activists during the Egyptian revolution in 2011, said in a television interview:

> if you want to liberate a society, just give them the internet. If you want to have a free society, just give them the internet. (CNN 2011)

That view might be true to some extent, in specific historical settings, and in relation to some specific media ecologies. But we also know that if the communication of the revolution goes on Facebook, the power to shut Facebook down, and the communication of the revolution with it, lies in the hands of a small number of people with the right credentials. Writers such as Morozov (2011), Rebecca MacKinnon (2012), and Virginia Eubanks (2011) remind us that the use of digital platforms will not necessarily lead to democratic revolutions all over the world. Similarly, just because it is easy to use social media platforms, this does not make everyone an activist. And in cases where social media becomes a significant part of the public sphere (such as in the case of #MeToo), it is likely that this excludes many, many more people than it gives voice to (such as, for example, all those abused women globally who don't have access, or maybe even the digital literacies, to gain from that movement). If everyone in the world was on Twitter, and everyone was an avid and literate user of hashtags, we might have a case. But only a small fraction of the global population is on Twitter, and the majority of people there don't use hashtags with any particular agenda in mind. One might legitimately ask: The wisdom of which crowd? The intelligence of what collective? Furthermore, doing democracy in online and datafied settings also entails risks for computational propaganda, and for the spread of misinformation and disinformation (Bennett & Livingston 2020).

DISCUSSION

In the next section, I will argue – maybe not very surprisingly – that the reasonable perspective on the relation between the internet and social change lies somewhere in the balance between the pessimistic and optimistic positions. But before reading on, give some thought to your own views on this subject. Do you agree firmly with one of the perspectives, while clearly disagreeing with the other? If not, which aspects of the respective perspectives do you find the most compelling and why? Do you find the debate obsolete or antiquated? Is one perspective more relevant than the other in some cases or contexts, and if so, how and when?

MIDDLE GROUND

As with all sociality, the effects of the internet come down to the individual, relational, and contextual aspects of the interaction. Robert McChesney (2013: 4) agrees that both the celebrants and the sceptics are heading down a dead-end street, when they instead could just take the best of what each position can offer. This is of course a sensible and pragmatic position.

Due to its decentralised structure, and because of the volume of its networked publics, the internet has an enormous potential for transforming society. But sometimes this potential is undermined, leading to what McChesney (2013: 5) describes as 'a world, at worst, where one could logically wish the computer had never been invented'. Morozov (2013: 21) presents a similar argument, pointing to the problem that 'the Internet' is all too often treated as a mythical entity:

> As it happens, Internet skeptics and optimists share quite a lot of common ground; both depend on some stable notion of 'the Internet' to advance their arguments. Remove that notion, along with its simplistic assumptions about the

inherent benefits of openness or publicness, and the pundits are suddenly forced to confront complex empirical matters.

Morozov definitely has a point here, and it is not only internet centrism which is problematic, but also the technological determinism that both the optimistic and the pessimistic perspective are often guilty of. Like McLuhan, who saw the medium as being the message, many writers and commentators often seem to disregard – or at least place within brackets – the crucial fact that digital media are themselves medi-ated. They are filtered and shaped by the context in which they are used, by culture, and by ideas. Digital media are shaped by society. Castells (1996: 5) writes:

> Indeed, the dilemma of technological determinism is probably a false problem, since technology is society, and society cannot be understood or represented without its technological tools.

So, he means that we must deal with media as environments and environments as media, as I have argued in the first chapter of this book. We must then deal with quite 'complex empirical matters', as Morozov pointed out in the quote above. Counterintuitive as it might seem, the digitisation of society is just as much a social and cultural process as it is technological. As Castells (1996: 2) writes, the 'social changes are as dramatic as the technological and economic processes of transformation'.

In his book *The Future of the Internet and How to Stop It* (2008), legal scholar Jonathan Zittrain is both optimistic and pessimistic about this. He is optimistic because the internet can be 'generative'. By this he means that the internet, both at the level of individual users and at the network level, has a capacity to 'produce unanticipated change through unfiltered contributions from broad and varied audiences' (2008: 70). But this was mainly because the early internet had a 'chaotic design' which fostered innovation and disruption. Today, Zittrain (2008: 3) says, the internet is becoming a network of control with 'sterile appliances' tethered to it. Commercialisation and regulation have made it harder for people to identify as contributors and participants. Similarly, Lanier celebrates the early internet for giving rise to unique and special expressions of identity, not like the formulaic and template-driven identity expres-sions promoted by web 2.0. Everyone's Facebook page looks roughly the same, while personal homepages in the late 1990s were much less uniform. Today, there is a risk that we lose the individual human dimension to our online selves (Lanier 2010). Both Zittrain and Lanier do indeed like the internet, but not the direction of its development. Zittrain (2008: 150) argues that the 'mainstream success' of the internet has brought in people without connection to 'the open ethos' that was characteristic of the early web.

Legal scholar Lawrence Lessig also identifies the increased regulation of the inter-net as the main threat to its future. In his book *Code* (Lessig 2006), he writes that while it was true that the original internet could not be controlled or regulated, since then, innumerable systems for identification, authentication, and for managing credentials have contributed to pushing the internet along a regulatory path. His conclusion is that, even though one might be optimistic about the potentials of the internet, it is becoming more and more regulated, not least under the influence of commerce. Tim Wu, another legal scholar, describes how information technologies have typically progressed throughout history from being somebody's hobby to becoming somebody's industry. This means also, he claims, that media typically go from being 'a freely accessible channel to one strictly controlled by a single corporation or cartel' (Wu 2010: 6). Digital media is no exception, since it is also in the process of transitioning from being an open to a closed system. Such transitions do not always have to be linear either, because media systems may be cyclically opened, and closed again.

Thierer argues that many of the perspectives introduced in the debates over the internet are elitist. Many of them tend to overstate the severity of the problems they identify, and thus formulate static rather than dynamic views. Instead, Thierer (2010) suggests that a perspective based on 'pragmatic optimism' is best. He argues that the future is always messy, unstable, and unknowable, which means that we must embrace not exactly knowing what will happen. We must try to downplay extreme optimism as well as extreme pessimism in order to formulate a sensible perspective on when and how digital media contributes to a transformation of the social. As argued by Mullaney et al. (2021), uncritical techno-optimism is still alive and well, and we are currently suffering for many of the utopian and allegedly neutral views (i.e. techno deterministic ones) that have governed much of the digital industries during the last few decades. It is important to remember that digital society has changed significantly since the 1990s and 2000s, when many of the formative works in the area of internet research cited in this chapter were written. As introduced in Chapter 1, we now live in a deeply mediatised social reality, where the role of 'the digital' and of 'digital media' is different as it becomes more and more difficult to maintain a distinction between online/digital and offline/non-digital dimensions when analysing causes and effects of social change.

CHAPTER SUMMARY

After having looked, in Chapters 1 and 2, at how digital technology and social media have transformed society, this chapter has explored some of the debates over whether these transformations are good or bad. The general insight is that the discussions have been rather polarised. Some scholars have been optimistic and hoped for the emergence of collective intelligence and the generation of a cognitive surplus through mass collaboration and peer production. Others have been more pessimistic, and have feared that the developments outlined in the first two chapters of this book will lead to dehumanisation and superficiality, as well as to an over-reliance on technological solutions. One point of critique, which we shall explore further in Chapter 8, is that the continued capitalist logic that characterises digital society will threaten democracy. As I have shown in this chapter, however, the impacts of digital media and technology on society are multifaceted, and the most productive perspective to take is one that goes beyond technological determinism. This means realising that technology will have different consequences in different settings for different people, and that we as scholars must always evaluate those consequences empirically and in context.

FURTHER READING

Lindgren, Simon (2013). *New Noise*. New York: Peter Lang.
In my 2013 book on developing a perspective on what I call 'digital disruption', there are lots of theoretical discussions and case studies that relate to balancing between optimism and pessimism. My main argument is that the issue of how digital media affects society (and the other way around) must remain an empirical question, the response to which can vary from context to context.

Mullaney, Thomas, Peters, Benjamin, Hicks, Mar and Philip, Kavita (Eds.) (2021). *Your Computer is on Fire*. Cambridge, MA: The MIT Press.
This edited volume contains a number of timely essays on data, AI, platforms, networks, social power, and politics. Overall, the book points out some of the consequences of decades of a technological and digital utopianism, such as various forms of biases, inequality, and marginalisation. The book is based on the notion that technology cannot be trusted to control or fix society. It also has a focus on how these problems may be solved, or at least dealt with, in productive and more democratic ways.

Morozov, Evgeny (2013). *To Save Everything, Click Here*. New York: Public Affairs.
In his 2011 book, *The Net Delusion* (2011), Morozov argued strongly against technological determinism. His point was that technology is what people make of it. In the book recommended here, he criticises 'internet centrism' and 'technological solutionism' – the underlying ways of thinking that make 'the net delusion' possible.

4
INTERACTION AND IDENTITY

Key Questions

- What has generally been thought to be unique about computer-mediated communication when compared to historically preceding modes of communication?

- What are the key issues in the social psychology of digital society?

- How have the internet and social media changed the conditions under which we form our identities?

- What has been the role of relative invisibility and anonymity for how people have interacted and formed their identities online?

- To what degree is it possible to be truly anonymous in a digital society?

- What does it mean to, potentially, live in a post-anonymity age?

Key Concepts

Interaction * disembodiment * online identity * asynchronous communication * online disinhibition * invisibility * anonymity * post-anonymity

Despite the debates that were described in the previous chapter, the internet and social media, the key technologies of digital society, have in any case hugely transformed the conditions for mediated communication between people during the last thirty years or so. This goes for one-to-one, one-to-many, many-to-one, and many-to-many communication. The changes, however, have not only been quantitative, but also qualitative. In this chapter, I will focus on how computer-mediated communication has introduced a number of new features into the ways through which individuals and groups function together.

From the perspective of consumption, the internet and social media have given rise to new textual experiences, through new genres and forms such as online multiplayer computer games, YouTube clips, tweets, memes, animated GIFs, Instagram and Snapchat 'stories', TikToks, augmented reality interfaces such as Pokémon GO, and so on. Mobile phones, digital cameras, touchscreens, geographically aware wearables, VR helmets, and so on, also offer new ways of navigating and representing the world around us. As discussed in previous chapters, digitally networked media also alter patterns of social organisation and production, of distributing and consuming content, and contribute to a range of other dislocations and transformations in society.

As we shall see in this chapter, digital society also changes the parameters of *social interaction*. While the internet and social media might share some characteristics with earlier media in history, such as words written on paper or telephone conversations, they also bear specific characteristics that contribute to altering how we see ourselves and how we act when we socialise with others. While I have already touched upon these issues in previous chapters, this chapter sees us diving deeper into the social psychology of digital society. As was also discussed in the previous chapter, digital society is constantly changing, not the least through the accelerating process of datafication and the ever deeper embedding of digital technologies in our everyday lives. This means that while the opportunity for (relative) anonymity, which was one of the social psychological affordances of the early internet, is today being challenged.

The affordances of social media enable us to document, display, and share our lives, and to do this in more than one fixed and specific way. Identities are always open to negotiation and, as discussed in Chapter 2, a key element of being in society is the management of our identities in relation to others – showing some aspects, hiding others – depending on audience, context, and situation.

Furthermore, in today's world, identity is generally more of an open issue than in many previous historical eras. Of course, identities are always formed in relation to what position the individual has within the larger cultural and economic framework of society, and they are constrained by dominant sorting systems that might be rooted in class, gender, race, sexuality, (dis)ability, and so on. Still, there is considerable room for people in digital society to construct and perform different features (and even versions) of themselves. This is due to the relative fluidity of the digital environment, because, as McKenna and Bargh (2000: 62) write:

it is quite difficult for a person to effect changes in his or her self-concept when the surrounding social environment (i.e., one's network of acquaintances, colleagues, family, and friends) remains static. When an individual attempts to make such changes, his or her peers may be unwilling to accept, acknowledge, and provide validation for these new self-aspects, and unless and until they do so, the new role or identity does not become real for the individual. [...] Thus, interacting with others on the Internet may provide individuals with the opportunity to successfully implement wished for changes in their self-concept.

On the internet and in social media, people have the social opportunity and the technological tools for 'writing themselves into being' (Barton & Lee 2013: 84). By posting text, images, or video, by commenting on the posts of others, and when creating profiles, and so on, we are actively constructing who we are, or at least who we want to be seen as by others. The relative openness of many online settings allows for the projection of new or alternative identities, and for the extension of our offline selves in different ways. In practice, our identities will move between the online and the offline context in ways that blur the boundaries between the digital and face-to-face. Depending on which online context we interact in – which forum, which service, which mode of communication, which site, etc. – we might target our identity performances towards different audiences (actual or imagined). Managing and working with identity in such ways is 'a process of exploring and discovering new aspects of the self' (Barton & Lee 2013: 85). It is important to note, however, that our own self-presentations are not the only information that is available about us online. We may also be liked, tagged, mentioned, or discussed by others. This means that anyone looking someone up with a search engine will find 'a mix of what the person has put online and information placed there by others' (Baym 2010: 112). These dynamics are further complicated by the interesting tension between what the 'old' internet was and is – largely an *archive* of traces – and new forms of ephemeral media, such as instastories, which typically exist for twenty-four hours, or Snapchat posts that may only live for seconds. Yet again, in our datafied times, one of the biggest worries may be that we are being traced, tracked, and our data stored and used or exploited in a multitude of ways, by a wide range of actors, in an infinite array of settings (Livingstone 2019).

ACTIVE USERS, MUTUAL RELATIONS

When computer-mediated communication is defined in relation to older and other forms of communication, the characteristic that is most often highlighted is its *interactivity*. Media that are interactive offer their users the ability and potential to directly intervene in the content in different ways. Traditional mass communication is not very interactive at all, whereas telephone conversations are highly interactive, but with a very small audience. In digital society, the internet and social media enable interactive forms of communication among large numbers of people.

First, people can interact with the content of digital media. Even though the internet has plentiful content that can simply be passively absorbed, it also offers a variety of content that enables, or even demands, that the user actively does something with it, or to it. The things that we can do range from navigating, playing, experimenting, and exploring, to actually creating things such as images, videos, status updates, comments, tags, edits, and so on.

Interaction

Interaction is one of those concepts that is often used, but is seldom very well defined. From a sociological perspective, as stated by classic social psychologist George Herbert Mead (1934), interaction is what goes on when people do things in relation to each other. Social actions were defined by Weber (see Chapter 2) as behaviour that is oriented towards the behaviour of others. Mead (1934: 45) draws on that perspective when writing about 'the social act' as 'the interaction of different forms, which involves, therefore, the adjustment of the conduct of these different forms to each other, in carrying out the social process'. In other words, interaction is mutual. It goes in both, or many, directions. This mutuality may come from how the communication medium is structured, from the communication setting, or from how users think and act. Interactivity will be seen in somewhat different ways, and is studied from different perspectives, depending on which of these dimensions one is interested in. If we use the perspective introduced in Chapter 1 on media as environments, and environments as media, these dimensions flow together. In sum, when a communication environment is interactive, it implies that participants can control – modify the form and content of – the environment, and that the roles of sender and receiver are interchangeable.

Even if the word 'interaction', or 'interactivity', might be used to refer to things like human–computer interaction, and in fields such as multimedia and game design, I use it in this book to refer to a change in the nature of media 'audiences' or users. Because even if people in the pre-internet age could have interactive relationships with analogue media such as books, films, radio shows, and television programmes, the coming of digital media extends this interactivity. In other words, we focus here on the 'social interactivity' of digital media – their ability to enable groups and individuals to communicate with, and relate to, each other (Baym 2010: 7). New media researcher Martin Lister and colleagues (2009: 50) write that even though different users will not all share the same experience of any specific content, they collectively construct 'the text' through their discussions about it. The internet and social media enable such processes of making meaning to include larger groups of people and ever more refined ways to transform the content.

Furthermore, people can interact with each other in new ways through digital media. In 2004, just before the major breakthrough of social media, including YouTube, Facebook, and Twitter, informatics scholar Mikael Wiberg wrote about the emergence of an 'interaction society'. He felt this to be a more fitting description of the present times than 'the information society'. This was because the focus of computing was shifting around the turn of the last century from information, storage, and processing towards social interactions. The major shift was that the use of digital tools and platforms as a clearly delimited practice, as well as a field of expertise, started to become a pervasive and everyday activity. Wiberg (2004: 4) writes:

> While computing in the 1970s was about several persons working together around one single machine to make it produce an exact result, today's computing is about several persons interacting with each other via several computers and, as such, it enables them to maintain and develop their social networks. Here, it becomes clear that also the role of the technology has changed from being in the frontline of our attention to now becoming a more pervasive technology that enables us to do new things without directing our attention to the technology *per se*. How many people think about how the phone operates 'under the shell' while they are having a phone conversation?

Users were increasingly making connections, managing contacts, and coordinating and collaborating with each other, through new technologies such as mobile phones, pagers, email, and instant messaging systems. Obviously, these technologies are what was soon to evolve into what we talk of today as social media (see Chapter 2).

FROM BODY TO CONTENT

These interactive patterns are key to understanding how the widespread use of digital media and the internet changed the fabric of society around the end of the 20th century. This was obviously the case, even though perspectives differ on how dramatic the change was. The transformation was not only about the tools and platforms – email, online forums, chatrooms, the web, blogs, social network sites, etc. – but about the emergence of new social and cultural phenomena and patterns. While people have always been communicating, and, for example, emails are quite similar to analogue letters in many ways, phenomena such as 'the online forum', 'the social network site', 'the tweet', 'the link', and 'the like' are purely digital, and have changed the nature of communication, and thus culture and society. Today, as different forms of direct messages (SMSs, DMs, texts, comments, or even simply likes or emoji) have largely taken over the function that email played on the early internet, people rarely write lengthy messages anymore. Instead of communicating by fewer and longer letters, electronic or otherwise, we now communicate in more frequent, but much shorter, and relatively ephemeral snippets, snapshots, and reactions.

DISCUSSION

Think of things that you do online digitally and what their offline or old media counterparts would be. For example, an email is a kind of letter, a video call over the internet fills many of the functions of the traditional telephone call, and watching a video on YouTube is somewhat similar to watching TV. What other parallels can you think of? What about tweets or instastories, or things such as 'likes' or emoji reactions? This exercise makes you reflect on what things the internet simply enhances or simplifies, and what things are unique to it. The bottom line is: Which social things that you do in digital society would you *definitely* not be able to do in *any way whatsoever* in a non-digital world?

Sociologist Tim Jordan (2013: 1) writes about how internet technologies gave rise to 'different identities, bodies and types of messages'. In society before electronic media, people who communicated at a distance – while not being face-to-face, that is – used written language on a variety of media. Things like signatures, personal seals, particular salutations, or recognisable styles of handwriting and language use compensated for the physical body not being tangibly present. Once the telephone was introduced, new means of substituting for the presence of a physical body became relevant, such as the sound, intonation, or other characteristics of someone's voice. Jordan explains how these methods stand in contrast to what happens with communication through digital media. He argues that in communicative practices that are dependent on the internet, the identity markers, and the traces of the non-present body are much more unstable.

While the handwriting or voice of a person has a natural connection to their physical body, things like email addresses, Twitter usernames, or nicknames used on messaging services do not. In this context it becomes more and more important to be able to decipher the style of messages. The symbolic content, Jordan says, becomes more important than the physical body (or stand-ins for it) for stabilising the communication. Newly evolving forms of 'internet speak', or the use or non-use of things like emoji, become more and more important for identifying who is the sender and receiver of a message. In the case, for example, when someone's email is hijacked by spambots, it will most of the time be rather easy for human recipients who are familiar with the owner of the mail account to decode this. If we suddenly start receiving body-part enhancement or Viagra advertisements from someone we know does not normally send across such things, the style of communication, content themes, the visual and textual form, and other markers and means for stabilising communication will reveal the hijacking.

The key social shift which is identified here is that from the body and the voice to style and content. Pre-internet communication and social interaction used the body, or substitutes for it, to validate the mediated interaction between people – to make sure that one knew who one was communicating with. On the internet, however, messages are legitimised through the style and content of communication. In today's society, both of these potentially dissonant communicative practices co-exist. When we meet people face-to-face or talk to them over the phone, we recognise them by their body and voice. But when we text or email the same people, we recognise them by the style and content of what they communicate digitally.

Because of this difference, early accounts of interaction on the internet often had a tendency to focus on the *disembodied* character of the medium. The point was repeatedly made that the internet made it possible for people to make believe that they were anyone, or anything, they liked. It was also largely assumed that anyone receiving the communication lacked the information or resources needed to validate the identity of the person(s) they were engaging with. The character of internet anonymity versus visibility has changed significantly since then, and I shall return to that issue towards the end of this chapter.

NO ONE KNOWS YOU'RE A DOG

In the 1990s, Sherry Turkle wrote about how we were increasingly constructing our identities in a 'culture of simulation'. Her point was that:

> [people online] become authors not only of text but of themselves, constructing new selves through social interaction. [Digital media] provide worlds for anonymous social interaction in which one can play a role as close to or as far away from one's 'real self' as one chooses. (Turkle 1995: 12)

A very often cited cartoon from *The New Yorker* magazine in 1993 depicted two dogs in front of a computer and the caption: 'On the Internet, nobody knows you're a dog'.

Wikipedia (2021a) credits the cartoon as being a key moment in the introduction of the internet into the minds of people other than government engineers and academics. The disconnect between 'real' and 'virtual' identities was indeed crucial to early understandings of digital online interaction. The main idea was that as users of digital media leave their physical bodies behind, they can freely choose and construct their *online identities*. This was also seen to allow users to escape any expectations and norms that are tied to our 'offline selves'. Philosopher Sadie Plant (1997: 46) wrote in her book *Zeros + ones* that:

> Access to a [computer] terminal is also access to resources which were once restricted to those with the right face, accent, race, sex, none of which now need be declared.

Donna Haraway, a scholar of science, technology, and gender, had made similar points in her 1991 'cyborg manifesto' when she suggested that since the late 20th century, we are all 'fabricated hybrids of machine and organism' (Haraway 1991: 150). Writing from a feminist standpoint, she even claimed that we might now be living in a 'post-gender world'. Like Jordan, she argued that identity is no longer manifested with reference to anything 'natural'. Instead, *cyborg identities* are 'permanently partial' and contradictory (1991: 154). In general, then, communication on the internet was seen as establishing a distinction between an embodied self and disembodied – potentially multiple – digital selves or identities. Some have also claimed that the connection between the two sides can be very fluid. Cultural critic Mark Dery wrote in *Flame Wars* (1993: 2–3) about:

> the upside of incorporeal interaction: a technologically enabled, postmulticultural vision of identity disengaged from gender, ethnicity, and other problematic constructions. Online, users can float free of biological and sociocultural determinants, at least to the degree that their idiosyncratic language usage does not mark them as white, black, college-educated, a high-school dropout, and so on.

If one looks at the ways in which many people use digital media today – to connect with each other and share things on platforms like Instagram, Snapchat, or Facebook – it is easy to see that our identities are not as free-floating after all. We tend to communicate and interact quite a lot with people we already know outside the digital setting, and our offline identity is often obvious from our profiles. The story was a bit different, however, a few decades back. Internet researcher danah boyd (2014) describes how the early adopters of the internet and the web (in the 1980s and 1990s) often entered online spaces without knowing the other people there. This was before social network sites with systems for 'friending' or 'following' certain individuals.

The dominant forms were instead things like chatrooms, newsgroups, and bulletin boards, all of which were organised by topic rather than if participants knew one another or not. Depending on whether you were interested in computer programming, electronic music, or football, you would enter a different space – largely to connect with like-minded strangers. This is still the case today when people use open forums such as Reddit, or enter chats such as those on, for example, Discord servers. In such settings, there has always been some room for experimentation by entering into different social roles and identities. Today, however, an increasing number of platforms are organised around connections between individuals rather than topics. As boyd (2014) has it, it was around 2003 – with the major breakthrough of blogging and social network sites – that the online landscape shifted from being topically organised to being organised around social connections between people. In pre-social media online forms of communication, such as bulletin boards and forums, people were brought together by shared interests even though they might not share any other connection either online or offline. In the age of social media, however, connecting with friends rather than interests came to the forefront.

I have underlined in previous chapters that digital media and their uses today are embedded in 'real-life' social settings, and boyd's description is yet another illustration of that. While early internet sociality was more about entering chatrooms and forums with a more exploratory mindset or even at random, today's internet is increasingly anchored in, and entangled with, the physical world. As the internet has become ever more used, the uses are more and more founded on social and economic processes that were pre-existing. This means that the degree of anonymity afforded by the digital world does not really facilitate the creation of fantasy selves. Instead, it forms a foundation for making connections, building trust, and establishing relationships in the 'real world' (Hardey 2002: 583). In other words, if people don't know whether you're a dog or not, they might be less interested in interacting with you.

OUT OF SYNC

Even though people's interaction over digital media today mostly is not as disembodied or fluid as some might have expected, social interaction on the internet and through social media still differs from other forms of interaction. With audio and video long since being an integral part of the internet, and with services such as Skype, Facetime, Zoom, and a large number of others enabling real-time audio and video communication, it can be argued that the online and digital interaction of today can indeed be very similar to offline and analogue interaction. Computer-mediated communication may now happen in real time, and you can potentially see the person(s) you are talking to, so that you are able to take in non-verbal cues, and so on. This is all very good and practical, but it does not cover all of the traditionally 'internet' ways of relating to each other, such as the use of written language online, emoji, digital imagery, and tags, or by liking and sharing on platforms, which are much less embodied. Indeed, the parameters of interaction are altered to some degree when it happens through the natively digital forms of things like forum posts, blog posts and comments, likes or shares. So what, then, does the digital do with sociality?

One of the first things that tends to be brought up when it comes to characterising digital sociality is the fact that it can be *asynchronous* – it does not *need* to happen in real time. Even if people may use texting, chats, direct messaging, emails, and discussion forums for communicating at a steady pace, or to respond to each other the very moment that they receive a message, these digital communications do not have to take place in real time, in the same way as an offline conversation or an online video call must. Many digital tools and platforms allow for delays. In some contexts, one might respond within seconds or minutes, while at other times one may take hours, days, months, or even forever to reply. These possibilities for asynchronicity lead to a 'conversational relaxation' (Walther 1996: 26). This gives users time to be more strategic about what they say, and how, which also enables more refined forms of self-presentation and self-censorship. An important aspect of digital asynchronicity, however, is that communication is still comparably quite fast. It has all the advantages of postal mail, but without the associated days or weeks of waiting. It may be worth reflecting upon how the liberating aspects of asynchronous communication – that they allow for responding whenever it suits *us* – at the same time can be anything but liberating as they tend to increasingly demand that we respond swiftly on all of the occasions when it suits *others*.

The space of flows

In the 1984 book *Neuromancer*, science-fiction author William Gibson popularised the term 'cyberspace'. This was his name for a 'non-space', a 'consensual hallucination experienced daily by billions of legitimate operators' of 'every computer in the human system' (Gibson 1984: 128). It can also be defined as 'the notional environment in which communication over computer networks occurs' (Lexico 2021). In other words, things that are 'cyber' relate to the imaginary and non-physical (sometimes called virtual) place where digital media communication and interaction happens. It is the non-space where the message is when it passes from sender to receiver. Such views contribute to a mystification of digital media. Having been 'understood' in science fiction before its breakthrough in the real world, the internet and its related social activities have often evoked people's imagination. But the idea of something akin to cyberspace can also be theorised in a more sociological way. A crucial concept in Manuel Castells' definition of 'the network society' (see Chapter 5) is 'the space of flows'. It refers to the fact that as communication technologies develop, being in the same place at the same time becomes less important for social interaction. We no longer need to share places and moments in time. We can still do things together. This is because physical places, and moments, are now 'connected by electronically powered communication networks through which flows of information that ensure the time-sharing of practices processed in such a space circulate and interact' (Castells 2009: 34).

Asynchronicity makes it possible for very large groups of people to have sustained interaction. Asynchronous communication also means that we don't have to deal with the immediate reaction of those we are interacting with. Psychologist John Suler (2004: 323) argues that this makes users disinhibited. The possibility of moving in and out of a conversation – returning when we are ready and prepared – and the absence of 'a continuous feedback loop that reinforces some behaviors and extinguishes others' enables us to feel safer, and to formulate our thoughts more freely.

Asynchronous online interaction can also be more democratic than face-to-face interaction. It can contribute, at least in some contexts, to minimising the role played by status and authority. Suler argues that this has to do with how authority figures express their status through their physical presence – 'in their dress, body language, and in the trappings of their environmental settings'. When we communicate online, those cues are largely absent, meaning that the impact of the authority is reduced. Suler (2004: 324) continues:

> Even if people do know something about an authority figure's offline status and power, that elevated position may have less of an effect on the person's online presence and influence. [...] Although one's identity in the outside world ultimately may shape power in cyberspace, what mostly determines the influence on others is one's skill in communicating (including writing skills), persistence, the quality of one's ideas, and technical know-how.

A similar point was made in a study of video teleconferencing in the 1970s, where the conclusion was that status hierarchies and informal leadership emerged much faster and clearer in face-to-face groups than in mediated groups (Strickland et al. 1978: 593). Suler's overarching argument is that people will say and do things online that they would not say and do in offline and face-to-face settings. He writes of *the online disinhibition effect* – the effect that people tend to be less restrained and to express themselves more openly online. Obviously, this has its advantages and disadvantages: it might enable blatant hate speech, as well as it may promote participation, intimacy, and self-disclosure. So once again, digital communications bear the double-edged sword of potentially bad versus potentially good outcomes, which you will recognise from Chapter 3.

DISCUSSION

Think about situations when you choose between different modes of communication to interact with friends, businesses, teachers, experts, politicians, etc. What influences your choices? When do you rather text than voice-call your friend, and when is it the other way around? When would you rather chat online with your doctor than have a face-to-face appointment? Would you use social media or email to get the attention of a political leader? Such questions help you identify what is useful about different tools and platforms. For example, a group of internet researchers found in a study of Snapchat that the platform gave users emotional rewards, while it did not offer them any deeper social support. The participants in the study viewed Snapchat as a lightweight platform for sharing experiences spontaneously with people who they already trusted (Bayer et al. 2015). What other characteristics of other platforms can you think of?

OUT OF SIGHT

Another idiosyncrasy of digital sociality is that it has the potential to make us relatively *invisible*. This is no pure invisibility, however. It is about a *potential* for *relative* invisibility or anonymity. As I will discuss further towards the end of this chapter, the internet indeed in many ways makes us less rather than more invisible, and a key feature of social media culture is that it focuses on visual presentation and self-expression (see Chapter 6) – on showing our faces, bodies, and lives rather than hiding them. Nevertheless, there are also different degrees of, and potentials for, not being seen and not seeing others on the internet. Especially in the early days of the internet, when a much larger share of the communication was purely text-based than today, many researchers focused on these issues. The related theories have a broad social psychological relevance and are definitely applicable today in relation to some of the strategies and activities that people engage in online.

When we use services such as Facebook, Twitter, and YouTube, we often cannot be directly seen by others, nor can we see who else is there at the same time. Similarly, people who happen to be viewing the same website or looking at the same Instagram photo at the same time are also largely invisible to one another. A person's, relative, presence may sometimes be revealed through the person having recently 'liked' or commented on something, or through similar signals or proxies. And even though some sites, platforms, and services have indicators that display whether people are online or not (or when they were most recently online), they are still physically invisible (even though sometimes represented by a profile photo or other avatar). Furthermore, even if we are in a voice-call, or sharing instant messages at a rapid pace with someone, there is still an element of invisibility there. We don't see the face of the person in the call, and we don't hear the voice of the one we are texting with. Even in video calls, the non-verbal cues – as they are mediated – are of a different quality from the directly experienced non-verbal cues. So, indeed, the internet like any medium will convey some things and obscure others.

According to something called 'social presence theory', the sense of awareness of an interaction partner is very important for the social effects of any communication medium. The theory suggests that increased social presence leads to a better perception of the person with whom we are communicating (Short et al. 1976). As discussed earlier, the lack of non-verbal cues and of other information about the communication partner, and the social context of interaction, has been thought by some to increase uninhibited communication, such as being aggressive or using foul language (Culnan & Markus 1987: 429). Still, it is a general insight from previous research on digital media that people often disclose more intimate and private things in computer-mediated communication when compared to face-to-face communication (Joinson 2001). In contrast to how interaction happens in a classroom, for example, online invisibility means we don't have to worry about our physical appearance or the sound of our voice as we communicate. Indeed, in 2020, as the COVID-19 pandemic caused an explosion in online teaching via services such as Zoom, there were pedagogical debates about whether students should be required to indicate their presence by having their cameras turned on or not. For a teacher or other speaker, having an audience with their cameras turned on has some obvious advantages. On the other hand, with cameras and/or microphones turned off, they don't have to deal with verbal or non-verbal cues or reactions from their audience. No frowns, no shaking heads, and no sighs, but, on the other hand, no big smiles, oohs and aahs, or applause either. But maybe a replacement 'applause' or 'thumbs up' emoji. Still, as in a confessional box, or much as the traditional psychoanalyst is supposed to be positioned behind the client, the lack of eye contact and face-to-face visibility alters the social psychology of the interaction context. As Suler (2004: 322) writes: 'Text communication offers a built-in opportunity to keep one's eyes averted.'

As McKenna and Bargh (2000: 64) put it: 'physical appearance does not stop potential relationships from getting off the ground'. In online interaction, other and less superficial aspects – such as similarity of values and interests, or conversational style – can determine attraction to a larger extent than in some cases of face-to-face interaction. In the best of worlds, relationships that would never have come to be in 'real life' can be fostered through the internet. McKenna and Bargh were also able to show in a study that people who had met on the internet before they met face-to-face liked each other better than people whose first encounter was face-to-face.

In addition to the fact that digital interaction can enable invisibility – a form of visual anonymity – it can also warrant other forms of *anonymity*. One such form is discursive anonymity, which is the situation when things that are written and posted can't be attributed to any specific and known source (Qian & Scott 2007). Of course, digital interaction is not the only mode of communication where it is possible to avoid identification. But the multitude of communication channels on the internet, in combination with the separation of users in space and time, makes it relatively easy to evade identification. With anonymity as a protective cloak, people tend to take more risks, and to express more directly what they truly think or feel. Once again, that online disinhibition. With identities concealed, we may share more intimate confidences earlier in potential relationships, and develop closeness faster than we would in face-to-face offline relationships. In fact, a number of studies undertaken in the 1990s demonstrated that people tended to forge strong friendships based on high levels of self-disclosure on the internet (Henderson & Gilding 2004: 490). Yet the same mechanism – the fact that we feel less restrained by social norms – might also lower the thresholds for expressing views and behaviours that are racist, sexist, homophobic, and so on. Anonymous interaction can be liberating, but positive as well as negative beliefs might be acted out and reinforced under such conditions.

IN THE DARK

Anonymity can be both good and bad for social interaction. As experimental psychologist Philip Zimbardo showed in the infamous Stanford prison experiment, anonymity in groups can lead to de-individuation – the process by which individuals unknown to each other, and with concealed identities, become immersed in a group dynamic – a state where people can be impulsive, blatantly aggressive towards one another, and even sadistic (Zimbardo 2007). On the internet, the 'illusion of large numbers' might make us overestimate how many people share our views (McKenna & Bargh 2000: 64). We might see, for example, the number of views of a YouTube video or the number of times a tweet has been retweeted and make a rough translation between such numbers and the general legitimacy of the content.

When anonymity removes personal responsibility and generates a perceived loss of individuality, it can also lead to people becoming more altruistic and more willing to help others. In digital society, then, anonymity can be a force of unity and solidarity as well as of fragmentation and nihilism. This is a longstanding debate. Some claim that anonymous interaction in digital media is a major cause of hate speech, racism, sexism, etc., while others like to focus on how anonymity online can facilitate things like grassroots political action in places where censorship and surveillance make such mobilisation difficult. The bottom line is that de-individuation is not necessarily bad; it just makes people more affected by external cues. If the impulses coming from outside are bad, people may behave more badly if they are anonymous than if not. Similarly, if the cues are good, the behaviour can be good too.

In the evocatively titled paper 'Deviance in the Dark' from 1973, experimental social psychologists Kenneth Gergen, Mary Gergen, and William Barton explored how people function together under conditions of 'extreme anonymity'. They put the people who took part in their experiment in a dark room for about an hour. The participants did not know or see each other before the experiment, and they were not introduced to one another afterwards. Their interaction was recorded with infrared cameras and audio tape recorders, and the participants were interviewed about their experience after-wards. Then the researchers repeated the experiment with other groups and with the lights on. The results were that people in the light room found places to sit at 'appropriate' distances from one another. They kept these positions for the entire hour, and kept a continuous and focused conversation going. Many respondents reported that they became bored after a while. In the dark room, on the other hand, people were moving around fluidly and entered into a more explorative mindset. These subjects were less bored, and more open. Many of them reported afterwards that they had been talking about 'important' things. They had felt 'free' and 'serious' at the same time, half of the subjects had hugged someone, and nearly everyone had accidentally touched someone else. In a variation of the experiment, where people in the dark room were told that they would be introduced to each other once the session was over, subjects were less explorative and more bored. The researchers found that these results challenged previous studies that had shown that anonymity fed aggression. They wrote:

> Both laboratory and field studies have demonstrated that when a person is without markers or personal identity, when he or she becomes deindividuated in the researchers' terms, the stage is set for increased aggression. Faceless people are more likely to harm each other. [...] Yet few of our subjects found anything displeasing about the experience of anonymity. Most gained deep enjoyment. [...] Anonymity itself does not seem to be a social ill. When we are anonymous, we are free to be aggressive or to give affection, whichever expresses most fully our feelings at the time. There is liberation in anonymity. (Gergen et al. 1973: 38)

This insight is quite similar to what Howard Rheingold (1993: 27) wrote about cyberspace twenty years later. He claimed it was

> a place that people often end up revealing themselves far more intimately than they would be inclined to do without the intermediation of screens and pseudonyms.

In Simmel's classic essay 'The Stranger' from 1908, he wrote about a social form which unifies closeness and remoteness. This makes for a certain form of interaction. As the stranger is not bound by constituents and predispositions, (s)he

> often receives the most surprising revelations and confidences, at times reminiscent of a confessional about matters which are kept carefully hidden from everybody with whom one is close. (Simmel 1971: 145)

This tension between closeness and remoteness is indeed a trait of many relations in digital society as well. On the internet, there are several possibilities to maintain anonymity at the technological level. Users might connect via servers that conceal their actual IP address, use anonymous email or messaging services, or use other forms of anonymity-enabling hardware and software. With some of these methods it is next to impossible for anyone, even with the right expertise, to reveal the true identity of someone. With others, the protection might not be as secure as the user would hope.

However, from a sociological perspective, the most interesting part of online anonymity is that even those who interact online with little to none of these protective layers tend to feel that they are more anonymous than in some offline settings as well. This is because when we post on a forum – even if it is easy to see the IP address behind our username – or when we upload a tweet – even if we have information about who we are on our Twitter profile – we might feel two things. First, that our activities will be drowned out by the multitude of other interactions going on at the same time, and second, that no one will bother to investigate us further, at least, not very thoroughly.

DISCUSSION

Think about this interesting contradiction. On the one hand, some forms of social media use are celebrated for making it possible for people to come together as swarms where individuality is obscured. The coordinated actions of campaigns like #BlackLivesMatter and #MeToo illustrate this. But even aside from such movements, the relative anonymity of some digital social platforms makes for powerful forms of counter-power deployed by consumers, workers, young people, and so on. On the other hand, some forms of social media use are lauded because they enable people to express their individuality and manage their identity. This is the contrary of being anonymous. So, reflect upon whether you feel that social media are primarily an anonymous or a non-anonymous set of tools for communication. How do you navigate between different degrees of disclosure depending on context? When you *feel* anonymous, do you think that you really are anonymous, technically speaking? And what about the other way around?

HYPERPERSONAL INTERACTION

Anonymity is of course not new, but before digital society, people generally only had the opportunity to be anonymous in random, occasional, and impersonal forms of interaction. On the internet and in social media, anonymity can be maintained in interaction that is not just brief and on a one-time-only basis. In some online environments, people can communicate over a period of time, get to know each other well, and share intimate things, while still keeping their true identities relatively or partially concealed. Furthermore, there is also an ongoing debate about whether the internet and social media offer any real anonymity, as users are increasingly mapped, tracked, and watched by governments, as well as corporations, who use the data for purposes ranging from surveillance to marketing.

Anonymity is not definite, since it might vary in degrees, and is shaped by the technology used to communicate. The legal name and address of a person can identify them uniquely, while a picture accompanying a name is more limited. With access to nothing but a nickname, identification is even harder, and so on. Media researchers Hua Qian and Craig Scott (2007), writing about blogs, make a distinction between being anonymous, pseudonymous, or identifiable. This sliding scale of disclosure means that communication in digital media allows much greater flexibility in how we construct our identities when compared to what is possible in face-to-face encounters (McKenna & Bargh 2000: 62). The ability not to always have to deal with face-to-face interactions opens up many possibilities for tweaking and altering the ways in which we present ourselves to others. While social psychologists have long pointed out that our self-presentation, even in the pre-digital world, has always been selective and strategic (Goffman 1959) – where we choose to show some things and hide others, or even try to deceive – the internet has offered a new and quite hands-on toolset for this.

Joseph Walther, a researcher of the social and interpersonal dynamics of computer-mediated communication, found that what he called *hyperpersonal interaction* could be developed online. This is a notion that may account for why some forms of inter-action through digital media are sometimes marked by higher levels of emotional intensity and self-disclosure than face-to-face interaction. He explained that people communicating digitally – with fewer cues than in face-to-face communication – might succumb to an over-reliance on the information that they have. We might assume that the people we are interacting with are more similar to ourselves than they actually are, which may in turn generate feelings of closeness and lead to an idealisation of them. As discussed earlier, at the same time we also tend to manage our identities online in order to optimise the public image of ourselves. Because of this, Walther (1996: 27) claims, an intensification loop of 'behavioral confirmation' can be set in motion. When we idealise our interaction partner, they will respond to this by further optimising their self-image, and so on. This might explain why some communications online with what ought to be seen as relative strangers might become surprisingly intimate. Walther (1996: 28–29) writes:

> At the level of the sender, CMC [computer-mediated communication] partners may select and express communication behaviors that are more stereotypically desirable in achieving their social goals and transmit messages free of the 'noise' that otherwise comes with unintended appearance or behavior features. At the other end, CMC receivers take in these stylized messages, construct idealized images of their partners and relationships, and, through reciprocation, confirm them. These processes may be further enhanced when the minimal-cue inter-action is also asynchronous; freed from communicating in real time, users are released from the pressure to meet.

In other words, computer-mediated communication seems to be able to make inter-action either impersonal, or increasingly (hyper-)personal, and possibly anything in between. Walther writes that digital media alone do not decide which one of these forms of interaction are realised in any given situation. Rather, the internet and social media afford opportunities for people to communicate in different ways depending on the structural constraints or opportunities that are in effect in a given situation.

AFTER ANONYMITY

Early internet research was mainly focused on text-based digital communication, and therefore had a strong focus on the potential for internet users to be anonymous to varying degrees – as discussed throughout this chapter. As also discussed in this chapter, the potential for relative forms of anonymity and invisibility still remains in several online practices and settings. But the whole argument can also be turned on its head. The rise of web 2.0 and social media has in fact led to a decrease in the importance of anonymity online. Social media, when compared to the earlier forms of internet sociality, are based more on users being visible to each other, where our identities tend to be grounded to a larger extent in relationships with the offline friends that we also have contact with online. In the 1990s, when the web was new, the theories that were developed about online identity tended to focus on anonymity, fluidity, and openness.

It is more and more obvious today that people's online identities are not separate from their 'real identities'. So, maybe what we do on the internet and in social media can extend or augment, rather than replace or fully alter, our offline personas. Communications researcher Allison Cavanagh (2007: 121) argues that in order for the internet to function as a social network – as it does to a considerable extent today – the identities of participants need to have a certain degree of stability. This is how trust is built between people online. In fact, already in Henderson and Gilding's (2004) study it was found that people rarely maintained anonymous identities online. Instead, they used pseudonyms (the same username across platforms and over time), or their real identities, and built a reputation around that.

This development has no doubt been intensified in recent years, and this is because we live in an age of post-anonymity where:

1. Truly anonymous places online are becoming rarer.
2. Social media encourage visibility rather than anonymity.
3. Our data are tracked and traced by others, and by ourselves.

First, places where one can operate with a concealed identity are becoming increasingly marginal online. It is no coincidence that a hacktivist movement called *Anonymous* appeared during the first decade of the 21st century. This was a group whose activism largely drew on ideas rather than identifiable individuals, and which experimented with masks, graphics, voice changers, and text-to-speech software to appear as a truly anonymous, social force (Ferrada Stoehrel & Lindgren 2014). On conventional social media platforms, such as Instagram, Facebook, Twitter, YouTube, and TikTok, the content posted tends to be associated with user identities – profiles – that are persistent. A stream of content comes from a user who is identifiable to a certain degree. Some services are *non-anonymous*, such as Facebook, and actively demand that you use and validate your real name and officially true identity (Wikipedia 2021b). Others, such as Twitter, are *pseudonymous* and demand a persistent identity, even though it is possible to conceal who is actually behind the account by using burner email accounts and/or taking other steps to wipe out tracks in the process of registering and posting. In addition to such services, there are still *anonymous* services, such as, for example, Whisper or 4chan (Mondal et al. 2020). This means, clearly, that any form of true anonymity exists today only on sites and services that users specifically seek out for that reason. Mainstream social media are largely non-anonymous or pseudonymous and lack the full set of characteristics that are indicative of anonymous communication and interaction. Recent debates about data harvesting and user monitoring have, however, contributed to an increased interest among certain groups to use chat services such as Telegram or Signal to evade surveillance carried out by companies or governments (Abu-Salma et al. 2017).

Second, the social media landscape of today is largely based on a norm of being visible and expressive rather than invisible and anonymous, while the early internet use had a focus on content consumption, and on knowledge sharing within special interest groups. As shown in a study by Cotter (2019), professional social media users – influencers – are increasingly playing a 'visibility game', the goal of which is to gain influence via authenticity, and to play into how algorithms work in order to be as non-anonymous as possible. While a minority of internet users are actual influencers, this logic of visibility cuts deeper into the logic by which social media function today. One of the organising principles of social media platforms is popularity. van Dijck and Poell (2013) argue that '(p)latform metrics are increasingly accepted as legitimate standards to measure and rank people and ideas; these rankings are [...] in turn reinforced by users through social buttons such as following and liking'. This is related to the insight that there may not be much interest among many internet users in being anonymous, but rather to play into the attention economy of the platforms. As described by Harsin (2015: 329), significant parts of social life unfold in a 'highly affectively charged attention economy of constantly connected cognition'. Add to this the fact that more and more services, such as banking, shopping, education, travelling, reading, parenting, and taking care of one's health, are nearly impossible to maintain without being on the internet with a validated, non-anonymous, identity. As argued by Couldry and Mejias (2019: 7), the logic of global capitalism demands for human beings and things to be connected. There are also forces that try to resist this dominant logic through periods of 'digital detox' (Syvertsen & Enli 2020), or even by leaving social media altogether. In the book *Ten Arguments for Deleting Your Social Media Accounts Right Now*, Jaron Lanier (2018: 149) encourages his readers to:

> Quit 'em all! Instagram and WhatsApp are still Facebook and still scoop your data and snoop on you. Don't tweet about how you quit Facebook or post to Facebook about how you quit Twitter.

Third, in this age of datafication, the online traces that we leave behind are tracked, harvested and exploited, by corporations and governments that don't want us to be anonymous. Quite the opposite, they want to know as much about who we are as they possibly can. As has been debated vividly in recent years, during the hype surrounding so-called big data, and in relation to phenomena such as computational political propaganda and targeted advertising, there lies potentially huge power, and immense risks, in that most of what we do can today be registered and stored. Internet researcher John Cheney-Lippold (2017: 3) points this out, and writes:

> If you don't believe me, open your computer and roam the web for five minutes. In a period of time only slightly longer than the average television commercial break, you will have generated, through your web activity, an identity that is likely separate from the person who you thought you were. In a database far, far away, you have been assigned a gender, ethnicity, class, age, education level, and potentially the status of parent with x number of children. Maybe you were labeled a US citizen or a foreigner. There's even a slight chance you were identified as a terrorist by the US National Security Agency.

Even if we don't directly experience this data collection, as it happens out of our sight, it still feeds back to us, and it affects our sense of not being anonymous. Moving around the internet and social media, if we, for example, see obviously targeted ads that reflect some of our interests or our recent browsing behaviours, it is easy to feel as if we are not lurking in the shadows. They know who we are.

CHAPTER SUMMARY

While Chapters 1–3 addressed broader societal changes following from the rise of digital technology and the coming of a digital society, this chapter has focused on the particular social psychology of digital society. I have introduced the interactive character of online platforms and focused on how social interaction through digital media differs from other forms, for example face-to-face interaction. Key issues in these discussions relate to how we build trust in communication environments that are relatively disembodied, partly asynchronous, and potentially anonymous. While some of these factors may disinhibit social behaviour, it must be noted that disinhibition can work in different directions, for example to promote both hateful and supportive behaviours. The chapter also raised issues, to be revisited in Chapter 10, about how datafication – alongside other causes – are pushing us towards an age where online anonymity is increasingly hard to come by. While this present chapter has mainly addressed social processes at the micro-level of interaction, and while Chapters 1–3 were more targeted towards the macro-level of society, the next chapter will look at how the digital society functions at the intermediary level of social groups (communities and networks).

FURTHER READING

Amichai-Hamburger, Yair (2017). *Internet Psychology: The Basics.* London: Routledge.

This book by Amichai-Hamburger provides a great overview of the social psychology of the internet as a space for communication and interaction. He breaks this down into seven factors: (1) Feeling of anonymity; (2) Control over level of physical exposure; (3) High control over communications; (4) Ease in locating like-minded people; (5) Accessibility and availability at all times and places; (6) Feeling of equality; and (7) Fun of web surfing. The book is an excellent starting point for further exploring the issues discussed in this chapter about how the internet affects social relationships.

Turkle, Sherry (1995). *Life on the Screen: Identity in the Age of the Internet.* New York: Simon & Schuster.

Turkle's modern classic from 1995 is a key reading about how people interact with computers and what the effects are of that interaction. It reads partly as a historical document, with discussions about the relationship between humans and machines, that are very characteristic of the 1990s. Still, her analysis of multi-user online environments spawns ideas that are still useful, about misrepresenting oneself, and about the relationship between online and offline.

McKenna, Katelyn Y. A. & Bargh, John A. (2000). Plan 9 from Cyberspace: The Implications of the Internet for Personality and Social Psychology. *Personality and Social Psychology Review,* 4(1), 57–75.

Henderson, Samantha & Gilding, Michael (2004). 'I've Never Clicked This Much with Anyone in My Life': Trust and Hyperpersonal Communication in Online Friendships. *New Media & Society,* 6(4), 487–506.

Suler, John (2004). The Online Disinhibition Effect. *CyberPsychology & Behavior,* 7(3), 321–326.

These three early 2000s papers are important for understanding the social psychology of digital society. McKenna and Bargh analyse how social interaction, social identity, and relationship formation may be different on the internet than in real life. They focus on anonymity, and on the lessened importance of appearances, distance, and time. Suler lists and discusses the different factors of online communication that interact to create a disinhibiting effect. And Henderson and Guilding specifically explore the issue of how trust is developed in online communication.

5

COMMUNITIES AND NETWORKS

Key Questions

- What are (online) communities and what social needs can they fulfil?

- What are (social) networks?

- What are the key differences between communities and networks?

- What is the social network revolution and how does it relate to digital media?

- How do the notions of 'network society' and 'networked individualism' overlap and differ?

Key Concepts

Communities * networks * imagined communities * third places * network society * networked individualism * mass self-communication

As we saw in the previous chapter, the key technologies of digital society have transformed the conditions under which people interact with each other. However, society is not only comprised of one-on-one connections between individuals. Individuals also function together in groups, communities, and networks.

People have connected and clustered together in groups since the beginning of time, and sociologists have been thinking about patterns of social relations and about how technological changes affect social cohesion since the early days of the discipline in the 19th century. Communities and networks are not new things, but the internet and social media have enhanced and altered the processes by which they are formed, and also enabled some new patterns of human association. The internet and social media offer new opportunities for people who do not share a common locale to form relationships of collaboration and bonding. Online, one does not have to look far to realise that many users clearly strive to go beyond the narrowly private sphere, reaching out to each other in different ways to create, or affiliate with, a variety of online groups.

There was much debate in early internet research about whether the groups that people form with the help of digital tools and platforms can be seen as 'real' social groups or not. These discussions questioned whether 'online communities' can have similar characteristics and fulfil social functions equal to those of 'real communities'. Critics argued that the large-scale, fragmented, asynchronous, non-face-to-face character of online interaction (see Chapter 4) make online communities more isolating and less genuine than their offline counterparts. The philosopher of technology Albert Borgmann (1999: 165) likened the early internet to life in a log cabin – small-scale, coherent, transparent, comprehensible, intimate – and the developed internet to a skyscraper:

> Many of the intimate engagements that a log cabin enforces are not just unnecessary but entirely impossible in a highrise building. You simply cannot take the stairs to your office, haul all the water you need, make your own heat, nor even open a window. Like the coherence and intimacy of the log cabin, the transparency and comprehensibility of [early computer-mediated communication] are distant memories.

But even though some critics have argued that the internet cannot foster 'real' communities, others have claimed otherwise. Like the things discussed in the previous chapter, about how digital media might foster closeness and intimacy, many online groups tend to develop a strong sense of belonging and group membership. Groups of individuals that interact through the internet and social media, gathering around shared interests, and in which the sense of unity and support is strong, have been called online communities, or sometimes virtual communities. Such groups are often driven by a shared passion for some form of common interest (Rheingold 1993). In this chapter, I discuss perspectives on online communities and their relationship to the notion of social networks. Even though the two concepts are sometimes used interchangeably, they have some important differences.

While communities are more closed, bounded, and embedded, with a significant number of members knowing each other relatively closely, social networks are more fragmented, open, and partial. Communities are often focused on a certain topic, interest, or identity, while social networks are rather centred on the different sets of connections that can provide an individual with things like information, friendship, support, and social status. If one looks at the field of digital media research, it becomes clear that the distinction between communities and networks is largely dependent on perspective: 'communities' can be analysed as 'networks', and 'networks' can be conceptualised in terms of 'communities'. Over time, however, some researchers have claimed that society at large has come to function increasingly according to a logic of networks, rather than one of communities, and that computer-mediated communication has played an important role in this shift.

A SENSE OF COMMUNITY

As you will remember from Chapter 2, Ferdinand Tönnies saw '*Gemeinschaft*' (community) as a vital part of human existence. Society ('*Gesellschaft*') is merely a lifeless aggregation of individuals, unless a sense of community holds people together. The glue, he argued, was created through common languages, common beliefs, and common interests, which generated feelings of kinship and togetherness. Community is defined in different ways in different contexts and by different writers, but Tönnies' basic idea is at the centre of most theories about community. This basic idea is that the mere existence of a form, forum, or place for people to interact is not enough to be sure that community exists.

For community to emerge, an element of warmth, sincerity, or even cosiness is required. The classic cultural studies figure Raymond Williams (1985: 76) wrote that 'community' is a 'warmly persuasive word to describe an existing set of relationships' which 'seems never to be used unfavourably'. Likewise, echoing Tönnies, geographer and sociologist James Slevin (2002) defines communities as 'cosy realities' of social relationships based on fellowship, understanding, locality, and shared responsibilities. In a similar vein, sociologist Lori Kendall (2011: 309) states that community has a 'feel-good fuzziness' about it. It evokes thoughts on shared values, empathy, affection, and consensus. Sociologist Amitai Etzioni and computer scientist Oren Etzioni (1999: 241) define community as having two vital attributes:

> First, it is a web of affect-laden relationships that encompasses a group of individuals – relationships that crisscross and reinforce one another, rather than simply a chain of one-on-one relationships. […] Second, a community requires a measure of commitment to a set of shared values, mores, meanings, and a shared historical identity – in short, a culture.

Communities have existed for as long as humankind itself, and throughout history, technologies (railways, radio waves, airplanes, cellular networks, etc.) and media (the alphabet, paper, video cassettes, television, etc.) have facilitated the creation and maintenance of these communities. The evolution of the internet and social media are no exception. Going online makes it possible to establish and nurture shared symbols, to transmit shared stories and histories, to manifest our interconnection, and so on. This can be done through building affinity groups that work towards a common goal, which may be fighting racism or sexism, or the appreciation of certain books, movies, or artists. Building such groups is often a very positive thing, both for individuals and for society. Being part of a group of like-minded people gives us a certain psychological strength, which can be a resource also beyond the particular group, and in settings that are of a less online character (Bargh & McKenna 2004). While this chapter is mostly focused on introducing communities and networks from this more optimistic perspective, it is important to remember (cf. Chapter 3) that all traits that make the internet into a unique social environment (cf. Chapter 4) in positive respects can also work in opposite ways, for example by fostering negative communities. Amichai-Hamburger (2017: 73) writes:

> On the Internet, the aggressor can find soulmates to share any particular hatred and any campaign of harassment – against people of any ethnicity or religion, for example. These friends will provide positive reinforcement, which acts as a reward for the violence expressed toward the hated group. Alliances tend to forge among aggressors, and individuals among their number may be seen as heroes defending their cause.

It is in such settings that Amichai-Hamburger describes, where hate and aggression build through the power of community, that different degrees of radicalisation can take place (Fernandez et al. 2018; von Behr et al. 2013). Loners seeking to make social connections need 'only to echo the prevailing aggression, and the group responds with messages of welcome, with positive reinforcement, and with the offer of a sense of shared identity' (Amichai-Hamburger 2017: 73). The warm fuzzy feeling of belonging to a community may therefore even make individuals express agreement and loyalty with groups for the single reason of the reward that comes in the form of a sense of belonging.

Imagined communities

Benedict Anderson (1983) famously wrote about nations as 'imagined communities', and thereby wanted to underline that a sense of community relies largely on people 'imagining' – as in feeling, thinking, and talking – their communities into existence. The point he made, and one to underline here, is that the strength of a community is derived from the ways in which its members maintain the sense of their community through symbols and language. As most online community members will never know most of the other members closely, and are even less likely to meet them in person, the community mainly exists in people's minds. Social reality tends to be quite messy, but we are disposed to imagine that communities are more clearly delimited and bounded than they really are. Anderson also thought that we, in our imagination, overstate a sense of comradeship in our communities, while understating inherent inequalities, exploitation, and hierarchies. This is an important point, because it is easy to see that all communities are imagined in one sense, at least to the extent that they are produced, maintained, and reproduced through a range of symbolic strategies (feelings, flags, icons, traditions, etc.).

In his seminal book *The Virtual Community*, Rheingold (1993: xx–xxi) saw the emergence of communities online as a natural and inevitable process:

> [W]henever CMC [computer-mediated communication] technology becomes available to people anywhere, they inevitably build virtual communities with it, just as microorganisms inevitably create colonies […] CMC enables people to do things with each other in new ways, and to do altogether new kinds of things – just as telegraphs, telephones, and televisions did.

Communities can be formed in many ways on the internet. In its early uses, in the late 1990s and early 2000s, the concept of 'internet communities' was sometimes used to refer to entire sites. These were early variations of what later came to be called social network sites, in which the entire site was seen as being a community that one could join and be part of (Skog 2005). On today's internet – and also from a general sociological perspective – it is more fitting to see community as being a property of certain forms of social interaction, which can be underpinned by different forms of technological infrastructure. Communities can indeed still form on social network sites. For example, Facebook Groups, which are devoted to special interests, can function as communities, even though such groups are not communities by definition. In some Facebook Groups, a sense of community among participants may arise, while in others it may not. Communities are also likely to form in settings such as discussion forums, where, for example, the interaction and communication in many of the topical sub-forums (so-called subreddits) on Reddit have community features.

Community can also occur in more fluid settings, such as around a particular hashtag, for example #PhDchat or #MadWriting, or among certain users of large-scale hashtags, such as #BlackLivesMatter or #MeToo. The 'hashtag publics' (Rambukkana 2015) that take shape in this way have been seen as 'ad-hoc' in the sense that they can form in the exact moment that they are needed. When someone uses a new hashtag in a post, its existence is announced to the followers of its originator, and can be used and disseminated from there. But not all social groups that form around a certain hashtag are ad hoc (Bruns & Burgess 2011: 7). Some of them may not be huge and loosely-knit assemblages of people, but rather have a community element to them. In other words, communities can emerge in a wide range of digital settings, such as in comment threads that follow the posts of certain personalities on Instagram, TikTok, or YouTube, or on Discord servers for certain games, and so on.

The basic criteria, sociologically speaking, for us to be able to talk of something as a community is that people – at least a core group of them – are returning to one and the same place, and that they recognise one another – at least from time to time. Community demands a degree of continuity and familiarity. In relation to the contents of this chapter, it is also important to note that the wider range of infrastructures, platforms, and affordances that enable communities to take shape are oftentimes the same platforms that also enable networks. This is a key point of this chapter: people come together and connect socially. Sometimes this gives rise to communities, sometimes it produces networks, and often hybrid forms of the two. Learning more about the sociological terminology that surrounds these two concepts still makes it easier to analyse processes of interaction and communication in the digital society. But remember this: 'community' or 'network' is not a property of the particular platform. Just as a particular café can foster a community of regulars who enjoy each other's company and social support, so can some places on the internet. At the same time, some cafés are just cafés.

Rheingold (1993: xx) defined an online (or virtual) community as a type of social aggregation that emerges on the internet when 'enough people carry on […] public discussions long enough, with sufficient human feeling, to form webs of personal relationships'. Online communities can be defined simply as groups of individuals who interact around a common interest, where the interaction is mediated or supported by internet technology. Such communities can differ from one another due to a variety of contextual factors. Relationships between members may be of different types and strengths (friendship, exchange, unequal, mutual, etc.). The content and character of the communication will also vary, as will the motivations of members to be part of the group.

A general motivation for joining and staying in online communities, as discussed above, is fulfilment of the basic social need of feeling part of a group, and being gratified by the sense of emotional and cognitive connection. In other words, no matter what the topic or profile of the online community, people enjoy hanging out there because they get a sense of attachment and belonging through their shared communication practices. Through such practices, social norms will by necessity emerge, be negotiated, and then transmitted through shared behaviours. This means that power structures and hierarchies will also take form. Indeed, it may also be a motivating factor for some members to join online communities so that they may acquire status through their membership, and can influence, or even dominate, others. In some cases, one and the same community will be able to help with a wide variety of things. In other situations, people will turn to different communities for different types of information and support. These may be communities of which they see themselves as members, or not, or of which they aspire to become part. The availability and feeling of relative anonymity (see Chapter 4), of some online communities offer the opportunity for people to turn to others for comfort, security, or to boost their self-esteem during stressful times. At the same time, community members who are able to support others might be gratified by this activity. Helping others leaves you with a feeling that you are needed.

Constance Elise Porter (2015: 168) lists a few motivations that people might have for being part of online communities. One such reason is to just relax, hang out, play around, and have fun. Another motivation might be the opportunity to engage in identity experimentation and self-expression, as was discussed in Chapter 4. Yet another driving force is to acquire certain forms of information, which can be useful for solving problems and making decisions. People may turn to communities on the internet for information about anything ranging from crucial life decisions, such as that of moving across the world, becoming a parent, or making a gender transition, to more everyday things, such as cooking, working out, or finding nice desktop backgrounds for their computers.

Another reason to seek out online communities might be to build relationships through interaction with others. Such relationship-building will often be a by-product of other types of interaction. Some communities might indeed be solely focused around people socialising and befriending each other. But more often, some of the people who seek out a community with a certain focal interest – say, a sports team or computer programming – will gradually build productive relationships that go deeper than, and beyond, the initial focus for membership.

COMMUNITIES AS THIRD PLACES

In the early 1980s sociologists Ramon Oldenburg and Dennis Brissett introduced the notion of 'the third place'. They defined the home as people's 'first place' and their workplace as the 'second place'. They argued that there was a decreasing range of arenas for social participation in society, and that people were stuck in an everyday loop of flitting back and forth between the two places. They wrote that: 'Neither place, nor even the two together, seems to provide satisfying experiences and relationships for people' (Oldenburg & Brissett 1982: 266). Oldenburg and Brissett (1982: 267) felt that people were in need of 'third places' – places outside the home and the workplace that could provide people 'with a larger measure of their sense of wholeness and distinctiveness'.

Such third places could be, for example, coffee-houses, barber shops, gyms, libraries, parks, or streets. Oldenburg and Brissett emphasised that simple escape from the demands of family and work – something that has historically been easier for men than women to achieve – was not the main point of these places. Rather, the goal of using third places is that they are primarily about socialising with each other. They are based on what Simmel called 'sociation'. Simmel (1950: 43) wrote that:

> Certainly, specific needs and interests make [people] band together in economic associations, blood brotherhoods, religious societies, hordes of bandits. Yet in addition to their specific contents, all these sociations are also characterized, precisely, by a feeling, among their members, of being sociated and by the satisfaction derived from this.

The point here is that people generally enjoy hanging out, just for the sake of hanging out. Simmel, as well as Oldenburg and Brissett, write in a way that seems to assume that the third places are for men exclusively. Simmel writes of 'brotherhoods', and Oldenburg and Brissett about 'fraternal orders'. This sexist perspective can, at least in part, be explained by the prevailing structure of labour market and family patterns and policies at the times when they were writing – Simmel in the early 1900s, and Oldenburg and Brissett in the 1980s. Today, even though gendered power structures prevail, people of all genders access third places. Furthermore, when people come together outside the home and the workplace, social roles and qualifications become much less important. Simmel (1950: 46) continues:

> Wealth, social position, erudition, fame, exceptional capabilities and merits, may not play any part in sociability. At most they may perform the role of mere nuances.

Oldenburg and Brissett (1982: 278) describe third places as creating a free space for expression. While we are taught that conflict does not belong in the family, and that we must stay balanced and professional at work, third places 'encourage and, indeed, thrive on emotional expressiveness'. Furthermore, third places have an unpredictability and diversity that first and second places often lack:

> One can never be certain exactly who will be there; can never predict what the chemistry of a particular 'mix' of people will create. One can, however, count on it being lively for the third places are arenas for active participation with others. (1982: 274–275)

Third places are theorised, in other words, like communities, as being sincere, emotional, and free. Oldenburg and Brissett developed their theory while worrying – much like Robert Putnam in his book *Bowling Alone* (2000) – that social changes (globalisation, mobility, generational shifts, etc.) and media (predominantly television) caused a dramatic decline in community involvement. Putnam (2000: 408) said that society desperately needs communities and public spaces that 'will encourage more casual socializing with friends and neighbours'. He was not very optimistic about what the internet can achieve along these lines, but what he asked for is obviously similar to Oldenburg and Brissett's third places. Putnam largely blamed disengaging media for the decline in community. This is in line with the literature about so-called pseudo-community, which claims that mediated connections between people are impersonal. James Beniger (1987: 356) wrote of how 'mass media have fostered the growth of pseudo-community over the past quarter century'. His perspective, even though formulated in the late 1980s, seems to assume that with the development of new interaction technologies we will increasingly 'experience the superficially personal relationships of pseudo-community, a hybrid of interpersonal and mass communication – born largely of computer technology' (Beniger 1987: 369).

DISCUSSION

The theories about online community argue that it is possible to build close relationships online with people that we have never met in person. They also claim that we can achieve a 'real' sense of being in a 'place' when using the internet and social media. In our everyday lives we mostly move about our different networks of offline as well as online connections without analysing this any further. But, as an experiment, try to think about the relationships you have with people online but with whom you have never been in the same physical location. Or think about 'places' you go to digitally – social media platforms, sites, forums, feeds. Ask yourself: Is it clearly the case that all such relationships and places are less genuine, rich, intimate, or sincere than your offline ones? If yes: why? If no: why? Compare your purely digital friendships and places with their offline or hybrid counterparts. What does the digital mode of interaction remove, or add, to a relation or setting? Are there any satisfactory ways to compensate online for the lack of in-person interaction?

In a study of multiplayer online role-playing games, Constance Steinkuehler and Dmitri Williams found that hard-core gamers who had reached a stage where long-term collaborative activities and large-scale collaborative problem-solving endeavours were the main activities, gaming was in fact quite work-like for the participants. For the more casual gamers, however, the games seemed to function as 'new (albeit virtual) "third places" for informal sociability' (Steinkuehler & Williams 2006: 903). They argue that those who claim that computer-mediated communication can't foster 'real' community are wrong. This is because such a view fails to see the nuances in what 'community' can mean. So while these researchers found that online multiplayer games can potentially function as third places, one might ask whether this goes for social media in general. Can the likes of Instagram, Twitter, online forums, and so on, be third places? Obviously, they have the potential to be, but that potential is not always realised. If one enters into a bar or goes to church, one makes the choice to participate in some respect – or at least to be seen by others. Online, however, as discussed in Chapter 4, we can sometimes choose to be invisible to some degree. And if we don't participate, we don't further any sense of community, or contribute to creating a milieu as a third place. Geert Lovink and Ned Rossiter (2005: n.p.) claim that:

> In the information society passivity rules. Browsing, watching, reading, waiting, thinking, deleting, chatting, skipping and surfing are the default conditions of online life.

If they are right, perhaps only a minority of people will create – because it takes active creation – communities or third places for themselves on the internet and on social media. A Facebook Group, a Twitter hashtag, or a discussion thread on a forum might be a third place for one user, while it is nothing even close to that for another. So, once more, the key to understanding the actual societal effect of digital media is an understanding of the wider context of their use. Sociologist Craig Calhoun (1998: 373–374) writes that:

> CMC [computer-mediated communication] is an enormously powerful bundling of technologies, rich in possibilities. It is convenient and also generative, giving rise to new practices of social interaction, new patterns in the production and dissemination of culture. [...] But not all technological possibilities become social realities, and the directions of actual change depend a good deal on existing institutions and distributions of power and resources.

Online versus offline community

Critics of theories of online communities have argued that many such perspectives are too much focused on what happens online. Because of this, the critics argue, they fail to see that most interaction that happens on the internet involves both an online and an offline component. For example, some research has shown that while participating on the internet and in social media can increase the feeling of community online, it does not necessarily compensate for the lack of offline community (Kendall 2011: 320–321). While online communities can bring together people who share a common interest, they do not make it any easier for people to get to know others 'in the multiplicity of their different identities' (Calhoun 1998: 392). To get a complete picture, one must look at how interactions on the internet fit together with all the other parts of people's lives. This is because computer-mediated communication does not happen in a separate reality. Rather, we bring with us all our social baggage – our gender, our socio-economic status, our cultural resources, our age, our offline connections with others, etc. – to our online interaction with others. This complexity raises questions about whether 'online community' really is viable as a concept. On the other hand, perhaps part of the criticism fails to see what Rheingold emphasised already in 1993, that digital media breathes a *new* form of life into a *new* form of community. Perhaps digital media are not as good at resurrecting old forms of community as they are at giving rise to entirely new social forms. Some perceive online community as less 'genuine' than offline community, but maybe 'our notions of the "genuine" are changing' (Jones 1998a: 21).

THE TURN TO NETWORKS

In the early days of the internet, being part of a group online meant connecting to chat rooms, BBSs, newsgroups, or being a member of an email list. These places were separate from each other, and sometimes required quite elaborate processes to connect to, for example, through dial-up modems and dedicated software. Under such circumstances, it is easy to see how the notion of online, or even 'virtual', community became popular. Going online meant entering a certain 'room' of your choosing by logging on, then staying in that room for a period of time, and then logging off. Today, the boundaries between online and offline are increasingly fluid, thanks to the advent of web 2.0 and the arrival of social media platforms like Facebook, Instagram, Twitter, and YouTube. The online and the offline have also become ever more entwined because of the fast-paced development in wireless connectivity and portable devices such as smartphones and smart watches.

When we examine how people socialise through digital media today, we decreasingly see a gravitation towards communities with clear boundaries and an obvious home base on a particular platform. Communities are perceived by researchers to have some sense of permanence or consistency, but as the landscape of digital and social media is ever-changing and increasing in complexity, the notion of online community seems less and less fitting for describing the means through which people connect with each other digitally. Should any aggregation of people on any social media platform be seen as a community? At what level of recognisability and continuity are communities formed? Is Twitter a community, or is it a hub for thousands of communities? Is every user's Facebook home feed a representation of a community? Rhetorical questions like these point out that a clear definition of community is hard to maintain in today's dynamic media landscape.

Because of this, internet research in recent years has tended to be more interested in talking about social networks than about communities. This does not mean that a *sense* of community, as discussed above, is nowhere to be found online. People can indeed cluster together in formations that foster common norms and where close bonds are established between individuals. But when we talk about the overarching logic of the internet and social media today, 'networks' is often a more fitting concept than 'community'. In practice, less than spending time in bounded social spaces, we use tools like Instagram, Twitter, Snapchat, Facebook, YouTube, and various messaging platforms to maintain different sets of relations and interact with loosely-knit sets of social ties. This multitude of connections can provide us with different things – a sense of community being one. In today's digital society, people tend to relate to a number of fragmented social networks, rather than being embedded in clearly delimited social groups.

Lee Rainie and Barry Wellman (2012) point out that there is a tendency to see the world either in terms of groups (as in the community perspective) or as individuals. Either people belong to relatively tight social formations, or they operate mainly on their own. In between, Rainie and Wellman argue, is the important middle ground of social networks. A social network perspective is focused on socially connected individuals and the patterns of their relations. A social network, then, is seen as a set of two or more entities, such as individuals or organisations, among which some form of exchange – of friendship, ideas, information, etc. – is going on. This, of course, does not have to be a digital network. An individual is often part of many different networks. These networks in turn have structures which influence the ways in which both individuals and the network as a whole behave. Rainie and Wellman (2012: 40–41) write that:

> In all but desert islands and laboratory situations, people are constantly entering and leaving networks, and these networks are complex structures with clusters, cleavages, and separate ties.

So, even if people often feel and think that they are acting quite independently, they really are embedded in, and influenced by, social networks that provide different constraints and opportunities. This means that these networks are 'environments' or 'structures', as discussed in Chapter 1. Social network analysis as a research method (see Chapter 12) is interested in phenomena such as whether a network is hierarchical or democratic, and in mapping the flow of information among members to measure the influence of particular members over others.

Like communities, social networks have been around for as long as society has existed. This is because they are a product of the basic human desire to form various types of associations, or groups. Obviously, this applies to many animals as well, and even at a microbiological level, in metabolic or neural networks. Networks are a fundamental part of nature. Historians J. R. and William McNeill (2003) have shown that 'human webs' have existed throughout the history of human life. First, in the form of exchange between hunter-gatherer tribes, and later, in the continuous local interaction between agricultural settlements, around 12,000 years ago, and in the first metropolitan cultures, around 6,000 years ago. Those connections were made through things like transportation, handling animals, and the exchange of goods.

The human web was spreading even further, and became tighter, with the rise of the bureaucratic empires in places such as India, China, and the Mediterranean. Technologies such as hub and spoke wheels, better roads, writing, and ships with larger capacity, contributed further to the establishment of these webs. The period between 1450 and 1800 saw a dramatic rise in urbanisation, and information circulated much faster and much cheaper than before. In the last century and a half, the global web has been thickened with the increasing volume and velocity of communication, and more efficient means of transport. First, there was the evolution of a 'mass society' – marked by the mass audiences of early mass media – and later, a network society where internet and social media are merely the latest technologies for making connections. Communications scholar Jan van Dijk (2006: 23) writes of this period of the human web:

It is no longer only quantitatively extending across the globe and becoming more voluminous, but it is also qualitatively changing the infrastructure and working of current societies. This comes to rest upon social and media networks of all kinds and at all levels of society.

Simmel: Classic network sociology

Simmel was the first sociologist to write explicitly in terms of social network dynamics. He did this in his comparison of 'dyads' (groups of two people) and 'triads' (groups of three people). He wrote that two-person groups were different from groups that were of

(Continued)

larger sizes. Dyads are marked by more intense emotions and fragility, while triads are more emotionally modulated, and can persist even if a member leaves and is replaced. Simmel's main theoretical contribution was that social structure, in network terms, is important by itself regardless of the particular individuals that compose the groups. He wrote:

> Where three elements, A, B, C, constitute a group, there is, in addition to the direct relationship between A and B, for instance, their indirect one, which is derived from their common relation to C. The fact that two elements are each connected not only by a straight line – the shortest – but also by a broken line, as it were, is an enrichment from a formal-sociological standpoint. Points that cannot be contacted by the straight line are connected by the third element, which offers a different side to each of the other two [...] Yet the indirect relation does not only strengthen the direct one. It may also disturb it. (Simmel 1950: 135)

I shall return to these ideas from a more methodological perspective in Chapter 12.

Social network analysis as a theory and method started to gain momentum in the 1960s, and there has been a surge in such research in the last few decades (see Chapter 12). But generally, social networks are not new. Craig Calhoun (1998: 380) wrote:

> The Internet is the latest wave of new communications technology to bring dramatic predictions of transformation in community and political activity. Its importance is unassailable, but we misunderstand it [...] if we exaggerate its novelty rather than situate it within a continuing series of transformations in communication and transportation capacities that have shaped the whole modern era.

What Rainie and Wellman (2012) call *the social network revolution* is not a result of digital media. There has been a broader change in society, they argue, in how people relate to each other more generally. Throughout the last hundred years or so, people have become less and less restricted by things such as nation, village, and neighbourhood, as they gravitate more and more towards a multitude of different social networks. Rainie and Wellman (2012: 22) write that group boundaries have weakened, and that 'flexible manoeuvrable connectivity' has increased. Once again, this is not about the internet and social media in particular. Rather, a number of things, such as wider-ranging travel, a growing number of mass media channels, secularisation, the transformation of work and the labour market, and demographic patterns (smaller families, fewer marriages, etc.), have contributed to this transformation.

NETWORK SOCIETY

Taken together, it has led to a situation where clearly defined and bounded groups and organisations have been supplanted by informal networks of involvement that are more *ad hoc*. There has been a shift from group-centric societies, in which most of one's friends are likely to know one another, to a network-centric society, where most of our network connections don't know each other. Sometimes we overlap the different networks of which we are part, and sometimes we handle things by keeping some of our relationships compartmentalised and apart from each other. Some scholars have seen this shift as being of equal importance to that of the shift from agrarian to industrial society. As you might remember from Chapter 1, Manuel Castells has popularised the notion that we live in a *network society*. His definition of the network society goes as follows:

> A network society is a society whose social structure is made of networks powered by microelectronics-based information and communication technologies. By social structure, I understand the organizational arrangements of humans in relations of production, consumption, reproduction, experience, and power expressed in meaningful communication coded by culture. (Castells 2004: 3)

Even though, Castells argues, networks constitute the fundamental logic by which all kinds of life function, with technological change, and the evolution of communication technologies, networks have become more efficient than the 'vertically organized command and control structures' that dominated in the pre-digital age (2004: 5). According to Castells, it is because of computers and the internet that network society becomes fully realised. Previously, networks were an important part of social life, but now they have become *the* most important part. In Castells' view, this goes way beyond a social network revolution where people start to connect in new ways. For him, it is about the whole of society. Industrialism, he writes, is 'subsumed by informationalism' – a new form of social organisation where all human activity, economy, politics, warfare, social movements, etc., follow a networked logic (2004: 8). And while the internet and computer-mediated communication shift society into overdrive, none of it would have happened had it not been for a number of other social processes. In Castells' description, the network society is the result of:

> the accidental coincidence, in the 1970s, of three independent processes [...]: the crisis and restructuring of industrialism [...]; the freedom-oriented, cultural social movements of the late 1960s and early 1970s; and the revolution in information and communication technologies. (2004: 15)

The network society, in Castells' interpretation, is not only about the increasingly networked character of people's social connections. It is also about a large-scale and complete transformation of how society is organised. Network society is organised around globally interdependent networks of production, consumption, business, politics, and so on. He writes of a 'grid of networks organizing/dominating the planet' that includes some individuals, groups, nations, or regions, while excluding others (2004: 24). Anyone who wants to exercise control over others in this world of networks must be able to command two basic mechanisms: the ability to 'program' (affecting the goals and modes of operation of networks), and the ability to 'switch' (connecting different networks to ensure their cooperation). The real power-holders, however, are the networks themselves. Successful programming and switching will lead to the emergence of a new form of subject, which operates in ways similar to those theorised by philosopher of science Bruno Latour (2005: 46) in actor-network theory, the key point of which is that 'an actor is what is made to act by many others':

> An 'actor' in the hyphenated expression actor-network is not the source of an action but the moving target of a vast array of entities swarming toward it.

Simply put, networks aggregate people's actions thereby becoming a form of aggregated actors in their own right.

ONLINE SOCIAL NETWORKS

Social networks were not invented together with the digitalisation of society. But social networking demands some sort of mediation in order for our relationships to stretch beyond the local realm of connections that we can make and maintain through the medium of face-to-face speech. The written word, the telegraph, and the telephone are examples of media technologies that have been important for maintaining social networks since their invention and popularisation. The internet and social media obviously extend and amplify the reach of people's connections. As internet researcher Steve Jones (1998b: xv) put it, the internet is 'a "backbone" through which networks link up with each other'. Online networks that provide a material environment for social networks make new forms of sociality possible.

In short, the internet supports social networks and social networking. The very point of the internet is that it consists of computers that are networked together. This makes for a suitable infrastructure for communication in social networks too. In the early days of the internet, computer-supported social networks were already emerging among individuals who were interacting through networked computers. So indeed, the online communities discussed earlier in this chapter can be seen as networks as well. In fact, Rheingold, a key theorist of online communities, wrote in the second edition of *The Virtual Community*, about Wellman, a key theorist of online social networks:

> If I had encountered sociologist Barry Wellman and learned about social network analysis when I first wrote about cyberspace cultures, I could have saved us all a decade of debate by calling them 'online social networks' instead of 'virtual communities'. (Rheingold 2000: 359)

The networked character of online interaction became even more visible and pronounced with the major breakthrough of social network sites such as Friendster in 2002, LinkedIn and MySpace in 2003, and Facebook in 2004 (see Chapter 2). In a seminal paper, Ellison and boyd (2007: 211) define *social network sites* as:

> web-based services that allow individuals to (1) construct a public or semi-public profile within a bounded system, (2) articulate a list of other users with whom they share a connection, and (3) view and traverse their list of connections and those made by others within the system.

They agree however, that the specific parameters and terminology will vary between different sites. These platforms make it possible for users to articulate their social networks and to make them visible to themselves and to other people, who may or may not be part of these networks. They call the sites social network sites – rather than social networking sites – as they argue that the primary activity is not to engage in networking to find new connections, but on simply self-presenting one's already existing social network. Not everyone agrees with this, but claim instead that people actually also do networking on the sites, initiating new relationships. Porter (2015: 166) argues that the socio-technical features of social network(ing) sites allow members to articulate and maintain as well as establish and extend their network of relationships. This is because these platforms have both a 'connection capability' (to invite and be invited to networks) and a 'communication capability' (to provide, view, and manage content).

While social network(ing) platforms have these specific characteristics, it is hard – and unnecessary – to maintain a distinction between these on the one hand, and online communities on the other. Indeed, many online communities are of a networked character, and in many social networks, at least in parts of them, a sense of community might be present. Porter argues that many online social networks, at least the ones that are sustainable, are becoming more and more community oriented. It seems that, like social bonds, sharing and mutuality is needed for online social networks to survive for longer periods of time.

Not too much, not too little

In an interesting study, digital media researcher Petter Bae Brandtzæg (2012) found that neither the most active, nor the least active, users of social networking sites – this is what he chose to call them – were unable to reap the potential rewards of the platforms. In a series of surveys, 'Sporadics' (low-level users) and 'Lurkers' (passive users who did not contribute or interact) reported low levels of face-to-face interaction and offline acquaintances as well. The most intense users ('Debaters' and 'Advanced' users), especially males, reported high levels of loneliness. The in-between category of 'Socializers' (those using the sites mainly for interaction with family and friends) felt less lonely and were more engaged in face-to-face interaction as well. Brandtzæg's conclusion was that social networking sites work best when they build on strong and pre-existing offline relationships.

NETWORKED INDIVIDUALISM

The quantitative and qualitative evolution of the human web, together with the emergence of the internet and social media, has brought about, Rainie and Wellman (2012) argue, a new *social operating system*. They use the metaphor of an operating system because, similar to computer systems, societies have networked structures for how people connect, communicate, and exchange information. These structures provide opportunities and constraints (see Chapter 1), procedures and rules, and through these, they shape society. The operating system in mass society was concentrated around units like communities, households, and workgroups. The new social operating system, by contrast, is personal. They call it *networked individualism*, as it puts the individual at the centre of the different networks that she or he draws on in different contexts, and for various uses and gratifications. Rainie and Wellman (2012: 12) write that:

> people are not rugged individualists – even when they think they are. Many meet their social, emotional, and economic needs by tapping into sparsely knit networks of diverse associates rather than relying on tight connections to a relatively small number of core associates.

Networked individualism, as defined by Lee Rainie and Barry Wellman (2012), reflects the social transformations that have taken place throughout the 20th and 21st centuries, where people have increasingly shifted away from tightly-knit communities. In networked individualism, each person sits at the centre of her or his own set of networks. Rather than being members of external entities, such as a church or political organisation, networked individuals command their own unique and ego-centric networks. These networks are unique in the same way that every person's experience of a social media platform, such as Instagram, will be individualised in the form of a personal feed. If Instagram was a traditional community, all members would share the same space, and have the opportunity to interact with all others in the community. Yet, despite the individual customisation, the content that any one indi-vidual sees on Instagram will largely overlap with what *some* others can see. Many connections are shared, but everyone is in the middle of her or his own network. That the networks are *egocentric* – with the individual at the centre of a personalised set of networks – does not necessarily mean that people will act in egoistic ways.

The networked individual lacks any one single 'home' community, but has partial membership in multiple networks, meaning that there are a variety of social ties to rely on (Rainie & Wellman 2012). Therefore, the new operating system demands that people develop new skills and strategies. They must network actively to maintain ties, forge alliances that are useful, and remember which parts of their networks can be mobilised for what ends. People must also deal with the instability and volatility of networks, since there is frequent turnover and change. In other words, networked individualism is liberat-ing, since it loosens the grip of communities that might be limiting, but it also takes effort. Rainie and Wellman are optimistic, however, that the internet and social media will help the networked individuals to maintain and nourish their social ties. Geert Lovink (2008: 241–242) also believes that networks don't automatically become powerful. He argues that the informality of online networks is often celebrated, but that they must be actively organised to function in productive ways. In what he calls, 'the age of disengagement', 'the default user is the lurker' and 'engagement is the state of exception'.

DISCUSSION

If you have an account on a social media platform (Instagram, Twitter, Facebook, etc.), use that as a starting point to think about the different networks you are connected to. Looking through your list of accounts that you follow and are followed by, you might be able to iden-tify people as belonging to certain networks, such as family, childhood friends, classmates, neighbours, people you work with, or have worked with, friends from an organisation that you are a member of, friends that you have found online due to some common interest, and so on. Reflect on the different roles of these networks in your life. For what needs do you turn to the different connections that you have? Are there any overlaps between the networks, or are they largely separate from one another? Do you have any key friends that bridge your different networks?

111

FIELDS OF TOGETHERNESS

Ultimately, the most important question is not whether 'communities' or 'networks' best describes how people interact online. As you will have realised when reading this chapter, the notion of community was more popular in early internet research, while thinking in terms of networks has become more common in recent years. This has to do both with changes in how society, the internet, and social media function, and with a more general trend in research towards an intensified interest in networks. In practice, as pointed out by communications researcher Maria Bakardjieva (2003), a continuum of different forms of being and acting together is constantly emerging online. For some aspects of this *virtual togetherness*, thinking in terms of the boundedness and emotional exchange of communities is more fitting, while others will be better understood by employing the perspective of fragmented and sprawling networks. In order for research to move forward, we must also stay open to the construction of entirely new concepts for understanding new and unexpected variations of digital media use that will emerge in the future. Bakardjieva (2003: 310–311) writes:

> Users approach the medium […] from a variety of situational motivations, needs and ideologies. In doing that, they generate a rich repertory of use genres, each of which needs careful consideration and evaluation on its own merits.

Similarly, anthropologist John Postill (2008) thinks that there are problems with the dominance of 'the community/network paradigm'. Instead, he suggests that turning to, and developing, theories about *social fields* might be the way forward. The important point that both Bakardjieva and Postill are making is that the either-or of community versus network may be limiting for research. Concepts like community, network, togetherness, or fields might be helpful to a varying degree, in different situations, to help make sense of how people interact and connect in digital society. But in the end, they are just theories. As I have argued in another book, it does not really matter what we call our object of study, as long as we are able to map and understand it in practice:

> The only way to comprehensively deal with technological, cultural, and social aspects of the Internet without remaining in a purely philosophical domain is to empirically analyze what actually happens. (Lindgren 2013: 143)

CHAPTER SUMMARY

In this present chapter, I have built further on the discussions that were introduced in Chapter 4 about how micro-level interactions play out in digital society. We have looked at how digital media platforms can play an important role in how people relate to others and come together, consciously, or consequentially, in different social agglomerations. I have introduced the concept of 'communities', both rooting it in classic social theory and drawing on more recent writings about online communities. I have also introduced the partly overlapping but also different concept of 'networks' to describe logics for how people cluster together in somewhat more mechanistic terms. While 'community' and 'network' are words that can be used to describe social groups in any era throughout the age of the internet, this chapter has also explained that we may be moving in the direction of a larger reliance on networks at the cost of communities. The notion that we live in a 'network society' has been influential in social science, and a number of parallel developments in technology and society have put a stronger emphasis on networks, both in empirical and conceptual terms. The chapter has also briefly addressed the fact that other concepts, for example that of 'fields', may be more useful as they can clearly include both community and network dimensions.

FURTHER READING

Rheingold, Howard (1993/2000). *The Virtual Community*. Cambridge, MA: The MIT Press.
Rheingold's book from the early 1990s, exploring and explaining how people connect in communities on the internet, is a modern internet research classic. The key argument is that community online can be as real and as multifaceted as any offline community. The revised edition from 2000 contains an additional chapter where the author revisits and develops some of his earlier ideas in light of the intense developments in online communication.

Rainie, Lee & Wellman, Barry (2012). *Networked*. Cambridge, MA: The MIT Press.
In spite of its rather one-sided empirical focus on the United States, Rainie and Wellman's book *Networked* is one of the most excellent recent books about the internet and society. The two researchers write in an accessible way, with lots of everyday case examples, and yet manage to develop new theory with their ideas of a new social operating system driven by networked individuals.

Castells, Manuel (1996). *The Rise of the Network Society*. Malden, MA: Blackwell.
Castells' book from 1996, actually the first volume in a massive trilogy, is a seminal work about the rise of the network society fuelled by the growth of computers and the internet. The book introduces a range of theoretical concepts for discussing the global and

(Continued)

large-scale transformations that are brought about through the coming of an 'informational economy' which leads to new forms of social exclusion and polarisation. Castells writes of a world organised around digital media where basic categories such as time and space are renegotiated.

Ellison, Nicole B. & boyd, danah (2007). Social Network Sites: Definition, History, and Scholarship. *Journal of Computer-Mediated Communication*, 13(1), 210–230.

One of the most cited research articles in the history of internet research, written by Nicole Ellison and danah boyd, was actually an introductory paper to a themed set of papers in the *Journal of Computer-Mediated Communication* in 2007. The authors describe the key features of social network sites, give a historical overview, and propose a definition. The social media landscape has changed since 2007, but the article is still useful, and effectively a classic.

VISUALITY AND VISIBILITY

Key Questions

- How does the evolution of digital society relate to visual culture?

- In what ways have new visual phenomena, such as selfies, emoji, GIFs, and memes, introduced new elements into social interaction?

- What does it mean that selfies are a 'technology of the self'?

- What are 'videos of affinity' and what is their social use?

- How can the social meaning of images and videos online be analysed?

Key Concepts

The visual turn * postmodernity * selfie * technologies of the self * performativity * affinity spaces * videos of affinity

This chapter is about how being on the internet today is largely a visual experience. While early social media tools and platforms, such as BBSs, Usenet, and the early web, were largely text-based, images and videos are key to today's digital society. On platforms like Instagram, Twitter, YouTube, and TikTok, we may also enter our personal photos and videos into flows that blur private and public boundaries.

In her book *Hamlet on the Holodeck*, digital media researcher Janet Murray (1997: 153) writes of how 'the interactor, whether as navigator, protagonist, explorer, or builder' makes use of a 'repertoire of possible steps and rhythms to improvise a particular dance among the many, many possible dances'. This is her poetic way of saying that on the internet, people engage in a vast number of different subgenres where different *narrative pleasures* are developed. From one perspective, platforms like Instagram and YouTube are simply online archives where one can find virtually any type of photo or video. Instagram users post images and stories in a wide range of styles and genres, and so is also the case with YouTube videos. But there are some subgenres on there that are of specific interest in relation to the topic of this book – how people relate to each other, and the world around them, in digital society. Two examples of such genres are selfies and personal YouTube videos, both of which we shall explore in more detail in this chapter. The latter will be approached using anthropologist Patricia Lange's notion of 'videos of affinity'. Aside from the ability to share pictures and video clips, the internet has also given rise to a number of other unique visual phenomena, such as avatars, emoji, memes (for example, in the style of so-called image macros), GIFs, and the particular type of 'stories' (Snapchat stories, Instagram stories) that combine several of these formats.

THE VISUAL TURN

There is sometimes talk of a *visual turn* in the social and cultural sciences, meaning that there has been increased interest in how images and visuals, photos and videos, affect how we experience culture, and how we interact with each other. Writer and film director Jean-Louis Comolli (1980: 121) wrote about how society is driven by representation:

> If the social machine manufactures representations, it also manufactures itself from representations – the latter operative at once as means, matter and condition of sociality.

He felt, in other words, that society – 'the social machine' – is thriving on the production and consumption of images and depictions. He claimed even that this was the very basis of sociality. Images, paintings, symbols, and visualisations are what hold society together, and has done so since the very beginning. But Comolli (1980: 122) further argues that 'the second half of the nineteenth century lives in a sort of frenzy of the visible'. This is the same point made by many theorists who are associated with so-called postmodern thinking, such as sociologist Jean Baudrillard, who used concepts like *hyperreality* and *simulation* to argue that representation and reproduction were key mechanisms in postmodern society. The idea is that, since the last few decades of the 20th century, there has been an explosion of visual culture, where pictures and video have assumed a dominant position. This is a consequence of the development of film and cinema, television, colour printing, advertising, video, computers, and so on.

Postmodernity is what happened when modern society, as we knew it during the 19th and 20th centuries, entered into a form of cultural crisis during latter part of the 20th century. Things like the 'grand narratives' of history, the idea that things could only get better, and the belief that there was always only one truth no longer seemed convincing to many people. Still, no viable alternative had emerged. This led to culture becoming ironic and artificial. Communications scholar Nicholas Mirzoeff (2013) claims that it was specifically a *visual crisis of culture* that made the postmodern condition emerge. While modern society had a strong tendency to picture and visualise things, the spoken and written word were still privileged as illustrations of ideas during that era. In postmodern culture, the increased focus on the visual challenges this hegemony. Mirzoeff (2013: 4) writes that:

> While print culture is certainly not going to disappear, the fascination with the visual and its effects that was a key feature of modernism has engendered a postmodern culture that is at its most postmodern when it is visual.

In digital society, the interaction and communication between people through the use of images on platforms like Instagram and Snapchat and through videos on platforms such as YouTube and TikTok are prime examples of this cultural tendency towards a prominence of imagery. Digital cameras and smartphones have thoroughly changed the role of visuals in everyday life, as well as in culture and politics. Sociologist Kiku Adatto (2008) says that we live in 'the age of the photo op'. Just as with other social forms, such as the communities and networks discussed in the previous chapter, the focus on capturing, watching, and sharing images and audiovisual content is not something entirely new. But rather, the pattern has been intensified in digital society.

Ever since photography and film were invented in the 19th century, their realism has fascinated people. As these have become widely used technologies, and as photos and videos have become increasingly easy to capture, reproduce, and circulate, (audio)visuals have become more and more prominent elements of society and culture. But today it is not necessarily the realism of imagery that fascinates us. Adatto (2008: 7) writes that: 'Today we pride ourselves on our knowledge that the camera can lie, that pictures can be fabricated, packaged, and manipulated.' She argues that in a mediated culture, people even come to develop an affection for the artificial element of what they see, as they start to appreciate images as images (see the discussion of memes in Chapter 2). This is even more valid, as we also live in the age of image editing software, where 'photoshopping' has entered our vocabulary as a lexical verb. Easy-to-use tools allow anyone to alter images with fast results, for purposes ranging from humour to deception.

Adatto maps the history from TV shows like *Candid Camera* in the 1960s – where the camera was hidden – through *America's Funniest Home Videos* in the 1990s and

117

onwards – where most filmed subjects were aware of the camera's presence. Today, on social media, a popular format for online photos is the 'mirror selfie' where the subject is not only conscious of the camera, but where the camera(phone) itself is clearly seen in the image – sometimes styled with smartphone covers that express identity.

The visual turn demands that new perspectives are developed to understand the new modes of expression, as the model of textuality might no longer be working. Philosopher Régis Debray sees the history of society in terms of 'mediaspheres' – the shifting environments where messages are transported. Debray (1996: 26) argues that each 'mediological period' has its 'collective personality or psychological profile'. We live now, he says, in the 'videosphere', an era of computer graphics and audio-visual content which is marked by an 'instantaneity/ubiquity of messages' (1996: 28). In this age, which has come after the logosphere of speaking and writing, and the graphosphere of printing, we are 'rediscovering the values of the bodily' (1996: 36).

He argued that we are rediscovering the possibility of expressing things with our bodies after a long historical phase where words and letters have been dominant. In addition to this, one can also claim that the smartphone age means that visuals are increasingly captured in everyday settings and in places like bathrooms, bedrooms, and kitchens. The traditional media photography shots of talking heads in news studios, or of styled and prepared presenters or actors, is challenged by a rich stream of personal and vernacular photos and videos.

SELFIES

As discussed in previous chapters, digital society has brought along changes in how people express themselves. This development is intensified as networks sprawl and technology becomes increasingly portable. One such new form of visual self-expression is the *selfie*, a photographic self-portrait shared on social media. The coming into being of the selfie is based on hardware – smartphone cameras – as well as software – social media platforms – that sit at the centre of today's social world.

The popularity of selfies might have to do with the more general tendency towards visual fascination, as described in the previous section of this chapter. It could also be interpreted as an expression of today's culture as being individualistic, focused on identity work, superficial, or even narcissistic. But the explosive growth of the phenomenon also has to do with the global saturation of phones with cameras, and with the large-scale introduction of front-facing cameras on such phones. In fact, that feature, occurring for the first time in 2003, was originally intended for video calls but was soon adopted by users for taking stills at arm's length. The first use of the word 'selfie' is said to have been in Australia. In September 2002, a young man posted a photo of his damaged bottom lip, writing in a forum post on the site of public broadcaster ABC: 'sorry about the focus, it was a selfie' (ABC 2013).

Of course, self-portraits are not new. People have depicted themselves through various techniques and media since the beginning of time, and, naturally, even users of the very early cameras in the 19th century sometimes turned the lens towards themselves. But these photographic self-portraits were still mostly random events, at times simply taken to use up the last frame of a roll of film. As a recognisable and codified genre, however, the selfie is a product of digital media, and it has introduced several new elements into social interaction.

The Oxford Dictionaries named 'selfie' as the word of the year in 2013, defining it as 'a photograph that one has taken of oneself, typically one taken with a smartphone or webcam and uploaded to a social media website'. Their editorial director Judy Persall explained that 'selfie' had already emerged as a tag on the social photo site Flickr back in 2004, but the word became widely used in mainstream media around 2012. She also explained that the usage of the '–ie' suffix likely has to do with the term having been conceived in Australian English (Oxford Dictionaries 2013). Communications researchers Katharina Lobinger and Cornelia Brantner (2015: 1848) argue that selfies have indeed 'become their own genre of visual self-representation with its own conventions, representational techniques, and poses'. Photographically speaking, the recognisable attributes of selfies – such as the often-visible arm of the photographer bearing witness to how the photo was made – make their production process visible.

Communications researcher Aaron Hess talks about the selfie as an 'assemblage' – a grouping together – of four different elements. First, the self. The photos present a version of ourselves, whether staged or not. Second, physical space. The place where they are shot – at home, at school, at a restaurant, outdoors – also expresses something. Third, the device. The actual camera(phone), the perspective, the way we hold our arms, and so on, also affects the selfie. And fourth, the network. Selfies presume that a networked social media audience will receive it, and thereby it invites us to liking and sharing it.

Selfies are no doubt a form of social action (cf. Chapter 2) that happens in some form of social context with some sort of intention. It is a crucial trait of selfies that they are shared through online social networks. One might therefore say that the selfie is social by definition. And as it is fundamentally social, it also has to do with people's need for affirmation – something that can only be fulfilled in interacting with others (Ehlin 2015: 22). In comparison with traditional self-portraits, selfies are also generally much more spontaneous and casual. The latter are predominantly taken and shared by people whom we would not conventionally define as artists.

The selfie is consciously social. It is created to be viewed, in the present, and when we look at a selfie, we are aware of this intention. Internet researchers Theresa Senft and Nancy Baym (2015: 1589) write that it is part of the character of a selfie that it initiates a number of relationships. The most obvious of these is the one between viewer and viewed, but they also point to how selfies set in motion relational processes between images and the software used to filter and share them, between users and the architecture of social media platforms, and between the subject as simultaneously being photographer and the photographed.

Selfies offer many possibilities for people – human actors – to be active, in selecting, framing, filtering, and so on. But selfies also engage what Latour (2005) would call non-humans. The creation, display, circulation, and monetisation of selfies occur through a number of technological artefacts, such as cameras, servers, algorithms, screens, and so on. Senft and Baym (2015: 1589) argue that once a selfie enters the internet, it instantly becomes part of an infrastructure that detaches it from its original time and place of production.

Using the words of cultural studies theorist Stuart Hall (1972), the selfie is 'encoded' by its sender in a certain way (drawing on thoughts, aspirations, attitudes, posing, filtering, and so on), to be 'decoded' by its receivers in either preferred, negotiated, or oppositional ways. Such decoding can happen only in the mind of the receiver, or by responses in the form of actions that are digitally social, such as likes, comments, or remixes. In other words, taking and sharing selfies entails a whole complexity of looking and framing both inwards and outwards.

We might think of selfies in the first instance as pictures of lone individuals. Indeed, celebrities who are active on social media – and whose celebrity largely rests on this fact – have contributed to shaping the genre. But the social aspects of selfies also go beyond the mere sharing of solo images. For example, taking selfies together with others – with one person holding the camera and one or more individuals sticking their heads into the frame – can be used as a means of showing which groups one belongs to. Political and religious leaders figure more and more often in shots with other authority figures, as well as with 'ordinary' people. Visually framing and sharing one's relations with school friends, family, celebrities, or authority figures, in the form of selfies, is a type of self-presentation which is unique to digital society.

Selfies also raise questions about social norms (Miltner & Baym 2015), such as: Who can take a selfie? When and where is it appropriate to take them? More generally, there has been a debate over the inappropriateness of selfies taken in some places and situations, such as at grave sites, the Anne Frank House, the Holocaust Memorial, at Chernobyl, in front of burning houses, hostage situations, together with homeless people, and so on. Furthermore, some have worried that the increased use of selfies in politics is 'turning politicians into teenagers' (Dooley 2014), and that 'the tyranny of selfies' will transform the political climate for the worse (Merica 2016). Such reactions may have to do with selfies still being a relatively new phenomenon around which social norms are in the process of being formed. Other observers have argued that selfies can have many positive functions, such as helping in self-exploration, making connections, and balancing beauty ideals (Rutledge 2013a).

Still, it has also been claimed that selfies are related to body dysmorphic disorder (McKay 2014), and news media have highlighted the phenomenon of 'selfie deaths' following from people taking risks in trying to capture the perfect selfie in front of a train, on top of a building, at bull runs, and so on (Rizzo 2015). A new genre like this might need new perspectives altogether to be fully understood. Still, it is natural that we initially react by falling back on norms that have been formed around other forms of photography. Media psychologist Pamela Rutledge (2013b: n.p.) writes that 'the sheer volume and publicness of selfies defies any models we have', so we tend to think that they 'violate social rules of self-presentation and therefore something's wrong'. She continues:

> If the people in selfies aren't famous or being paid to pose, then it must indicate a moral failing and they are labeled bragging, attention seeking, self-focused or narcissistic. (Rutledge 2013b: n.p.)

Like Rutledge, social media researcher Anne Burns (2015) thinks that a 'common sense' understanding of selfies is that they are narcissistic. The very word 'selfie', she writes, hints at a form of egotism. Furthermore, people tend to understand selfies in terms of their subjects being vain and overly preoccupied with their appearance. McLuhan (1964: 41) anticipated this when writing about how people in the age of electronic media 'become fascinated by any extension of themselves in any material other than themselves'.

Part of why selfies have been seen as a social problem has to do with generational divides. Media technologies, platforms, and practices that are new to us often set in motion *media panics*. Therefore, each generation of adults will question the media use of younger generations. Young people's media use is different from the forms that were known before, and therefore it can generate worry. Much like popular print media in the 19th century, film in the early 20th century, rock music in the 1950s, and so on, selfies today are seen by some researchers and commentators as potentially dangerous to society. Media panics are polarising reactions that blow the possible consequences of the new technology out of proportion. Drawing on sociologist Stanley Cohen's (1972) theory of so-called 'moral panics', media researcher Kirsten Drotner (1999) traces the history of media panics from the 18th century up until the age of the internet.

So, what is the purpose of selfies? Media and fashion researcher Lisa Ehlin (2015: 13) writes:

> If I post a selfie (a shared social media self-portrait) I desire to reach out, enable contact. I watch myself anew in a form of endless self-fashioning. Images are personal, yet implicit.

But selfies not only show what we look like, but also where we are, what we are doing, who we think might be watching, and who we want to be. Wendt (2014: 8) speculates that: 'Perhaps, our preoccupation with Instagram is simple: it offers us infinite versions of ourselves, as though each picture promises a better version.' In taking and sharing selfies, versions of the images can be created through the different filters included in photo-sharing apps, which enable experimenting with different styles that allow us to see ourselves in new or different ways. This can also be associated with the possibility of viewing ourselves from the outside, as digital culture researcher Jill Walker Rettberg (2014: 27) describes how the raw and revealing character of selfies, alongside the practices of running them through retro – and other – filters, gives the image 'a distance that makes them new to us':

> We see ourselves and our surroundings as if we are outside of ourselves, through a retro filter or in the same poses and layouts as we see fashion models or homes in magazine spreads. (Rettberg 2014: 27)

But the openness of the possibilities for being whomever we might want is limited. As with most other visual culture, selfies are definitely associated with the politics of gender. For example, one of the popular selfie poses is the mouth-pouting 'duck-face', especially prominent among female subjects. This gendered pejorative term refers to selfie takers who 'suck in their cheeks to highlight their cheekbones, which tends to push the lips out in a manner that appears duck-like' (Katz & Crocker 2015: 1866).

The way in which selfies are used and talked about can contribute to maintaining compliance with gendered social norms, and also govern under what circumstances men or women can participate in social and political settings online. As selfies are part of society and people's construction of identities more generally, not only gender, but also other social divisions have an effect as well. Sociologists Apryl Williams and Beatriz Aldana Marquez (2015) have found that many white men don't take selfies as they are seen as 'unmanly'. Latino and black men, on the other hand, were more positive to taking and sharing selfies. Those research results point to selfies having a potential for self-empowerment, as well as for expressing alternatives to hegemony. More generally, selfies, while in part reproducing social stereotypes related to power, can also potentially be used to take control in various ways. Philosopher Michel Foucault (1988: 18) wrote about something called *technologies of the self*,

> which permit individuals to effect by their own means or with the help of others a certain number of operations on their own bodies and souls, thoughts, conduct, and way of being, so as to transform themselves in order to attain a certain state of happiness, purity, wisdom, perfection, or immortality.

Selfies, or social media in general for that matter, can be seen as such a technology, which we use for framing, filtering, presenting, and sharing ourselves. While selfies, on the one hand, are enforced by, and enforcing, social power and norms, they may also enable performances that resist such things (Losh 2015: 1649). In other words, the fact that selfies might be seen as superficial photos that express things such as problematic beauty ideals does not exclude the possibility of them being powerfully progressive. Philosopher Judith Butler (1990), one of the originators of queer theory, has argued that identities are performances. Her concept of *performativity* suggests that nothing within our identities is fixed, so people maintain their gender identity, like any other aspect of identity, by repeatedly performing it in similar ways. If people start doing things differently, society can gradually change. The problem is, however, as Butler argues, that the performances are not always conscious, and that some performances are repeated so often throughout culture and media that they appear 'natural' or 'true'. Still, this is just an illusion and the seemingly fixed identities – gendered, racialised, and other – can be subverted and reinvented through the accumulation of alternative performances.

VIDEOS OF AFFINITY

Affinity spaces is a name for a type of social setting that sometimes takes shape online. The term was coined by linguist and educational psychologist James Paul Gee (2005), who suggests that rather than communities (see Chapter 5), we should talk of spaces of affinity in order to capture current forms of digitally social affiliation. In affinity spaces, people come together because of a feeling of similarity or like-mindedness. Gee says that such ways of relating to, and connecting with, each other have become increasingly prominent in today's digital world. Affinity can be defined as feelings of connection between people. Anthropologist Bonnie Nardi (2005: 99) writes:

> A feeling of connection, as stated, is an openness to interacting with another person. Affinity is achieved through activities of social bonding in which people come to feel connected with one another, readying them for further communication.

Affinity in this sense is based on other things than broad categorisations such as nationality, ethnicity, class, gender, disability, and so on. In her research on YouTube, Patricia Lange has, among other things, been interested in how the visually enhanced communication through YouTube videos relates to establishing affinities. In a study mapping the patterns and principles by which video creators get the attention of viewers, she introduced the notion of *videos of affinity*. She underlines the social aspects of communication by means of YouTube videos, specifically focusing on how videos are used socially to generate feelings of connection between people. In her two-year ethnographic study, she looked closely at videos that seemed to try to establish some sort of 'communicative connection'. Lange (2009: 71) writes that:

> Videos of affinity attempt to maintain feelings of connection with potential others who identify or interpellate themselves as intended viewers of the video.

In order for the creator of a video to be able to 'interpellate' (address) the potential others, he or she needs to capture their attention. However, Lange continues, attention does not come for free. Rather, it is an achievement that requires work, and the point here is that this work is done visually – through video. The definition of videos of affinity is that they are focused on the present, that they aim to create feelings of connection, and that they fulfil the function of maintaining a certain communication channel as open and active. The videos seem to say: I am (still) here! This is what I look like! I am in this room! This is my life at present! You can still subscribe/like/comment on what I do! We continue to be connected! In that sense, these videos are social actions that foster communities or networks.

In other words, videos of affinity are not meant for everyone. Even though anyone can watch them – as long as they are posted as public videos – they typically are interesting only for certain groups of people who desire a connection – who feel an affinity – with the topic, attitude, values, or maker of the video. Lange (2009: 83) writes that these videos often lack any traditional form of content. Such videos are often neither original nor very 'interesting' – in the most common sense of the word. Instead, they tend to be stereotypical, stylised, and draw heavily on in-jokes and other jargon.

Historically, we can think of the genre of home movies – analogue or digital – traditionally recorded by fathers during specific rituals, such as graduations, birthdays, weddings, and Christmases, often simply as a means of remembering the occasions. In some sense, these are videos of affinity: they connect the family members, relatives, and friends who get to watch them. Home movies are also mildly interesting to a wider audience – not counting the genre in its own right created through the wider dissemination of bloopers and failures captured (accidentally or not) in such settings. The proliferation of affordable digital cameras and cameraphones, however, has made it possible to capture more personal things and smaller everyday moments. At the same time, the internet and YouTube have changed the ways in which the videos are distributed. Instead of small-scale home viewing, there is potentially massive global sharing. Personal media can be spread by, and to, heterogeneous and dispersed groups of people. Lange argues that this can disrupt the traditional father-driven – patriarchal, middle-class, nuclear family-oriented – forms of home movie making, by showing different locations, identities, and values. Still, young video bloggers and other non-conventional creators are unfortunately and undeservedly often criticised for sharing pointless stuff.

So videos of affinity are not primarily about documenting things in order to be able to remember them in the future. Instead, even though, from a technical perspective, they are recordings of something that has already happened, they fulfil the function of getting across the feeling that a particular moment – which might be large or small – is shared between the creator of the video and its viewers, subscribers, likers, and commenters. This 'work of connection', as Nardi (2005) would call it, might seem meaningless when taken out of context, but is very important in keeping a field of communication open within certain groups.

Lange (2009: 83) says that a video of affinity is not a 'cinematic end point', but rather 'a mediated moment in an ongoing social relationship'. The point of the videos is not their particular content, but their role of maintaining connections between people simply through keeping channels open. And videos of affinity do this largely through visual means, as they tend to revolve around evidence of the live body of their creators.

So even though the creators of the videos may be talking to the camera throughout, the creation of affinity – as Lange shows – relies on a number of aspects of visuality and visibility that are conveyed in the videos. Videos of affinity, often shot in home environments, tend to be spontaneous recordings – or maybe carefully staged to appear spontaneous. They are about sharing informal experiences, and often include laughs, the making of crazy faces, and editing with comic effects. The body is often at the centre of these videos, as they will likely be shot at quite close range, enabling close inspection of the facial attributes and expressions of the speaker. Nardi (2005: 114), referring to social presence theory, writes of how bonding and commitment is best promoted when people meet, and see, each other in person 'with the body in full view'.

In line with this, videos of affinity quite often feature their subjects eating or drinking in front of the camera. Having an apple, drinking water, coffee, or a cup of tea, while addressing the viewers, enhances the casual character of the videos. One will quite often see video bloggers discussing things such as whether they are tired, hungry, bored, whether they had (or need) a haircut, and in other ways providing social 'proof' of their (recorded) bodies. In other words, videos of affinity are social tools – drawing on visibility – that lack any traditional artistic, narrative, or informational content. Instead, they simply 'show' the online presence of individuals in order to establish communicative connections with others. In this sense, like selfies, they are uniquely and natively digital and visual social phenomena. Lange argues further that, while YouTube videos are often analysed around a simplifying division between professional versus user-created content, a focus on affinity allows us to see more interesting dynamics across such categories.

125

EMOJI

Another form of visual communication, which has been enabled by the internet are emoji. These small visual symbols, that we combine with other modes of visual and textual communication, are now ever-present, and play a very important role in the everyday digital interaction between people. They have quickly become so well integrated in the ways in which we communicate in chats and messages that we rarely think deeply about how they actually transform how we express ourselves.

The first 'smiley' symbol is said to have been created in the early 1960s by graphic designer Harvey Ross Ball to be printed on buttons to boost morale among employees at an American insurance company (Stark & Crawford 2015). Unrelated to its initial intended purpose, the button became a hit across the USA and the symbol started to spread throughout popular culture. By the early 1970s it could be found on a range of mugs, t-shirts, and stickers.

Yet another decade later, in the early 1980s, digital *emoticons* saw the light of day, as they were first used in forum conversations among a group of researchers at Carnegie Mellon University, who communicated through an online bulletin board, to indicate if messages were intended to be humorous or not. They did this by using :-) and :-((Fahlman 1982). While there are previous historic examples of experimenting with typographical symbols to mimic facial expressions (Evans 2017), this marked the start of the kind of use that emoticons have today. In some contexts, the words 'emoji' and 'emoticon' are used interchangeably, but literature in the field clarifies that emoticons (a combination of the words 'emotion' and 'icon') refer to representations of facial expressions that are composed entirely of regular ASCII characters. ASCII – the American Standard Code for Information Interchange – is based on a character set consisting of numbers, letters, and a selection of punctuation symbols (Giannoulis & Wilde 2019).

Emoji are an evolution of the ASCII-based signs, in the shape of the small images of facial expressions, common objects, animals, food, and so on, that we now use in online chats and messaging. Emoji originate in Japan, and the literal meaning of the word 'emoji' is 'picture word'. They were launched as mobile carrier SoftBank released a phone that supported 90 different emoji in 1997 (Burge 2019). Generally, however, the set of 176 emoji created by interface designer Shigetaka Kurita for the mobile phone operator NTT DoCoMo in 1998, has been recognised as the first emoji set. NTT DoCoMo also offered functionality that converted, for example, :) into ☐. In 2009, the Unicode Consortium, which is the non-profit organisation devoted to developing and maintaining a universal scheme for character encoding (Unicode), implemented 674 emoji pictograms in their standard. These became available for software developers in 2010, which enabled the widespread circulation of emoji across platforms and devices that we see today. The initial set of emoji is continuously updated and now includes around 2,000 pictograms (Unicode Consortium 2021).

Today, emoji are seen by some researchers as being the first truly universal 'language', or communication system (Evans 2017). Emoji are seen by language scholars as so-called paralinguistic elements, often used to end sentences, to somehow modify the meaning of the other text. Emoji can be used to emphasise, intensify, boost, or weaken the content alongside which it is used. For example, putting the winking-eye emoji at the end of a sentence will make the reader interpret the content as being ironic or meant as a joke. In many different ways, emoji can lend communication a certain tone or interpretation. Once we start using them, it can become quite difficult to stop. We may, for example, start to expect a smiling emoji to accompany messages for us not to feel insecure about the other person's intentions. Similarly, people who are not using emoji in messaging may be interpreted as being distant, angry, cold, or impolite, even if they are not. Just as capital letters can be used as a substitute for shouting, and multiple exclamation points can be used to indicate excitement, emoji are used to compensate for the lack of non-verbal cues in text-based digital communication. They help make people's intentions clearer, and to express emotions and other context, in situations where such things may be difficult to catch.

While it may be easy to see emoji merely as playful and fun additions to text messages, it can also be argued that their arrival in fact marks a substantial shift in how communication and writing works. As explained by Marcel Danesi (2017), a professor of semiotics and linguistic anthropology, the age of print communication was based almost exclusively on using alphabetic writing, whereas the digital age encourages 'blended writing', which is based on visuals, audio, and alphabetic units as well as non-alphabetic units of meaning.

But emoji are not only significant in the sense that they have brought about an interesting transformation in terms of how language and meaning-making works. They also have a socio-political significance. Like any other language, emoji don't have universal and uncontested meanings. Rather, their usage and meaning are strongly structured by social and cultural conventions. As digital communications researchers Stark and Crawford (2015) argue, emoji are 'codified', not only in a technical sense but also in a social sense. By this they mean that certain readings of emoji become dominant at certain times, and in given settings, but that these readings may also be contested and renegotiated. This also means that emoji may be misunderstood and misinterpreted.

In recent years, there has been an increased focus on the political aspects of emoji. As Unicode 8 was introduced 2015, emoji with different variations of skin tones were included. This followed from a debate about white racialisation of emoji, and the change was an attempt to expand the racial representation of the pictograms. Nevertheless, the debate over whether this change has alleviated the problem goes on (see for example Sweeney & Whaley 2019). Similarly, the gendered aspects of emoji have been widely debated, in terms of, for example, how various professions and activities are performed by 'male' or 'female' pictograms (see Barbieri & Camacho-Collados 2018). First, such debates, and their resulting changes in the emoji code, are illustrative of the important role played by new innovations in digital communication in how society and politics work. Second, they raise the question of how to see technology in relation to society. Implementing certain emoji will not transform society at depth. For example, expanding the range of skin tones in the emoji will not remove discrimination. Correspondingly, emoji are not without effect. We must balance our understanding of them to see the complex interplay between technology and the socio-political.

MEMES, GIFS, AND BEYOND

As this chapter has shown, visual content is an increasingly important part of communication through digital and social media. Many of the most popular platforms are explicitly based on visual communication as its main mode (TikTok, Instagram, Snapchat, YouTube), while others are based on combinations of text and images in a wide variety of forms (Facebook, Twitter). Furthermore, the very language of online communication – regardless of platform – is embedded in visuality. As discussed above, this is through the kind of iconography offered by emoticons and emoji, but also through memes (see Chapter 2), which are almost exclusively visual. Another ubiquitous example of visual communication that permeates digital platforms are GIFs – animated GIF (Graphical Interchange Format) digital images. Alongside emoji, these are an example of how digital messaging and social media not only mirror face-to-face dialogue but extend beyond it. GIFs, like emoji, are made possible by technological advances in the communicative system, and can be used in place of non-verbal behaviour (Tolins & Samermit 2016).

Not only everyday routine communication is affected by these changes. It resonates throughout public life, as visual media through selfies, GIFs, memes, online videos, TikToks, Snapchats, Instagram stories, and so on, are now key to how politics is enacted. As argued by Dean (2019: 256), we must see digital visual 'cultural production and exchange not as some frivolous activity on the margins of politics, but as increasingly central to how large numbers of predominantly young citizens experience politics'. This means that ways of communicating visually through social media – even if they may seem playful, harmless, or everyday – must be studied closely in order to gain a richer and more fine-grained sense of how they work.

Now let's try to make a closer analysis of the ways in which visual communication among users of digitally networked media can work to establish social connections. One out of many useful ways of doing so is to turn to the theory of linguist Roman Jakobson (1990), who famously defined six factors (1–6) of 'speech events' together with six functions (I–VI) of language. He said that in any speech event, there is always (1) an 'addresser' sending some sort of (3) message to (2) an 'addressee'. A video shared online, for example, might be addressed to certain groups of viewers that share the interests of the creator, but this does not preclude that many people who are not the addressees of the content may still watch it. The video will be decoded in different ways, depending on whether it is meant to speak to you or not.

The addresser uses the (I) *emotive function* of language to express his or her attitude towards what he or she is speaking about. Jakobson writes that this function works to create the impression of a certain emotion. Then there is the (II) *conative function*, which is directed towards the addressee, as in 'Please click below to subscribe to my channel!' or 'Post your questions in the comments below!'. The message itself fulfils what Jakobson calls the (III) *poetic function*, which depends on how the addresser uses language (convincingly, playfully, rhetorically, etc.).

Furthermore, the message is always sent in one (4) context or another, which the addressee can grasp and which helps in interpreting what is said. This has to do with the (IV) *referential function* of language in the sense that what is expressed always refers to something. A video of someone having tea and talking about school represents someone having tea and talking about school. The addressee will need to know of the contexts of 'tea' and 'school' – what they mean culturally – in order to understand. There must also be (5) a code – some sort of 'language' – shared, at least to some degree, by the addresser and the addressee. The fact that both addresser and addressee know what words, symbols, and things mean fills what Jakobson calls the (V) *metalingual function*. Finally, there must be (6) a contact – meaning some sort of channel of communication through which the addresser and the addressee can enter and stay in communication. Messages serving primarily 'to initiate, extend, or terminate communication' or 'to check whether the channel works ("Hello, do you hear me?" […] "Are you listening?")' (Lange 2009: 75) fill a (VI) *phatic function*.

One way to start thinking more in terms of the deeper meanings behind visual communication online is to use analytical strategies, such as the one described above, and to try to unravel the layers of meaning. Look up videos, or other visual content online, try to see them as a 'speech act' and try to unravel them. How is the addresser using the emotive function? What emotions are expressed and by what (visual) means? Can you identify the conative function being used? Is the addressee spoken to directly or indirectly? What contextual factors does one need to have knowledge of in order to make sense of this particular piece of visual communication? In what ways may it be filling the phatic function? You can continue like this, and will probably be able to find other ways of applying Jakobson's terminology as well.

CHAPTER SUMMARY

Having addressed the overarching issues of the digital society in Chapters 1–3 and having explored some of its more general social characteristics in Chapters 4–5, this chapter has shifted focus towards one particular trait of digital society, namely its emphasis on visuality and visibility. In recent decades both society and social research have taken a turn towards the visual. This means that society has come to rely more and more on easily accessible and spreadable forms of visual communication. As a consequence, social researchers have become more interested in visual analysis. The increasingly visual character of society and culture is not a consequence of digital tools and platforms uniquely, but they have no doubt – through the introduction of mobile cameras and platforms such as YouTube, Instagram, Snapchat, and TikTok – given it a boost. More and more social situations are visually documented, and this documentation is circulated among growing audiences. In this chapter, I have discussed some of the particularly digital phenomena that have emerged in the wake of the visual turn. We have looked at the visual genres of selfies and personal videos, and also addressed emoji as a new form of visual communication that has emerged on the internet. The chapter has also provided an example of a useful basic model for analysing such visual expressions.

FURTHER READING

Rettberg, Jill Walker (2014). *Seeing Ourselves Through Technology*. Basingstoke: Palgrave Macmillan.
Feminist new media theorist Jill Walker Rettberg's book about seeing ourselves through technology argues that selfies, as well as other forms of digital self-expression (not only visual), must be taken seriously. This means that they should be understood in a broader context of culture and power. For example, she discusses 'filters' in cognitive, cultural, and technological terms, and discusses how filter and algorithm literacies have become an important part of everyday life.

Wendt, Brooke (2014). *The Allure of the Selfie*. Amsterdam: Institute of Network Cultures.
In this small book, visual culture critic and photographer Brooke Wendt analyses self-portraits on Instagram to examine the hold that selfies currently have in society. She defines what a selfie is, situates it historically, and covers several key topics, such as poses, hashtags, and filters.

Lange, Patricia G. (2007). Publicly Private and Privately Public. *Journal of Computer-Mediated Communication*, 13(1), 361–380.

Lange, Patricia G. (2009). Videos of Affinity on YouTube. In Pelle Snickars and Patrick Vonderau (Eds.), *The YouTube Reader* (pp. 70–88). Stockholm: National Library of Sweden.

These two papers by Lange are important to the field of YouTube studies. In the first, she explores how participants on YouTube create and maintain their social networks by configuring who has physical and interpretative access to their videos. She makes a conceptual distinction between 'publicly private' and 'privately public' behaviour. The second paper is an introduction to the notion of 'videos of affinity'.

Giannoulis, Elena & Wilde, Lukas R. A. (Eds.) (2019). *Emoticons, Kaomoji, and Emoji: The Transformation of Communication in the Digital Age*. London: Routledge.

This edited volume contains contributions from a number of scholars who approach the phenomenon of emoji, and related types of symbols, from different academic perspectives. The book is an enlightening read when it comes to understanding how one particular kind of digital communication interplays with society and culture in complex ways and in a range of social spheres.

7

EMOTIONS AND AFFECT

Key Questions

- In what ways has digital society changed the social dynamics around emotions?
- How can theoretical concepts such as friction, stickiness, and grab contribute to explaining how emotions come to play a part in digital society?
- What are the mechanisms behind hate speech online, and why may digital hate campaigns be hard to battle?
- How can trolling be understood in terms of affect, and how does it impact society and politics?
- What does the cute cat theory tell us about the role of affect in digital society?

Key Concepts

The affective turn * affect/feelings/emotions * affective intensity * friction * flaming * trolling * lulz * cute cat theory * stickiness * grab * resonance * hate speech online

As much as the internet and social media have been discussed in relation to a visual turn in the social and cultural sciences (see Chapter 6), they are also important in relation to *the affective turn*. This turn, which happened in recent years, reflects a growing awareness in research of feelings and emotions for society and culture (Clough & Halley 2007). Of course, emotions have always been absolutely vital to how people function. But cultural and social research has avoided dealing with them for a long time, instead focusing on processes that have been perceived to be more neutral, such as representation, mediation, and signification.

The affective turn allows for new perspectives, some of which are highly pertinent in relation to digital society. While most sociological theories of emotions focus on things that happen between individuals who are co-present in social contexts, emotions are also important in the mediated chains of interaction between people through which norms and a sense of collectivity are formed. Durkheim (1912) aptly argued more than a hundred years ago that 'the force' of the collective is the result of people fixing sentiments (feelings) to things (symbols, objects, events, and so on).

In this chapter, I will look at how sociality in digital society is largely driven by different forms of affect. Social exchanges take place in networks where the friction between people and technologies gives rise to emotions of varying intensity. I will discuss research that sees *affective intensity* as a key driving force for digital sociality. Covering phenomena such as flaming, trolling, lulz, and cute cats, the chapter introduces the theoretical concepts of stickiness, grab, and resonance, which can help us understand some of the emotional aspects of digital society.

FRICTION AND AFFECTIVE INTENSITY

As you have already seen in previous chapters, questions can be raised about the extent to which, and how, digital society transforms the previously known ways in which people relate to each other and to society. Naturally, then, one can also ask whether interaction on the internet and in social media changes how emotions are formed and expressed between people. Is it possible, for example, to love or mourn online in the same ways, with the same intensity, as we do by other means? And if so, how do the parameters change when such feelings are expressed in digitally networked media? What does it really mean to 'like' something in terms of a 'like' button? And how do things such as asynchronicity and anonymity (see Chapter 4) change the social dynamics around emotions?

When thinking about these things, it is important to remember that questions of emotions and the media are not specific to digital media. It goes without saying that a phone call or something we see on television can make us feel things. But some have argued, however, that questions about mediation and emotions have become more acute in digital society. Sociologists Tova Benski and Eran Fisher (2014: 1) say that this is because the internet allows for 'more elaborate modes of sharing, communicating, performance, and display', which 'all are key ingredients of emotions'. The internet and social media, therefore, generate a new emotional language, new manifestations of emotions, new ways in which feelings bounce between people, and so on. We already touched on some of these emotional connections in the previous chapters' discussion about affinity, emoji, and so on.

The distinction between the words 'affect', 'feelings', and 'emotions' has been debated. Internet researcher Zizi Papacharissi (2015) says that it is essential not to confuse the three. She explains that 'affect' is an experience of intensity that can often be unconscious. It is a particular energy, mood, or drive, which may in turn generate a particular 'feeling' with someone. Possibly, that feeling can subsequently materialise in the form of an expression of emotion. In other words, affect comes before the individual, while feelings are personal experiences of affect. Emotions, on their part, are socially communicated feelings. Sociologist Imogen Tyler (2008: 88) takes another route and says that any absolute distinction between affect, feelings, and emotions must be refused as it is 'critically and politically useless'. So, it might be good to remember that these three words can be taken by some to refer to somewhat different things. There is no clearly established terminological consensus here, though. In this book, I will use them quite synonymously.

One way of understanding affect in relation to digital society is to use *actor-network theory*, a perspective that was mentioned briefly in Chapter 5. In this view, all subjects, human as well as others (hardware, software, gadgets, language, etc.) become what they are through their connections with other subjects. Basically, actor-network theory argues, as one might tell from its name, that actors must be understood through the networks of which they are a part. The networked connections are what make the actors come into being. Internet researchers Susanna Paasonen, Ken Hillis, and Michael Petit (2015) argue that as such networks are in a constant state of interaction, interplay, and becomings, they generate *friction*. That friction, in turn, generates affect, feelings, and emotions. They explain:

> An individual looking at a display screen, for example, is connected to a computer, itself an assemblage of hardware, protocols, standards, software, and data. Once connected to an information network by means of modems, cables, routers, hubs, and switches, the computer affords access to other computers, online settings, people, groups, and files. All this entails a rethinking of both human and nonhuman actors and how affect is generated and circulated. (Paasonen et al. 2015: 10)

While this sounds a bit abstract, another way of putting it is that things that people do on the internet, and in social media, are largely about affective attachments. Online, people articulate desires, deal with issues of trust, and foster interests, activities, and relationships that might be of deeply felt importance to them. In discussions through digital media, or when taking part in different types of content, we will laugh, cry, be seduced, become furious, or be interested. Paasonen and colleagues argue that online connections, as well as disconnections, are shaped by fluctuating and altering dynamics of love, desire, and wanting. Still, they say, many examples of internet research have presumed that digital tools and platforms are reasonably instrumental and neutral channels, through which the flow of information runs (at least relatively) smoothly. Some approaches also seem to assume that most users are quite rational and enlightened. Paasonen (2015) argues that this has brought about research perspectives that do not bring affect into the equation, and which therefore fail to account fully for the passionate character of many online exchanges.

It should come as no surprise, however, that emotions have been an important element of internet use ever since the early days of the medium. Discussion groups, social connectivity in general, and the motivations that make us share and circulate content, are all about intensities and sensations that are created in online encounters between people, digital platforms, images, videos, text, and sounds. But Paasonen (2015) argues that in spite of the crucial role played by affect in our experience of digital society, far too little research has been done in this area.

It is an important point for Paasonen that people's uses of social media are generally driven by a search for intensity. We are looking for some kind of 'affective jolt'. This desire for intensity, Paasonen argues, is what makes users of digital tools and platforms interested and motivated to move across sites, networks, and discussions. Interestingly, she also points out that even though the thrills we seek are often not delivered, there is in fact also an element of affect to the very boredom that might keep us moving steadily from one item of content to another, as we search for something. Paasonen argues that interactions in digital society are driven by what she calls *affective intensity*. Affect is a force that attaches people to certain communities, networks, topics, tools, and so on. It is affect that makes people use social media and pulls them back for more. Calls for support, aggressive outbursts, descriptions of harm and hurt, or waves of sarcasm or amusement are the types of actions and experiences that knit digital society together.

Paasonen makes this argument by referring to feminist researcher Sara Ahmed's (2004) notion of *stickiness*. In Ahmed's view, things might be sticky both because of enjoyment and antagonism – both positive and negative affect. But some commentators, such as Grusin (2010), have claimed that social media is generally biased towards fostering only positive affect. A good example of this would be that Facebook has a like-button, but no corresponding dislike-button (although YouTube has one). According to this perspective, social media operate in order to minimise expressions of negative affect, such as fear, shame, and disgust. Grusin further argues that the positive jolts of merriment and surprise generated by cute and odd cat videos are symptomatic of the relationship between social media and emotions more generally.

Stickiness

Sara Ahmed (2004: 11) has formulated the very useful concept of 'stickiness' to describe how some of the objects that are shared and circulated socially 'become sticky, or saturated with affect, as sites of personal and social tension'. Things can be sticky because they are loaded with affect. And sticky things can obviously stick to other things. Online we might find sticky videos, sticky images, sticky hashtags, or sticky discussion threads. As things go viral, they are stuck together by affect. The stickiness of such things might be measured by how often people reply or comment, share or like, or dislike, the content in question. For Ahmed (2004: 45), there is a '"rippling" effect of emotions; they move sideways (through "sticky" associations between signs, figures and objects)'.

Paasonen, on the other hand, claims that it is evident that mixed, as well as negative affect, does indeed exist online. She writes that like-buttons might be used in quite ambiguous ways, so that a 'like' is not necessarily a like in all contexts and for all users. Furthermore, she emphasises that many memes, or cat pictures, might seem harmless at first glance, but that they in fact might also have unsettling qualities. Paasonen et al. (2015: 29) states that:

> in uses of networked media, positive and negative affective intensities intermesh and cluster in complex ways to the degree that their qualities are difficult to tell apart and their intersections hard to precisely determine.

So, exchanges over the internet are affectively driven, but the type of affect that drives the exchanges can often be ambiguous. People connect, disconnect, share, and react because of emotions that they experience in doing so. These emotions might be both positive and negative, and are often much more intense than many early internet researchers expected. The internet, therefore, is a space where affect is both activated and expressed. Not only does it arouse and transmit emotions, but it also influences how those emotions are shaped and displayed.

DISCUSSION

Think about Grusin's view that social media in general tends towards expressing positive affect, and Paasonen's view that much of the content that may seem harmless can in fact

(Continued)

have unsettling qualities. Try to apply these perspectives to your own experiences of social media. Also, think about the balance between thrill-seeking and boredom that may drive or guide your clicking and browsing behaviours online. To the extent that you agree that 'affective intensities' are an important part of digital sociality, what positive and negative emotions can you identify as being central to what people do online? Are there emotional grey areas, or even all-new types of emotions, that can be experienced online?

GRAB AND RESONANCE

In order to account for the complex relationship between digital media and emotions, Paasonen suggests a shift away from a one-sided focus on representation. She means that if one only studies social exchanges and experiences from a textual perspective – just analysing written or other symbolic traces of what people have said or done – the sensory and embodied aspects of being digitally social are framed out. Therefore, she says, we must avoid 'logocentric' views, because they rely on linguistic models for understanding social life. So, instead of only looking at the posts that people have made, the photos they have uploaded or viewed, and the videos that they have created or watched, we must also think about how the content *affects* the users. This, however, is easier said than done, since it poses a delicate analytical challenge.

In media research and criticism more generally, there has historically been a tendency to devalue popular genres such as sentimental 'weepies', thrillers, and low comedy. This might have to do, some say, with the fact that such genres tend to be bodily felt rather than intellectually experienced. The same goes for many genres in internet culture. Paasonen (2011) makes her point in relation to a case study of online porn, which in spite of its widespread use, is still conspicuously under-researched. It is consumed by at least a quarter of all Western internet users, and was crucial for how the internet developed into a commercial medium. It is everywhere, but somehow it is still seen as marginal. This can at least in part be explained by its strong affective charge.

As Paasonen (2011: 2) explains, pornography attaches 'the viewing body to its affective loop: in porn, bodies move and move the bodies of those watching'. Furthermore, people's encounters with online porn involve intimacy. That intimacy can be desirable, surprising, unwanted, disturbing, and so on. But it is still intimacy. And this mechanism in digital society is applicable not only to the example of porn, but also for things ranging from pictures of cute cats that make our hearts melt, to shock sites with horrendous depictions of gore, which we can't erase from our minds. The content is physically experienced, and this poses problems for researchers who need to keep their analytical minds straight. Rather than watching content on the internet, Theresa Senft (2008) argues, people are 'grabbed' by its content. Senft writes of 'the grab' as a specific dynamic of spectatorship and participation that is characteristic of digital society:

> By 'grab,' I mean to clutch with the hand, to seize for a moment, to command attention, to touch – often inappropriately, sometimes reciprocally. To grab is to grasp, to snatch, to capture. Grabbing occurs over the Web in different ways during each stage of production, consumption, interpretation, and circulation. (Senft 2008: 46)

Being influenced by Senft's notion of the grab, Paasonen agrees that doing things with the internet and social media is quite different from engaging with television or cinematic fiction. In her studies of porn, Paasonen explains that from the narrow perspective of representation – what story it tells, what imagery is shown – online porn is largely the same as pre-digital porn. The difference now is in the technological makeup and the related modes of engagement:

> Users do not merely choose a video to watch, as one might do with VHS, DVD, or a pay channel. Instead, they search, browse (through sites, listings, and directories), bookmark, click, download, upload, leave comments, rate, log in, and compare. (Paasonen 2011: 259)

Such things render engagement with social media as having a stronger visceral character than many other, and previous, forms of media use. It is not that books, music, films, and television don't move us emotionally. Indeed, all of these media often do. Loud live music is certainly felt in the body, as is what we experience when watching a stunning 3D movie at a cinema. But many of the visceral experiences of non-internet media also happen at the representational level. In those cases, we are moved by identification – with the story of a book, the lyrics to a song, the symbolic power of a photograph, and so on. But in some settings – especially so with digitally networked and interactive media – something more happens. Paasonen suggests that we use the concept of *resonance* to describe this. Once again, using online porn as an example, resonance describes not only the force and grab of porn, but also how users attach themselves – stick – to the content. Resonance, for Paasonen, is about connections between affective content and affective audiences and how they resonate, or dissonate, with each other.

QUANTIFYING AND FLATTENING EMOTIONS

Also, in the area of computational research methods, there has been an increased interest in recent times in mapping people's emotions through what they post online.

This is illustrated by the explosive rise to popularity of the method called *sentiment analysis* (Mäntylä et al. 2018). While sentiment analysis has its roots in analyses of public opinion that were carried out in the early 20th century, and while it has been developed further in the field of computational linguistics, the internet has turned it into a very common method (see also Chapter 12). The goal of the different methods and techniques used in sentiment analysis is to find and extract subjective opinions and attitudes from language. A common application in business contexts, for example, is to computationally assess whether consumer reviews of a product or service are positive, neutral, or negative. With the coming of social media, sentiment analysis has been increasingly repurposed as a method for mapping people's emotions, or emotionally based opinions, in relation to a wide variety of areas. Sentiment analysis tools are increasingly developed in order to map sentiment based on particular internet abbreviations (lol, etc.) and to account for emoticons and emoji (Felbo 2017; Hutto & Gilbert 2014). While this may be useful in studies of, for example, reactions to YouTube videos (Lindgren 2012), or heated exchanges in politics (Lindgren 2019), these ways of quantifying people's emotions also raise additional issues. This is because tracking and quantifying people's emotions is not uncontroversial. Lupton (2016) writes about how 'emotion tracking' has become more frequently used in the area of marketing, where the goal is to measure the level of certain emotions – for example, excitement – in crowds or among individuals in order to tailor products and services. As people become increasingly connected to the internet via sensors, wristbands, and other devices, this kind of tracking (whether voluntary or not) becomes ever harder to avoid. By extension, Lupton argues, this development leads to a form of surveillance via data – *dataveillance*. This means that businesses and governments can monitor people's emotional states and opinions in powerful and potentially harmful or oppressive ways.

Furthermore, the affordances provided by different platforms decide which emotions can be expressed and how. Some platforms only have a 'like' function, others have both a 'like' and 'dislike' function, yet others provide different kinds of reactions. Facebook, for example, expanded its previous 'like' in 2016 with a new feature that allowed users to express emotions through a set of 'reactions': 'like', 'love', 'haha', 'wow', 'sad', and 'angry'. While there is often the opportunity to express more nuanced emotions through written content, images, emoji, and so on, categories such as the above contribute to an oversimplification and flattening of emotional expression. But this is not necessarily a shortcoming, but rather the intended function of these systems. As Auerbach (2019: n.p.) explains, 'the primitive level of user feedback encouraged by online services is a feature, not a bug. It is vastly easier for a computer to make sense out of a "like" or a "☆ ☆ ☆ ☆ ☆" than to parse meaning out of raw text'. In a datafied society, explicitly structured information is king. Data that has built-in rankings and categories is easily quantifiable, and will be more useful for algorithms and automation. The more nuanced expressions, emotional and others, which are inherent to unstructured data (images, video, full-text content), are less interesting to algorithms and risk slipping through the cracks in a highly datafied world.

FLAMING

Online social actions that express affect in the form of aggression, insults, and hatred towards other users are sometimes called *flaming*. Back in the 1990s, cultural critic Mark Dery (1993) defined flaming, or 'flame wars', as 'vitriolic' online exchanges that are conducted in public. He identified this type of discourse in discussion groups and emails, and argued that there is a 'wraithlike' nature to digital communication, which tends to make hostility escalate much faster online than in face-to-face situations. He wrote that 'disembodied, sometimes pseudonymous combatants tend to feel that they can hurl insults with impunity (or at least without fear of bodily harm)' (Dery 1993: 1). This is, of course, in line with the perspective discussed in Chapter 4, that the reduced social cues in computer-mediated communication can disinhibit people.

Aligning with the criticisms raised in relation to Suler's disinhibition perspective (see Chapter 4), other scholars who have researched flaming have underlined the importance of not jumping to the conclusion that it is a direct effect of computer-mediated communication as such. Communications researcher Joseph Kayany (1998) argues that flaming, rather than being an antisocial consequence of simply communicating through computers, has to be understood from the perspective of social context and group norms. Some political, religious, or otherwise 'sensitive' topics may have a tendency to bring out uninhibited expressions of hostility, and Kayany made the point that this is a facet of human communication in general, not just one found on the internet. Furthermore, there is the issue of definition as, according to communications researcher Philip Thompsen (1996: 302), 'a flame is not a flame until someone calls it a flame'.

In an experimental study, computer scientist Peter Moor (2007) analysed the role of perceived social norms on flaming behaviour in the context of posting text comments online. He found that users flamed more often when the commenters before them had done so. He concluded from this that people tend to conform to norms of flaming, meaning that if one person starts doing it, others will follow in their footsteps. Similar patterns of imitation, peer pressure, or escalation, may of course happen in the same way offline. But in many online settings, a fair amount of people will write just one comment and never return to the discussion again. This disables accountability, and might also contribute to people being more aggressive, since they don't have to wait around to take the consequences of anything they have said.

As we find in offline life, some forms of flaming can be done jokingly, as a form of friendly online 'trash-talking'. Even though the flames expressed can be received in different ways, whatever the intentions of the flamer (see the discussion about encoding/decoding in Chapter 6), the things said are not necessarily rooted in deeper sentiments of hate. However, they might still be, and regardless of the intentions of every individual person who is vilifying or attacking someone, these comments can sometimes add up exponentially to massive hate campaigns. This has to do with the specific dynamics of online debates more generally. When emotions are expressed in computer-mediated and networked modes of communication, the specific affordances as well as the limitations of the platforms seem to easily contribute to making affect sharper, while also reducing people into stereotypes.

Love online

Love, romance, and sexual attraction are among the feelings that are often discussed in relation to the internet and social media. Research on online dating and cybersex has generally argued that online relationships, if compared with their offline counterparts, tend to be more intimate and emotionally more intense (Ben-Ze'ev 2004). Consequently, different aspects of love online have been explored in a number of studies. A main focus for that research has been on self-presentation strategies in online dating, and many results have confirmed similar patterns to those discussed in Chapter 4; namely, that people can reveal a surprising amount of intimate details, as well as build trust, through computer-mediated communication.

ONLINE HATE

We must remember, however, as discussed in previous chapters, that these same affordances that can bring out affect sharpened into aggression can at the same time be essential for some people's opportunities and possibilities to peacefully express their identities and their views on the world. Law professor Danielle Keats Citron (2014) argues that it is not necessarily the case that the internet fuels hate or brings out the worst in us. She emphasises the importance of anonymity for empowerment:

> Political dissenters document governmental abuse on micro-blogging sites because they can disguise their real names. Teenagers share their concerns about coming out to family and friends on LGBT sites because they are not worried about being identified. Under the cloak of anonymity, new parents are more willing to be honest about the difficulties of raising children without worrying about being labeled a bad parent. (Citron 2014: 61)

At the same time, networked digital tools and platforms can obviously also facilitate the emergence of cyber mobs. Various extremist groups were indeed among the very earliest users of the first incarnations of the internet. Still today, it seems that people are more inclined towards antisocial behaviour, and joining bigoted mobs, when interaction happens online – relatively anonymously, asynchronously, and so on. Things may also get further amplified as online communication tends towards group polarisation. People who are inclined to turn to radical groups are 'nudged to greater extremes' if participation in such groups takes place online (Citron 2014: 63).

The same processes can contribute to making people who are generally not very radical or extreme in their views move towards more relentless views online. According to Citron, using the internet can thus radicalise people, pulling fence-sitters into either/or positions. Furthermore, the networked and viral character of online communication can significantly worsen the damage made by spreading the abuse both far and wide. There is also, Citron argues, a tendency to trivialise the feelings of people who become targets of hate and harassment online. In the 'Wild West' zone of free speech, which the internet is sometimes believed to be, anyone feeling hurt risks being seen as a hysterical 'drama queen', unable to realise that threats and attacks might be 'just words', satire, or a way for the alleged haters to simply pass time or beat boredom.

Communication on online platforms enables a range of different forms of *cyberbullying,* stretching from individual incidents to full-blown international hate campaigns. The concept of cyberbullying has often been used to refer to situations when bullying among peers, for example in a school or in a workplace, moves into the digital sphere. Definitions of the concept, however, emphasise that it covers any kind of systematic and repeated abuse, harassment, or insults to a person by digital means (Betts 2016). Such 'campaigns' that target individuals locally, and in a limited peer-group, in many cases represent nothing more than an extension of face-to-face bullying. However, cyberbullying has a set of unique characteristics – due to it happening digitally – which can make it even more harmful than face-to-face bullying by some measures. These characteristics relate to dynamics that have been discussed in previous chapters, such as, for example, the potential anonymity of perpetrators, its potentially broader audience, its pervasiveness (how it reaches its targets at home, and at any hour of the week), and so on (Betts 2016).

While the term 'cyberbullying' is often associated with cases where the targets face the same perpetrators both face-to-face and through digital communication, this is not necessarily the case. It is, however, more common, in those cases where targets have never met the perpetrators face-to-face and where the bullying is amplified as new perpetrators join in through the internet, to speak of online hate speech or online hate campaigns. These are cases when the bullying goes viral, and where a form of *online mob* joins in to magnify the campaign (Citron 2009). Many high-profile examples of online hate campaigns have targeted women in technology, including the developer and technology blogger Kathy Sierra in 2007 (Citron 2014), tech consultant Adria Richards in 2013 (the so-called *Donglegate* controversy) (Marwick 2013), game developers Zoë Quinn and Brianna Wu, alongside feminist media critic Anita Sarkeesian, in 2014 (the so-called *Gamergate* controversy) (Massanari 2017), and AI ethics researcher Timnit Gebru in 2020 (Schiffer 2021). All of these were cases where women pointed out various aspects of discrimination in the world of technology, and where the online mobs mobilised to try to stalk, scare, and silence them. More broadly, female politicians and journalists are also more likely to be targeted than their male counterparts, so too are minority groups in general (Gardiner 2018). In the 2017 UK election, Diane Abbott, a black MP, received nearly half of all abusive tweets posted in the run-up to election day, and other black and Asian women MPs were the targets of 35 per cent more abusive tweets than white MPs (Ging & Siapera 2019: 26). In other words, some of the affordances of the internet and social media clearly can function to maintain, and exacerbate, existing societal patterns of racial and gendered oppression.

TROLLS AND LULZ

It might not be very surprising that people love, hate, befriend, and fight each other on the internet and in social media. As society is increasingly also taking place in online settings, it seems a natural consequence that basic social forms, such as sociability, conflict, and dominance, come along with it. However, as I have discussed in previous chapters, digital society also gives rise to social forms that appear to be more specific to its modes of interaction. One such phenomenon is that of *trolling*. The existence of this ambiguous practice of posting inflammatory remarks, wrongful information, false accusations, or other content which aims to stir up emotions and generate strong reactions, underlines the complexity of online interaction.

Trolling is different from flaming, which translates into hostility, aggression, and insults. Trolling is a form of intentional provocation, entailing a broad repertoire of more nuanced practices: posting opinions that one does not really hold, being intently categorical, making comments that are abruptly off topic, and so on. Internet researcher and literary scholar Whitney Phillips (2015) is interested in this grey area of ambiguous behaviour online. She argues that many digitally mediated interactions fall somewhere in-between play – crass joking, identity experimentation, etc. – and hate – systematic bullying, hate speech, and other behaviours that are obviously damaging. So while far from all encounters on the internet can be defined in terms of trolling, the phenomenon nevertheless brings into view a hinterland of social practices, which can also contribute to wider understandings of how digital sociality works.

In her book on trolling, Whitney Phillips (2015) describes how the roots of the phenomenon were in newsgroups such as alt.tasteless and in the proliferation on the early internet of so-called shock sites. Such forums nurtured a nihilistic attitude towards content, and fostered a culture of pointing unknowing web surfers to shock-images that 'can't be unseen', or to completely pointless stuff. Subsequently, the infamous /b/ discussion board – a subset of the anonymous online forum 4chan – became a steady breeding ground for trolling. /b/, a 'random' board with a 'no rules' policy, became an incubator of sorts for making trolling into a coherent and recognisable practice. Internet researcher Lee Knuttila (2011: n.p.) describes the 'dirt and ore' of /b/:

> The derogatory specter which haunts /b/ stems from its habitually unpleasant discourse. There is minimal regulation of /b/, beyond the posting of personal information, images of child pornography and discussion of 'raids' on other Web sites. Even these nominal rules are regularly flouted. /b/'s enigmatic in-jokes, disparaging language, distressing gory images and unbound arguments are often matched with glimpses of astute political discussion, heartfelt moments of virtual friendship and sparkling banter.

The origin of the notion of trolling has been debated. The word 'troll' can make us think of the trolls of Scandinavian folklore. At the same time, 'trolling' may describe the fishing technique by which a lure is dragged behind a moving boat. Obviously both the mischievous character of mythological trolls and the activity of luring someone are functioning metaphors for the practice in question. Phillips (2015) found that internet trolls are a diverse group, ranging from individuals seemingly lacking in any form of empathy, or those being explicitly racist, sexist, or homophobic, to individuals who can be surprisingly respectful, even though they also engage in trolling.

Trolling refers to a whole spectrum of occasional as well as persistent behaviours, where some behaviours are very aggressive, and would legally count as harassment, while other are relatively harmless acts of misleading others for humorous purposes. In her research, Phillips found that in spite of a wide variety of trolls and trolling behaviours, there are still some consistent markers of what trolling is. First, she argues, a troll always self-identifies as a troll. In other words, there is no accidental trolling. Simply provoking others, simply flaming, or simply expressing racist, sexist, or homophobic sentiments does not constitute trolling. Nor does the act of disrupting online discourse with stupid questions. According to Phillips' definition, trolling is something that a self-identifying troll sets out to do.

Second, trolls are motivated by 'lulz'. This is a variation of the internet slang acronym-cum-word for laughter (lol). Lulz refers to a certain kind of laughter that is unsympathetic and ambiguous. It 'celebrates the anguish of the laughed-at victim' and expresses 'amusement at other people's distress' (Phillips 2015: 26). Trolling is done 'for the lulz'. The only reason for trolling is to extract lulz from a situation. But even though this means that trolls don't mean to do any real harm, Phillips (2015: 36) still underlines that 'lulz are predicated on asymmetry' as their pursuit means that trolls' targets become objectified pawns.

Trolling is based on the idea that nothing should be taken seriously. It revels in the attachment-free aspects of the internet and social media. Behind 'the mask of trolling' users are free to choose to what extent the things that they say and do reflect their actual personal beliefs or not. On the other hand, trolling depends on its targets not being anonymous, or at least being willing to disclose some of their offline vulnerabilities and attachments. While trolling is obviously both ideologically and ethically fraught, it still expresses something crucial about the mechanics of online interaction.

It might seem easy to dismiss trolling as aimless, immature, and unnecessary. But at the same time, trolls also develop skills in manipulating flows of communication or people's reactions – trolls are 'agents of cultural digestion' (Phillips 2015: 10). Trolling can also make us aware of overlaps that may exist between what we feel to be negative or positive, threatening or desirable. Phillips (2015: 11) argues that 'trolls are born of and embedded within dominant institutions and tropes, which are every bit as damaging as the troll's most disruptive behaviors'. Trolling points to the complexities of social actions online. People will do things with different motivations or aims, and these actions can get aggregated through networked media, and get intended as well as unintended consequences, which can be good and creative as well as hateful and destructive.

So, the concept of trolling can be defined as any online behaviour which aims to deliberately upset or start an argument with someone, especially when this is done in provocative and confrontative ways. Trolling, more generally, 'is the contemporary expression of an older attitude: of a historical spirit of disruption, disorder, challenge, play and humour' that targets social norms, social structures, and authorities (Merrin 2019: 203). Over the years however, the notion has become increasingly tied to the particular types of provocation that are hateful and most commonly related to far-right politics online. In this sense, while trolling *could* be a progressive force in relation to dominant social and cultural structures, the method has been by far the most successfully used by groups such as incels and the alt-right (Chang 2020; Wendling 2018). Such movements have proven to be outgrowths of troll culture (Hawley 2017). In its hateful incarnations – when it draws on misogyny, racism, Islamophobia, and LGBTQ+ discrimination – trolling becomes a threat to democracy rather than a potential tool for subverting oppressive structures.

The impact of trolling on politics and democracy became increasingly obvious in light of the 2016 US election which was won by Donald Trump. His followers in the alt-right were able to infiltrate the political conversation by mastering the art of trolling. While trolling had previously been known to be mean, but in many cases simply for the sake of provocation or to achieve a 'moment of nihilistic amusement' (Hawley 2017: 20), the alt-right gave trolling a clear political purpose. In a post-Trump world, trolling is no longer a phenomenon at the margins of politics. Rather, it has gone mainstream and contributes largely to shaping the political conversation. This is not only in the US, and not only among Trump supporters. As argued by rhetoric and communications researcher Jason Hannan, trolling is becoming 'the new normal' in politics, by imposing an environment where disagreements easily descend into battles where evidence and logic play second fiddle to popularity and shock. He writes that:

> Indeed, being too factual, being too thorough and meticulous in a disagreement on social media, is a recipe for 'tl;dr' ('too long; didn't read'). Lengthy, detailed disquisitions do not fare very well against short, biting sarcasm. They also do not fare well against comments that, however inane, rack up a far greater number of likes. In the mental universe of social media, truth is a popularity contest. And if a troll amasses a substantial following, that popularity can be put to malicious ends, including pushing falsehood as truth and responding to criticism with merciless abuse. (Hannan 2018: 220)

In the digital society, social media platforms combined with the speech act of trolling is pushing politics in the direction of a new language. This language is not based on any shared standards of logic, truth, and civility, and this opens up 'a kind of Wild West of communication' (Hannan 2018: 220), which poses significant challenges for democracy and justice.

AWW!

The largely popular social news and entertainment site Reddit is organised into special interest pages that are called 'subreddits'. As of 2015, the site has several hundreds of millions of visitors that take part in submitting text, images, and videos, and in 'upvoting' or 'downvoting' content on these pages. One of the default subreddits – this means that everyone who is creating a user account is automatically subscribed to it – is 'Aww'. Its focus is to 'post pictures, videos and stories of things that make you go, "Aww!" from utter cuteness' (r/aww 2021). The subreddit abounds with pictures and videos of adorable puppies, bunnies, kittens, and so on. It is allowed to post pictures of humans as well, but images of young and/or small furry animals are by far the most popular items to share.

Aww is one of many examples of how cuteness has become a 'powerful cultural medium', as argued by Japanese Studies scholar Mio Bryce (2006: 2265). This is expressed in relation to Japanese pop culture in the form of anime and other genres, expressions, or things that can be described as 'kawaii' (a specific form of cuteness), but also in the fact that there is an over-abundant interest in things that are cute in internet culture more generally (Wittkower 2012). Cuteness is, for example, an element of some internet memes, and most prominently of so-called LOLCats (Miltner 2011). The LOLCat meme, an image macro of one or more cats with humorous, misspelled, or grammatically incorrect captions, draws at least in part on an 'affective appeal of cuteness' (Shafer 2012). For some reason, images and videos of cats are in heavy circulation all over the internet. In many social media contexts, it might indeed seem as if it is 'kittens all the way down' (Lobato & Meese 2014).

Civic media researcher Ethan Zuckerman (2015: 134) has written that the contemporary internet was even designed 'in no small part, for the dissemination of cute pictures of cats'. Of course, he does not really mean that the internet was conceived as a vehicle on which to share cat photos. He uses cute cats as a metaphor for user-created, day-to-day content, and he argues that the post-web 2.0 internet is, on the whole, a space for regular people to make and circulate a mix of everyday things. Being interested in civic uses of digital media, Zuckerman argues that the social networks that are established and maintained among people who create, share, like, and comment on 'cute cats' has a latent capacity to be mobilised for political activism, should the need arise. This idea – sometimes called the *cute cat theory* – points out that publishing platforms that were designed to be used by activists or other specialists are often less effective than more widely used digital tools and channels:

> Internet tools designed to let ordinary consumers publish non-political content are often useful for activists because they are difficult for governments to censor without censoring innocuous content; because censorship of inoffensive content can alert non-activist users to government censorship; and because activism using consumer tools can tap the 'latent capacity' of non-activist users to create and disseminate activist content. (Zuckerman 2015: 132)

Another important dimension here, which is beyond the scope of Zuckerman's argument, is that this latent capacity often comes from the 'cute' stickiness – returning to Ahmed's (2004) notion – of the content that is circulated. The underlying potential for forceful action relies, in other words, on the affective appeal of the communication infrastructure. And apart from infrastructure, maybe it is also about the affective intensities stuck to the cute cats themselves which are mobilised for political purposes in these cases. As communications researcher Zizi Papacharissi (2015: 93) puts it, the platforms are already 'affectively disposed', and when this is the case *affective publics* can be mobilised.

In her research on political activism, Papacharissi argues that the internet and social media facilitate political expressions and formations that are grounded in affect. In line with the discussion above about the cute cats, Papacharissi says that people become connected by discourses that are affectively charged, and that feelings about both private and public issues and things are very important driving forces for networked publics. In other words, Papacharissi, like Paasonen, sees affect as a key element of digital sociality. Drawing on research that has been described previously in this book, about the means through which social media can facilitate people's feelings of engagement, Papacharissi argues that networked technologies create affective connections among people. This happens when 'affective gestures' call networked publics into being. Such affective gestures can take the shape of cute cat pictures as well as of explicitly political discourse, the point being that affect is not a bearer of any agenda, but simply of intensity.

> Thus, affective attunement demonstrated through liking a post on Facebook, endorsing an item in a news aggregator, uploading and sharing a YouTube video, or using a meme generator to create and share a simple message via a photograph is indicative of civic intensity and thus a form of engagement. (Papacharissi 2015: 25)

So, while the internet and social media can function as a space in which to express virtually any type of emotion – love, hate, anger, or the heart-warming feeling of looking at an adorable furry kitten – it is also interesting to think about what the affective character of digital media means more generally. Learning from perspectives such as those of Ahmed, Paasonen, Papacharissi, and Zuckerman, one conclusion would be that the very fact that people keep channels open by circulating everyday or random content that sticks, creates a powerful latent potential for mobilising networked publics for a variety of social and political reasons and aims.

DISCUSSION

You have read in this chapter about how online sociality is driven by affective intensities. Such intensities can come from feelings of 'aargh' (as in flaming), 'lulz' (as in trolling), 'eww' (as in being shocked or disgusted), or 'aww' (as in cute cats). As you have seen, some researchers think that there is a family resemblance to the emotions evoked by things ranging from the shocking to the cute. Now, go to a site such as imgur.com and browse through some of 'the most viral images on the internet'. To what extent can the images you find be understood in terms of affective intensity, grab, and resonance? What different emotions do the images seem to evoke? Can you construct a typology of the most common emotions? Try to reflect upon what function content like this has for social interaction and society more generally. You could also search the internet for 'reaction videos' – an emerging genre in its own right which documents and shares emotional reactions to content – and approach them from a similar perspective. Think about the social action of sharing reactions. What does it mean?

CHAPTER SUMMARY

While Chapter 6 dealt with the visual turn in (digital) society and research, this chapter has dealt with a parallel development in the shape of the so-called affective turn. On the one hand, digital culture and online platforms obviously have a certain impact on how affective and emotional content is produced, spread, and responded to. Building further on the notion of online disinhibition, which was introduced in Chapter 4, this present chapter has taken a closer look at how affect has tended to come into expression on the internet and on social media platforms. I have introduced a set of theoretical concepts, such as 'friction', 'stickiness', and 'resonance' to describe how the maybe seemingly neutral act of moving around the internet can, just as any other form of social interaction, easily become imbued with intense emotions. Furthermore, we have looked closer at a set of themes or dimensions of online affectivity such as flaming, hate-speech, and trolling, but also at the fascination of online culture with cuteness. The chapter has also addressed how popular metrics and methods (such as, for example, sentiment analysis), which approach emotional content on the internet and try to quantify it, often for commercial gains, may contribute to a flattening of how emotions are expressed and perceived.

FURTHER READING

Papacharissi, Zizi (2015). *Affective Publics*. Oxford: Oxford University Press.
Papacharissi's book about 'affective publics' looks at how political expressions online – both everyday, casual ones, and massive movements – are enabled by social media. This is because social media are a particularly good fit for expressing feelings of engagement. Affective publics, driven by storytelling, can feel their way through digital society.

Hillis, Ken, Paasonen, Susanna & Petit, Michael (Eds.) (2015). *Networked Affect*. Cambridge, MA: The MIT Press.
In this edited volume, a group of researchers address the relationship between networks and affect. Rooted in the emerging field of 'affect theory', the book covers how our interactions with websites, apps, forums, GIFs, and the like, allow us to experience a variety of sensations. It is about affective online encounters and the often contradictory and complex feelings that they may arouse.

Phillips, Whitney (2015). *This is Why We Can't Have Nice Things*. Cambridge, MA: The MIT Press.
Phillips' book on the relationship between trolling and mainstream media is the best book to date about the phenomenon. She argues that trolling is not as deviant as it is made out to be, but that it fits rather well with how the contemporary media landscape works. Trolling, she argues, can also be seen as a form of cultural critique.

8

POWER AND EXPLOITATION

Key Questions

- How do people's varying access to resources affect the extent to which they can exercise digital citizenship?
- How can network science help us understand why social networks tend to be hierarchical?
- How can power and authority emerge in an open and flat infrastructure such as the internet?
- What does it mean to approach digital society from the perspective of critical political economy?
- In what ways can the theories about 'digital labour' alter the dominant understanding of the meaning of digital media use?
- What is the relationship between gender, race, identity, and power in digital society?

Key Concepts

digital divide * digital citizenship * power law * scale-free networks * preferential attachment * charismatic authority * political economy * digital labour * playbour * the gig economy *cybertypes

The internet has been seen by some – in different ways during different parts of its evolution – as a 'Great Equalizer'. The optimists described in Chapter 3 expected digital media to challenge and redefine power structures by enabling people's self-liberation, bonding, organisation, and empowerment. At the same time, the digital world is definitely not without power relations. In this chapter, I discuss different aspects of power, dominance and subordination in digital society. For example, I focus on the notion of digital divides, and the related idea of digital competence – a set of skills that are related to people's capabilities and opportunities to make political use of the internet and social media. Furthermore, on the topic of power, scholars of network science have been able to show how the internet – at the structural level – is far from randomly connected. Rather, there is a rich-get-richer logic to its evolution, whereby those who have many followers, readers, or friends, will quickly gain even more. Those users who are marginalised will have a tendency to remain unimportant. In addition, with sociological theories about how social groups, by definition, demand some sort of social structure – and thereby some kind of, at least informal, leadership and authority – the outlook seems rather poor for the creation of completely open and democratic spaces online. While digital tools and platforms allow for a certain amount of renegotiation of the prevailing norms, values, and social stereotypes, there is a big risk – so many scholars warn – that we overlook the fact that deeply sitting power structures, rooted in political economy, are still largely influential in a digital world.

DIGITAL DIVIDES

It has been claimed that under the right circumstances the internet and social media can give people better opportunities to participate in society and politics. But while the internet may enable some people to be more politically active, online as well as offline, it might raise barriers for others. This is related to a debate about what has been called *digital citizenship*. The idea of digital citizenship refers to the opportunities and resources that a person has to participate online in society and politics. These resources are a combination of having access to the tools of participation, as well as having the right skills or literacy with which to use them.

In digital society, digital citizenship is turning to an increasingly large part of political citizenship altogether. So, in digital society, people's different degrees of access to digital citizenship can have important consequences for democratic participation. Just as public education has long been a facilitator for people to stay politically informed and active, networked digital media platforms are important to fulfil a similar role today. Around the world, government information and services are increasingly delivered over the internet. Furthermore, many political campaigns, as well as day-to-day discussions of political issues among citizens, take place online. Researchers have also shown that there is a positive relationship between online activity and political participation more generally. For example, internet use in general makes it more likely that a person will vote in elections.

Political scientists Caroline Tolbert and Ramona McNeal (2003) argue that the internet and social media – whether we see them as news media or as a set of communication platforms – have the power to update political institutions and to improve citizens' trust in governments. At the same time, they also worry that these same platforms have the potential to be biased, so that they expand the voter turnout rates only among people who are already politically engaged, thereby magnifying existing disparities in the electorate. The internet can function as a new form of civic arena, but it is one where all people are not equally present. We must remember, however, that the historical counterparts, in the form of non-digital arenas, did not have equal representation across the social spectrum either. The question is: Is the internet any better? In light of recent years' discussions about online disinformation and manipulation, for example in the run-up to big elections, the relationship between online activity and voting becomes ever more complex (Bennett & Livingston 2020).

Political scientist Karen Mossberger (2009) is among those researchers who have shown that systematic inequalities in the capacity to use digital tools – along dividing lines of education, income, race and ethnicity, age, and so on – persist in spite of the exponential increase in internet use. While she builds her argument on American data, similar patterns exist across the globe. The fact that someone has access to the internet does not mean that they have the skills to find or use information effectively, nor does it mean that they can harness the potential political power of these technologies for their own political, or other, goals and purposes. Being a digital citizen demands not only regular access to the internet, but also that the technology is put to effective use. Mossberger (2009: 173–174) writes:

> Digital citizens can be defined as those who use the internet every day, because frequent use requires some regular means of access (usually at home), some technical skill and the educational competencies to perform tasks such as finding and using information […] and communicating with others.

This means that fostering political debate and civil dialogue online demands us to be wary of who really gets the opportunity to take part. Sociologist Eszter Hargittai (2002) wrote in the early 2000s about what she called a second-level digital divide. The first-level *digital divide* is the division between those who have access to the internet and those who don't, and between those who actually use it and those who don't. While interesting, such evaluations become less relevant as more people gain access to the internet, and as more people use it actively. Focusing only on patterns of access and usage is a form of technological determinism (see Chapter 3), which fails to account for the big differences in use which actually exist among people who have access to the internet. So, the second-level digital divide is the division between people who have access to and use the internet, but who have different levels of skill in its use. On one level, there is the very technical access (physically having the gadgets, the software, and the connectivity), and on another level, there is the social access (the knowledge needed to benefit from those things). The social access, that is the skills which contribute to the division of people into groups of savvy and not-so-savvy internet users, has political consequences as it affords different people with different amounts of power. Hargittai and her sociologist colleague Paul DiMaggio (DiMaggio & Hargittai 2001) have suggested that digital divides can exist along five different dimensions:

- Technical means
- Autonomy of use
- Skill (internet competence)
- Social support
- Different uses

So, the first is that of *technical means*, as the quality and adequacy of hardware, software, and connections can limit the ways in which people put the internet to use. Users with slow connections and old devices will simply be unable to access certain information and spaces. The second dimension is that of *autonomy of use*, as different people will have different degrees of control over their use of digital social tools and platforms. Whether one accesses the internet at home, at work, in public places, and so on, will affect how autonomous and free the user is to do various things. Different contexts will permit different types of use. Formal and informal social rules may regulate the uses, and hard-wired things, such as filtering or monitoring content, can be in play in various ways, depending on the access point.

Third, there is the dimension of *skill*, mentioned in the previous section. Different users will vary in their knowledge and understanding of the logic of different types of tools and platforms, of how to navigate and interact effectively, and how to troubleshoot the variety of related problems, which always tend to arise. Taken together, DiMaggio and Hargittai call this 'internet competence'. Those with a higher degree of internet competence will have more political leverage as digital citizens. There is also a mechanism by which those who are already skilled in the use of digital technologies will become even more skilled, and vice versa. This is because internet competence is related to the degree of satisfaction that a user gets from using the tools. The extent to which the experience is found stressful or rewarding will naturally affect how much one persists in continuing to use these technologies and to acquire more skills.

The fourth dimension discussed by DiMaggio and Hargittai is *social support*. This is related to the degree to which users are able to draw on social support from more experienced users when they have reached the limits of their own skills. So, whether a user is embedded in a community or network (cf. Chapter 5) where peers can provide guidance and reinforcement will affect the extent to which they develop their own internet competence. Finally, the fifth dimension has to do with *different uses* of digital technology. Factors such as income and education, among others, will affect the range of purposes the internet is used for, and all uses are not equal. As DiMaggio and Hargittai (2001: 12) put it:

> The Internet prophets who foresaw that the Web would empower citizens, increase social capital, and enhance equality of opportunity probably did not have gambling or pornography sites in mind when they made these predictions.

Because of this, they argue, it is important to consider how different determinants, such as social class, race, ethnicity, age, and other identity elements, may affect why a person uses the internet. Some might be driven by economic factors (employment opportunities, education, consumer information, etc.), others by enhancing their political or social capital (e.g. following news, gathering relevant information, or engaging in civic dialogue). Others 'simply' use the internet for entertainment and recreation.

In 2020, both the concept of a digital divide and the research about it turned 25 years old (van Dijk 2020), but discussions about the far-reaching consequences of how different social stratifications intersect with the digital constantly need to be revisited and renewed. For example, various forms of digital divides were revealed for the digitally less connected or less skilled populations during the COVID-19 pandemic (Ramsetty & Adams 2020). Furthermore, as society becomes increasingly affected by digital automation and algorithms, the demand for new skills, such as 'algorithm awareness', grows. Gran and colleagues (2020) have discussed how people today are positioned as belonging to categories of, for example, 'the unaware', 'the uncertain', 'the affirmative', 'the neutral', 'the sceptic', and 'the critical' – all of which relate to the agency and power of the individual in question.

POWER = POWER

In 1968, sociologist Robert Merton wrote about the so-called Matthew effect in science. He showed how there exists a process by which things that already have achieved a certain degree of recognition tend to continue to build even stronger recognition while the visibility of less-recognised contributions remains low (Merton 1968). While Merton was discussing the area of science, the rich-get-richer pattern goes for many social areas, and also for the internet. When the net and the web were first taking shape, network scientists had quite simplistic ideas and expectations about the type of social structure they would find if they analysed this emerging communication system in closer detail. Physicist and network researcher Albert-László Barabási explains that when he started his research in the late 1990s, examining how webpages pointed to each other with clickable links, he thought that most sites would be equally popular. As with many other phenomena, he expected to find the classic bell curve structure, according to which most observations centre on an average value, and extreme highs and lows are very rare. Instead, however, he discovered a pattern where the majority of websites had very small numbers of links pointing to them, while a few extremely popular sites were referred to by an extraordinary large number of links. Barabási also realised that this pattern (a typical 'long tail' curve, as discussed in Chapter 1) followed a mathematical expression called a *power law*. Barabási (2003: 67–68) explains:

a power law is a continuously decreasing curve, implying that many small events coexist with a few large events. If the heights of an imaginary planet's inhabitants followed a power law distribution, most creatures would be really short, but nobody would be surprised to see occasionally a hundred-feet tall monster walking down the street. In fact, among six billion inhabitants there would be at least one over 8,000 feet tall. So the distinguishing feature of a power law is that there are many small events but that the numerous small events coexist with a few very large ones. These extraordinarily large events are simply forbidden in a bell curve.

Another example of a network which relies on a typical bell curve is a road map. A large number of cities will have a reasonable number of connections, while a minority will have very few or very many. By contrast, an airline routing map illustrates a power law: most cities have few connections, but some of them – the hubs – will have many, many more than the rest. It might be surprising to learn that Barabási's discovery that the internet was what he called a 'scale-free network', organised around a number of influential hubs (popular websites), was quite a revolution in network science. Previous network theories had largely seen networks as randomly connected, but the model developed by Barabási, together with his colleague Réka Albert, demonstrated that many networks may in fact have a set of large hubs that will be crucial to defining the topology of the network. While it is not very surprising from a sociological point of view that inequalities in terms of an uneven distribution of power, for example, will emerge in a relational system, this insight was novel from the perspective of network science.

The Barabási–Albert model, recognising the importance of hubs (centres of power), departed from two of the existing models that were popular before. Both the Erdős–Rényi (Rényi & Erdős 1961) model and the Watts–Strogatz (Watts & Strogatz 1998) model focused on the random connection of nodes and viewed all nodes as equal (even though nodes could of course be connected in various, random, ways).

Barabási and Albert's key genius idea was, in all of its simplicity, that 'in real networks linking is never random' (Barabási 2003: 86). Instead, networks, such as those established through the internet and social media, tend to self-organise as they grow and evolve. The focus on growth and evolution was also new, in relation to the Erdős–Rényi and Watts–Strogatz models, which saw networks as static. Those previous models did not account for new nodes being added to a network over time.

The process whereby a network grows is marked, Barabási and Albert argue, by *preferential attachment*. This means that nodes with more connections have a higher chance of acquiring new connections. According to this theory, a YouTube video with many views is more likely to get even more views, and a channel with millions of subscribers is more likely than other channels to get even more subscribers. Likewise, a tweet that has been retweeted a huge number of times will probably become retweeted even more, and a Twitter account with many followers will attract even more new followers. Barabási uses the example of film actors in his work, and points to the fact that actors with many connections in the industry (having been in many good films with other good actors) have a higher chance of getting new good roles. On the other hand, there is a catch-22 situation – an actor needs to be known to get good roles, but needs good roles in order to be known. This, returning to Merton, is also applicable for the scientific community, where highly cited papers are much more likely to be cited even more, and so on.

This relates clearly to what was said, in Chapter 1, about the concept of 'the long tail', according to which small things will survive more easily in digital society. Because of the networked multitude of people and interests, it has become less important – it was argued – to align with majority groups, dominant ideas, and popular taste preferences. The concepts of power laws and preferential attachment state that people's linking and clicking on the internet has a tendency towards the most popular things. In light of this, it may be interesting to reflect on how these two notions can co-exist. Is it possible to have a society where majorities and leaders both matter and don't matter at the same time? Is one of the perspectives right and the other wrong?

So, from the perspective of network science, the internet and social media have structural properties which encourage different forms of uneven distribution – of visibility, of clicks, of likes, links, and other social resources. As you will remember from the optimistic perspectives that were discussed in Chapter 3, the internet is assumed by some to be a more equal environment than many other social settings. This is because it is then believed to promote social networks where all nodes are equal. Those who subscribe to this view generally argue that in digital society people can engage more freely in social and political interactions and acts of sharing. They also say that, even though there might be some inequalities in access and skills, the online world is largely an arena where people can express themselves and organise in bottom-up, non-hierarchical structures, marked by participation and cooperation.

In other words, the internet is sometimes believed to be incompatible with hierarchy and automatically geared for democracy. However, the suggestion outlined above that those who are connected often seem to get even more connected is one of the reasons some people have come to increasingly question whether these assumptions about democratisation are really true.

AUTHORITY AND DOMINANCE

Digital communications researcher Mathieu O'Neil is among those who claim that the internet is in fact full of hierarchies. And this is not only because online networks are often scale-free. More importantly, O'Neil (2009) says, authority is a hugely important element of the social interaction in digital online networks. First, in order to be able to organise and express themselves, participants need to exercise some sort of quality control over what they are doing, and to organise their activities. Otherwise, he says, it will become 'an incoherent Babel'. He agrees, in other words, that online organisation is impossible without some sort of hierarchy emerging. So while Clay Shirky, whose optimistic views were discussed in Chapter 3, gave his book *Here Comes Everybody* (2008) the subtitle *The Power of Organizing without Organizations*, O'Neil argues instead that in order to organise with some power, at least some traces of organisational (power) structure will, by necessity, emerge.

Second, there is the issue of trust and reliability, which was discussed in Chapter 4. It is O'Neil's view that for online self-expression and organisation to work, participants also need to be able to somehow determine who is reliable and who is not, and understand which contributions are relevant and important. Third, he argues, the building of trust will in turn decide who should be part of the group, as issues of inclusion and exclusion need to be dealt with. O'Neil's explanation of how *authority* emerges online, in spite of the 'stateless' character of the internet, lies in his notion of *online tribes*. Such tribes are online formations based on direct forms of grassroots democracy, and on a feeling of closeness to others. But, because of the reasons presented above, authority is still an important dimension of such tribes.

O'Neil draws here on the classic sociology of Max Weber, whose view was that authority is a fundamental feature of all complex systems of human relationships – such as the internet. In Weber's view, the authority of a person is the result of other people agreeing that this person has a legitimate right to exercise power. Weber (1922/1978: 36) defined an authority as someone who 'is held to be legitimate and therefore meets with compliance'. O'Neil made the point that it is wrong to assume that just because the internet has a horizontal structure, which encourages many-to-many communication, it abolishes authority. Rather, he says, new forms of power and domination have arisen online. He updates Weber's classic take on the bureaucratic systems of modern industrialism, and suggests that power online is conferred through a new type of organisational arrangement which he calls *online tribal bureaucracy*.

This arrangement can be used to explain the structures of governance in groups that might seem at first to be anti-authoritarian. There is an interesting contradiction here between the dual requirements of an environment wanting to remain completely open, non-bureaucratic, and without hierarchies, but which at the same time needs some sort of system to achieve its goals. For example, Wikipedia is a peer production project which is focused on an open opportunity to contribute, and which seems to reject all forms of traditional bureaucracy. But O'Neil (2009: 172) explains:

> In reality, Wikipedia is clearly rules-based; it keeps written records of every possible transaction; and it is meritocratic […] in the old-fashioned way: through the recognition of effort. All these traits correspond to the bureaucratic model.

This is but one example in digital society that illustrates the point that even though democratic, peer-to-peer groups may aim to challenge or provide an alternative to different forms of domination, some form of authority always emerges from interaction. A key question, then, is how digital society can rest upon autonomy and authority at the same time.

DISCUSSION

Is it really true that we can't have groups without having leaders? Think of different social circles, ranging from less to more formalised ones, that you are, or have been, part of when interacting through digital media: friendship networks on Facebook, Instagram, or Snapchat, channels on YouTube, forum discussions that you contributed to, and so on. You can also think of offline social settings. Can you identify cases when interaction has been truly non-hierarchical and completely horizontal? In those cases, if any, what contextual factors do you think made that possible?

O'Neil (2009) makes the argument that whatever utopian hopes we might have for the internet and social media, groups will always need or have leaders of some sort. These are the *cyberchiefs* of the online tribes. However, O'Neil uses the concept of bureaucracy in a way that emphasises that such systems are not always centralised. Networked and collectivist initiatives may still be bureaucratic. In traditional bureaucracies, a key defining element is the separation between the organisational role and the concrete person. But, as O'Neil says, the new and unique characteristic of online tribal bureaucracy is the combination of what Weber called *charismatic authority* with the bureaucratic structure, thereby re-establishing the connection between roles and persons.

In his theory about social domination, Max Weber suggested that there are three types of authority. The definition of these types is based on what it is that makes them legitimate. He explained, first and second, that authority could be made legitimate either on a rational-legal or a traditional basis. In the first case, someone becomes powerful because they are appointed a title or hold an office of some sort (teachers, priests, CEOs, presidents, and so on). In the second case, it is tradition that legitimises authority (kings, queens, religious leaders, etc.). The third, and most famous, type of authority that he discusses is based on a person's charismatic qualities. This is a very powerful, yet temporary and unstable, form of authority, which will inevitably become 'routinised' and lose its attraction. Weber (1922/1978: 1112) wrote that people who emerge as charismatic leaders:

> were neither appointed officeholders nor 'professionals' in the present-day sense [...] but rather the bearers of specific gifts of body and mind that were considered 'supernatural' (in the sense that not everybody could have access to them).

So, applying this view on interaction on the internet and in social media, one can imagine how certain 'charismatic' individuals – or even topics or issues – emerge with authority in certain contexts, and for certain amounts of time. One might imagine this to be anything from YouTube stars with millions of subscribers, and hacktivist icons such as Edward Snowden, to individuals who launch a briefly very successful hashtag or viral video, or someone who becomes a key person in the micro-social setting of a specific discussion thread somewhere on the internet.

So, while online projects (ranging from full-on activist campaigns to other social 'projects', such as a hashtag or a single discussion thread in a forum) centre around charismatic leaders, who affect many and inspire them to follow, they still manage to maintain a formal equality between participants. Furthermore, digital society in O'Neil's view is marked by 'permanent conflictuality', a recurring sequence of action that proceeds in this way:

> a claim is made, the facts are examined, deliberation ensues. Eventually a resolution is reached and accepted. [...] Online tribalism has an equalising effect and systematically questions presumptuousness. (O'Neil 2009: 181)

In sum, O'Neil provides a rare and elaborated attempt to explain and bypass the deadlock between digital pessimism and optimism. On the one hand, he demonstrates that there is an inherently democratic character to social interaction and organisation in digitally networked media. It has 'an equalising effect' where resolutions are 'reached and accepted'. This is similar to what was supposed to happen in the idealised public sphere envisioned by Habermas (see Chapter 9). On the other hand, there is still no escape from the necessarily 'bureaucratic' character of social projects as such. There has to be some sort of structure and some sort of leadership – however widely defined – to create or achieve something.

So, when it comes to power and dominance in digital society, it is unavoidable that leaders and authorities emerge, even though some have optimistically imagined otherwise (cf. Chapter 3). But in fact, it is all but unexpected that digital media can support this timeless social form. Some sort of power structure or leadership is unavoidable. When writing of the forms of the social, Simmel argued that 'a group upon reaching a certain size must develop forms and organs which serve its maintenance and promotion', and furthermore that 'the structure of the group requires a certain quota of its members for leadership' (Simmel 1950: 87 and 107).

POLITICAL ECONOMY AND DIGITAL LABOUR

Issues of power and exploitation in our deeply mediatised age can be fruitfully approached from the perspective of *political economy*. Analysing the political economy of the internet, or of digital society as a whole, means focusing on how relations of power, grounded in how production and consumption are organised, shape all of its processes and outcomes. There is a complex set of power relations between mass media, digital/social media, and – importantly – the broader social, political, and economic structure in which they operate. It is difficult to gain a full understanding of digital society without taking these relations into account.

Communications and economics researcher Dallas Smythe argued, already in the late 1970s, that there was a need to employ more critical and marxist perspectives when analysing the complex role of media and communications in capitalist societies (Smythe 1977). Similarly, Fuchs and Mosco (2016) argue that the political economy perspective is key, as it directs focus to a number of important dimensions that are easily forgotten if we study the internet and social media with a too shallow focus on its mere surface expressions. Such dimensions include 'capital accumulation, media technology industry, media content industry/cultural industry, digital media industry, media and financialization, media and globalization, audience commodification, media concentration, media convergence', and furthermore 'media manipulation, media propaganda filters, advertising, public relations, commodity marketing, cultural imperialism', and finally 'ideological reception, critical reception, critical media use' and 'alternative media production spheres, alternative public spheres, media and social struggles' (Fuchs & Mosco 2016: 12–13). In sum, we must go deeper and be more critical when we study the digital society, and focus more on questions of economy and ownership, on who profits from what is going on, on who controls what people think and do, and on the digital society as an arena of continued historical struggles in capitalism. This means taking into consideration issues of ideology, monopolies, and labour power.

So, aside from the fact that any pure democratisation is very hard to achieve because leaders and authority always tend to emerge, a number of scholars in the area of critical political economy have also shown how digital society enables old forms of structural dominance to inhabit new forms online. One such old form of dominance is the capitalist exploitation of the value created by people's work. Indeed, the whole industry of digital media hardware and software is based on accelerated forms of global capitalist production, which include many different forms of labour and exploitation. For example, there are the low-paid digital 'knowledge workers' in the 'information industry' – programmers, technical writers, systems analysts, researchers, and so on (Drucker 1959). These are part of what economist Guy Standing (2011: 13–14) has called *the precariat*: a heterogeneous working class – a precarious proletariat – without any job security:

> The teenager who flits in and out of the internet café while surviving on fleeting jobs is not the same as the migrant who uses his wits to survive, networking feverishly while worrying about the police. Neither is similar to the single mother fretting where the money for next week's food bill is coming from or the man in his 60s who takes casual jobs to help pay medical bills. But they all share a sense that their labour is instrumental (to live), opportunistic (taking what comes) and precarious (insecure).

There are also, for example, all the highly exploited workers – and the slave workers – in developing countries who extract the minerals used as raw materials in producing digital hardware, as well as work under horrendous conditions in electronics factories, such as those run by Foxconn (Chan & Pun 2010). These are pressing issues that relate to the development of global capitalism more generally. Marxist media and information scholar Nick Dyer-Witheford (2015: 13) writes that 'the global economy depends on [...] informal, bonded, [and] slave labour, and other forms of shadow work, many of which, we would add, do not occur on digital networks'. Much of this relates to what has been called *the gig economy*.

But aside from all such labour, there is also the labour carried out by all users of the internet and social media. Some researchers argue that everyone who generates clicks and 'produces' things such as status updates, blog posts, tweets, Wikipedia entries, and YouTube videos can also be seen as part of an exploited workforce. Writers and researchers such as Christian Fuchs (2017) and Trebor Scholz (2013) have made the point that when users engage in creating content on Facebook, Twitter, in blogs, on various social content sharing sites, and so on, they carry out a form of digital labour which creates value, which can in turn be exploited by capitalists. Even though the users often do these things because they want to, because it is rewarding for them in one way or another, or simply because it's fun, it can still be seen as work. It is fun and work at the same time – a form of play labour, or playbour.

The logic suggests that the clicks and the content of users become a form of *data commodity* – a set of information about what users say and do online – which can be sold by social media companies to advertising clients, who can target their ads to the desired users accordingly. We have all experienced something along the lines of googling for a hotel in a certain place, or a shirt with a certain design, and soon find ourselves bombarded with ads for similar services and products whenever we turn online. Smythe (1977) wrote about this in terms of the *audience commodity*. He argued that people reading newspapers, listening to the radio, and watching TV were contributing 'work time' for which they were not paid, but which enabled media corporations to sell advertisements.

The proponents of the digital labour perspective suggest that the idea that the internet and social media provides a participatory, creative, and democratic environment is wrong. Fuchs (2017) argues that not only is it wrong, but it is even facilitating an ideology that celebrates capitalism. He argues that it is corporations and their capitalist logic that dominate digital society, which is definitely still a capitalist society. With a set of empirical examples, Fuchs also shows how this is the case: the most viewed videos (mostly music videos) on YouTube are produced by transnational media corporations, while politics on YouTube definitely is a minority interest. Popular political Facebook groups revolve around politicians who are already powerful, rather than around alternative political figures. Search results for 'political news' on Google yield results that are dominated by corporate news organisations. The most followed Twitter accounts belong to celebrities, and the short format of tweets promote simplistic arguments. Fuchs (2017: 127) concludes that:

> Such examples make clear that corporations and their logic dominate social media and the Internet and that the Internet is predominantly capitalist in character. [...] Social media do not automatically constitute a public sphere or participatory democratic space in a capitalist world. The dominant tendency is that corporations and capitalist logic colonize social media. Multimedia companies, celebrities and advertising dominate attention and visibility. Politics is a minority issue on social media.

But these things are not always visible to the user, who will gladly use his or her time to do fun things online, which will in fact mean that at the same time, they are being exploited. The boundary between play and labour has become fuzzy and there is an increased exploitation of play labour. It is a challenge for research and theories to grasp such complexity, and to try to come up with new knowledge about, and new perspectives on, these processes. As David Gauntlett (2018) has argued, while the exploitation thesis is true on the macro-level of digital society, it is much harder to evaluate this at the individual level. People may in fact be happy to freely create and share things, and few would probably see what they do on social media as 'work' for which they would expect to be paid. Gauntlett (2018: 169) writes that much of this labour is rather 'like the act of putting together a photo album, to show to friends, or the act of recording some music that you have composed, so that you can replay it to a fellow enthusiast'. So the idea of labour or even slavery may not be the best description of what most people experience when doing these things.

The digital labour perspective is one of those critical theories which say that people are somehow oblivious to the true nature of social reality – that they are indoctrinated or brainwashed, or at least that they have a wrongful perception of the character and consequences of what they are doing. At the same time, it is also one of those theories that appears to be right. Indeed, the analysis that a person posting content to a social media platform generates value for the companies who own the platform is correct. But Gauntlett is also right. Most people who create their own content don't feel that they have been cheated or enslaved. Rather, they may be rewarded in many ways by their creative process, big or small. Think of your own experiences with these things, and remember that even small things, such as posting a brief update or comment, are considered creative work (or labour) in this respect. How does this equation come together? Once again, we are in the situation where digital society seems to be two seemingly irreconcilable things at once. Who and what decides how the enslavement/creativity scale tips in each particular situation when someone makes something online?

RACE, GENDER AND BEYOND

Just as the political economy perspective reminds us that the material power relations of the 'non-digital' world exist in similar shapes also in the age of digital media, so do also racial, gendered, and other stereotypes live on and prosper in digital society – sometimes also worsened by online hate-speech and disinhibition (Chapters 4 and 7). It is not a secret, and not unexpected, that the history of sexism, racism, ableism, heteronormativity, and so on, continues into the deeply mediatised age.

As discussed in Chapter 4, a common view of the internet and social media is that they enable people to create and maintain fluid and flexible identities. Social relations in the online world have been predicted to be increasingly fleeting, transient, and fragmented, and this might potentially make things such as gender, race, sexual identity, ethnicity, (dis)ability, and so on into being something which is freely chosen to a large degree. In line with Judith Butler's perspective, as discussed in Chapter 6, new contexts for 'performing' gender open up in digital society. One might imagine how the 'virtuality' of many digital platforms can enable performances that are possibly not in as strict adherence to prevailing norms as performances in face-to-face situations. There is the possibility for more playful and subversive expressions that might have the potential to undermine existing perspectives on gender. Feminist author Laurie Penny (2013: n.p.) has explained that not so long ago people of the same ilk as the digital optimists discussed in Chapter 3 believed that the internet would mean a liberation from gender altogether:

> Why would it matter, in this brave new networked world, what sort of body you had? And if your body didn't matter, why would it matter if you were a man or a woman, a boy or a girl, or something else entirely?

But looking, for example, at digital media usage patterns, lots of research has shown that existing, traditional, gender norms and other stereotypes – relating to dimensions such as race, ethnicity, social class, sexuality, and abledness – align well with the many different uses of digital technology (Hargittai 2012).

Sociologists Eileen Green and Carrie Singleton (2013: 36) argue that 'rather than becoming dazzled by the shiny new vista that the digital age appears to open up', one must focus on the broader structural inequalities and the localised differences in how the digital works. Instead of repeating that things like gender and race do not matter in the digital age, we must look at how such things matter, in potentially new ways. According to the theory about *the social shaping of technology*, technology is (re-) shaped by the social while the social is (re-)shaped by technology (Williams & Edge 1996). It is from such a perspective, Green and Singleton (2013) argue, that we must look closer at the gendering of digital society, or the racialisation of digital society, and so on.

Digital tools and platforms are socially embedded and shaped by interaction and relations. This is as applicable to their design and development as to their utilisation and domestication. Some of the platforms may indeed allow for engagement in what cultural theorist Lisa Nakamura (2002: 14) calls *identity tourism*. This is a process whereby one can temporarily appropriate identities different from one's own in online settings (in games, for example). Nakamura says, however, that such tourism is not really about honouring diversity, but rather about playing with identities as 'amusing prostheses to be donned and shed' without any real consequences. It is obvious that gender, race, and other categorisations will continue to play a part in digital society. But it will do so in new ways. Nakamura thinks that instead of looking at 'stereotyping', we must focus on the process of cybertyping.

Cybertypes should not be understood simply as cultural stereotypes from pre-digital society, which have been translated into new media. Instead, they are the result of internet-specific processes where the cybertypes are created and defined collectively. But they are no less the product of hegemonic and regulating cultural norms. In her research, Nakamura (2002: 5) has shown that when presented with 'machines that offer identity prostheses to redress the burdens of physical "handicaps" such as age, gender, and race', people still 'produce cybertypes that look remarkably like racial and gender stereotypes'. Given a 'free' choice on how to present oneself – or others, or things – there is a strong tendency to make choices within the range of existing hegemonic discourses. It is more likely that someone will present as a sexualised geisha, which aligns with an existing orientalist stereotype, than as a three-legged owl-skunk, which would be something completely new and unexpected.

In spite of the existence of some utopian rhetoric to the contrary, race, gender, and other social categorisations, matter no less online than they do offline. All of us who spend time on the internet are already shaped by how these categorisations work in society and culture at large. We bring our knowledge, and experiences, and values with us. This means that even if some minorities or discriminated groups may have the appropriate digital tools to assume 'fluid' identities, most are still often rudely pulled back into the material realities of prejudice and discrimination. No matter how digital we become – no matter how deeply mediatised our reality becomes – the problem of social inequality and discrimination, of domination and subordination, will persist. However, this does not change the fact that the digital can alter our understandings of these processes, as well as give rise to entirely new forms of inequality. For example, sexism and anti-feminism has a very long history, but they take on new forms in the largely online *incel* culture, which is 'a particularly toxic brand of antifeminism [that] has become evident across a range of online networks and platforms [and which indicates] that the technological affordances of social media are especially well suited to the amplification of new articulations of aggrieved manhood' (Ging 2019: 638).

Digital media use in itself is also gendered. Deborah Lupton argues that the military connection in the early development of the internet (see Chapter 1), the gendered character of 'nerd', 'geek', and 'hacker' culture, and the old idea that you have to be good at maths (which is stereotypically seen as a male-gendered skill) to deal with computers, are all masculinised things that have had an effect on women's relationship to digital technologies. The idea of the archetypal computer user as a white (sometimes Asian) middle-class young man is a stereotype in itself. Computer 'geeks' are assumed to be physically unattractive, friendless, and socially awkward. While this idea may be limiting for some men and boys, it works more broadly to completely exclude many women and girls.

The arrival of social media and mobile devices has made digital technology widespread, ubiquitous, domesticated, taken-for-granted, and readily available in ways that have definitely removed most of its previous mystique. Yet still, 'actual' computer science is still largely a male domain. And while many people do not fit the stereotypes, and many are able to think beyond them, the bottom line is that a more nuanced understanding of inclusion and exclusion in digital society is generally needed. As we have seen in this and previous chapters, it is completely wrong to assume that social relations and identities have become entirely plastic and freely shapeable. The digitalisation of the social might have changed many things, but not the fact that mediated interactions are always embedded in social structures that exist before, after, below, and above the digital.

Using the example of feminism, the internet and social media have definitely contributed to the ongoing historical struggle to enhance women's agency. These technologies have opened up new possibilities for equality through a variety of emancipatory uses. This process has been documented by *cyberfeminist* scholars such as Donna Haraway (1991) and Sadie Plant (1997). However, sociologist Judy Wajcman (2004) is among those who are not impressed by the utopian idea that cyberspace is a virtual space of freedom and transcendence from the body, including gendered (and other) identities. She describes what she feels to be the utopian view of cyberfeminists:

> The message is that young women in particular are colonizing cyberspace, where gender inequality, like gravity, is suspended. In cyberspace, all physical, bodily cues are removed from communication. As a result, our interactions are fundamentally different, because they are not subject to judgements based on sex, age, race, voice, accent or appearance, but are based only on textual exchanges. (Wajcman 2004: 66)

Wajcman warns, however, that even though this idea of freedom and transformation may be exciting, we must make sure not to become hypnotised by it, since that may exaggerate its significance. She thinks that cyberfeminism seems to want to simply replace the need for thought-out programmes for promoting social and political change with technology alone. This is an example, Wajcman says, of the problem with technological determinism (see Chapter 3). She argues that 'an emancipatory politics of technology requires more than hardware and software; it needs wetware – bodies, fluids, human agency' (Wajcman 2004: 77).

The cyberfeminist perspectives may have been an important reaction to some more pessimistic views that construed technology as an inherently and hopelessly masculine domain. Instead, writers like Haraway and Plant stressed women's agency and subjectivity, and also the pleasures and playfulness that are immanent in digital technologies. But unfortunately, Wajcman says, this does not reflect reality. In reality, she says, empirical studies show that the most visited websites by women are shopping and health sites, and that women's use of social media reaffirms traditional views of femininity (focusing on things like beauty, fashion, family, and children).

While such patterns may not be universal and unchanging, Wajcman makes the point that it is impossible to generalise about women's experiences. However inspiring cyberfeminist ideas may be, she thinks that technology can still reproduce or even reinforce gender norms. And this goes for norms and divisions relating to other social categorisations as well (race, ethnicity, sexual identity, disability, age, and so on). The freedom to rework identities grounded in gender, race, and class, for example, must not be mistaken for the erasure of all kinds of divisions and equalities that may still be related to them. Tellingly, then, when the massive #MeToo movement was launched via social media in 2017 to raise awareness and share women's experiences of sexual abuse and violence, this was not a case of digital technology bringing about change and, in some cases, more justice. Rather, it was based in women's highly physical and materially situated experiences, which could be digitally retold and revisited through platforms with a longer reach and a stronger impact than those available to earlier movements. A digitally enhanced, rather than digitally enabled, uprising.

CHAPTER SUMMARY

In this chapter we have turned towards the more explicitly political dimensions of digital society, focusing particularly on issues of power and exploitation. As society has become digital, so has political life. We must therefore be aware of the divides that may exist, both in terms of access to technology but also in relation to the different skills that people have in using technology to participate and make their voices heard. I have explained in this chapter how there is a mechanism on the internet – as in most other parts of society – by which those who already are powerful can easily become even more powerful. Many studies of the internet show that a minority of users dominate discussions (political and others), while the vast majority are part of a 'long tail' with less power – at least individually – to have a political impact. The chapter has also built further on the discussions in Chapter 3 about how optimistic visions for a democratic internet have often been faced with the fact that the online world is by no means immune to hierarchies and differentials of power. Quite to the contrary, some such divisions may even become more pronounced online. This chapter has underlined the point that, even though digital society ('the network society', 'the information society', etc.) comes *after* industrialism, familiar capitalist logics of labour, class, race, and gender still prevail, and must be analysed from the perspective of political economy.

FURTHER READING

van Dijk, Jan (2020). *The Digital Divide*. Cambridge, UK: Polity Press.

Even though there has been talk about 'the digital divide' since the early days of the web, the insight that the digital world is rife with both old and new divisions is becoming more and more important, as the ways in which power is divided and exercised become increasingly complex. In this book, van Dijk discusses the state of digital inequality in the 2020s, and also explores potential solutions for how to tackle it. The book also addresses the important issue of to what degree digital platforms reinforce older or non-digital divides, and to what extent it may challenge those but potentially give rise to new inequalities.

Woodcock, Jamie, and Mark Graham (2020). *The Gig Economy: A Critical Introduction*. Cambridge, UK: Polity Press.

The book discusses the gig economy, and how it plays out across digital platforms such as Uber and Deliveroo. The platform work which underpins the gig economy is approached critically through a discussion of how new forms of precarious work emerge, while other forms of such work are being reshaped. The authors emphasise how, while 'gigs' are not a new form of work as such, we are now in a historical moment where this particular labour model is growing explosively and becoming increasingly normalised. The book asks what can be done to make the lives of gig workers fairer and more just.

O'Neil, Mathieu (2009). *Cyberchiefs*. London: Pluto Press.

O'Neil's book questions the celebrated self-organisation and autonomy of collaborative web 2.0 platforms by looking at how they actually work. Horizontal organisations and autonomy are celebrated in digital society, but any project must have rules and leaders in order to be efficient. O'Neil introduces the concept of 'online tribal bureaucracy' as a name for a type of organisation which is unique to the internet. A key question for the book regards how autonomy and authority can coexist on the internet.

9
ACTIVISM AND MOBILISATION

Key Questions

- In what ways do the theories about 'cybersalons' (Dean) and 'the private sphere' (Papacharissi) extend and alter the theory about 'the public sphere' (Habermas)?

- In what ways do social movements in digital society differ from previous social movements in history?

- What do theoretical concepts such as 'communication power' and 'connective action' add to our understanding of how political mobilisation works in digital society?

- Under what circumstances can the internet and social media make activism more powerful?

Key Concepts

Disruptive spaces * the public sphere * the private sphere * cybersalons * monitorial citizens * citizen journalism * networked social movements * communication power * personal action frames * connective action * repertoires of contention

It should be clear by now that the effects of digital media on society are neither universal nor unambiguous. As discussed in Chapter 3, and repeatedly throughout the other chapters, views vary widely with regard to the extent to which the internet has transformed society, as well as in what direction this has occurred. As reflected in Chapter 8, the consequences of digital society for power and participation are also a complex matter. However, research on more explicit forms of bottom-up digital activism – in the form of uprisings, revolutions, and protests – has demonstrated quite convincingly that digital tools and platforms *can*, under the right circumstances, be used successfully to challenge, provoke, and even overthrow prevailing power structures. This is illustrated, for example, through massive hashtag movements such as #BlackLivesMatter, #MeToo, and #FridaysForFuture. In other words, in spite of the tensions between digital optimism and digital pessimism, enough research has been undertaken on the subject of digital activism to claim that the internet and social media have some sort of capacity to create networks of resistance in order to counter dominant power structures. Digital media have contributed to the alignment of disparate social movements, and to challenging traditional forms of political representation. As poet and author Hans Magnus Enzensberger (1970: 15) wrote, the 'electronic media' can make people 'free as dancers' and 'surprising as guerillas'. Elsewhere, I have used the notion of *disruptive spaces* to describe those 'emergent online spaces that may function as a springboard for movements' (Lindgren 2013: 2).

A manifesto for the analysis of digital disruption

Adapted from *New Noise* (Lindgren 2013: 143–145)

Disruption is noise – a 'disturbance in the orderly sequence' (Hebdige 1979: 90). In digital society, an increasing number of online socio-cultural spaces are celebrated for being disruptive. Groupings and discourse stemming from these spaces may have the power to circumvent dominant flows of communication, to subvert preferred meanings, and to challenge power structures. An important task for digital social research is to evaluate the conditions under which this power is realised, or not.

Disruptive spaces are emergent online spaces that embody more or less conscious attempts at obstructing or providing an alternative to prevailing power structures. Sometimes these attempts are successful, and sometimes they are not. At best, the disruptive spaces are building blocks of an alternative public sphere. At worst, they are idealised technodeterministic fantasies.

The key to realising the potential of disruptive spaces lies in deploying what Enzensberger (1970: 26) calls *emancipatory use of media*. We need decentralised structures of communication where each receiver is also a transmitter, and where interaction and collective production creates a self-organising social system that mobilises people. As researchers of digital disruption, we must look for traces and examples of such media use.

The study of disruptive spaces demands that we adopt a *cyber-realist* perspective. This means acknowledging that in digital society there is a constant struggle between networks of domination and networks of liberation.

In this chapter, we look at a set of key concepts in relation to how the internet and social media can be, and have been, used as platforms from which to challenge the social order through radical politics. I provide a background to how digital media have been used by activists, and discuss concepts such as 'communication power' and 'connective action'. First, however, we shall dive into the discussion of what role digital media plays in offering a *public sphere* for democratic exchanges and deliberation. We will look at Jürgen Habermas' theory of the public sphere and discuss its relevance for digital society. Several tweaks and fixes have been suggested for how to update his theory for a digital age, such as the notions of 'cybersalons' and private spheres.

AN ONLINE PUBLIC SPHERE?

A functioning democracy demands that people are able to play an active part in society, being informed, critical, and responsible. As discussed in the previous chapter, the arrival of digital society has transformed the conditions surrounding participatory processes like these in several ways. Furthermore, as introduced in Chapters 4 and 5, people interact, develop their identities, form communities, and connect to networks in ways that alter many of the pre-digital social conditions around civic engagement politics. Today, the rapid technological and social changes in the media landscape have added greater complexity to political issues, spanning the local and global. People's identities have become more complex, overlapping, and sometimes in conflict, and this has added to the blurred boundaries between the public and the private spheres.

The internet, and its social tools and platforms for interaction and communication, has therefore contributed to changes in what sociologists have called the public sphere, and in political behaviours and activity in general. Craig Calhoun (1998) explains that these changes must be understood as part of a continuing series of transformations. You might remember Rainie and Wellman's (2012) view, discussed in Chapter 5, that 'the social network revolution' is not only about digital media, but about more long-standing social transformations of communication and social relations.

The discussion of democratic deliberation in civic society, and the question of who has the opportunity to participate, are longstanding issues within social and political science. Sociologist and critical theorist Jürgen Habermas is famous for having launched the concept of a *public sphere*. According to Habermas (1989), the public sphere is a social realm that channels civil society. It is an arena for conversations, exchange, and the formation of ideas and views. He developed his theory in the book *The Structural Transformation of the Public Sphere*, which was published in German in 1962 and translated to English in 1989, but the issues that it discusses have become relevant again because of the internet.

Habermas said that there had historically been a division, in language and philosophy, between two spheres: the public and the private. Before the 1700s, the focus in most societies was on 'representative publicity', a system where a king or lord was the only public person while all others were considered as private spectators. In England in the 1700s, however, the rise of capitalism brought on an increasing degree of 'rational-critical debate' among the literate public. People were responding to new cultural forms in literature and art, and discussed such things in coffee-houses and salons. Even though one did not talk about explicitly political issues, Habermas felt that this was a way for civil society to articulate its interests. He described the emerging 'bourgeois public sphere' as an arena mixing the two sides of private and public, as 'private' people joined together to form a 'public'. The public sphere, then, is a part of the private world that moves into the public domain. While there was an inclusive atmosphere in the salons and coffee-houses, access was still filtered by gender, class, race, education, and property ownership.

These citizen forums developed, according to Habermas, into a fully political public sphere which was institutionalised in the 1800s through the European constitutional states. But this incorporation of the public sphere into the democratic systems of states was not positive. Habermas saw this as the beginning of a process that was eroding and even erasing the public sphere. Media became cheaper and more powerful, and seemed to aim simply at the production of consensus rather than critical debate. Instead of an actual public sphere, there were instead manipulated media audiences.

In his book, Habermas wrote about how rational-critical debate among citizens had disappeared. The public sphere had been colonised by media, advertising, and entertainment. But, he contended, society needs a strong public sphere to keep top-down power and domination in check. 'Ordinary people' must be able to talk to each other and develop their opinions, as democracy demands an informed and critical public. At the time of his writing, Habermas was hoping for the return of a functioning and strong public sphere. And since then, the arrival of the internet and digitally networked social media has given some hope that we might be witnessing such a development. But as you will remember from Chapter 3, views differ as to whether this is really something to hope for. The internet and social media certainly blur some of the boundaries between the public and the private (which is not good according to Habermas), but they are also potentially a user-driven social realm for conversations and exchange (which is very good according to Habermas). Similar to how Habermas described the means by which discussions of art and literature in the salons in the 1700s gradually became political, Henry Jenkins (2006: 257) was hopeful when writing:

> Right now, we are learning how to apply these new participatory skills through our relation to commercial entertainment – or, more precisely, right now some groups of early adopters are testing the waters and mapping out directions where many more of us are apt to follow. These skills are being applied to popular culture first [but] may quickly get applied to political activism or education and the workplace.

So, the question raised by Jenkins was about whether one could in fact see all of the often playful and seemingly non-political things that people were doing online as a precursor to an emerging public sphere in the Habermasian sense.

In an analysis of Twitter, Christian Fuchs (2017) posed the question of whether this specific example of social media can be seen as a public sphere. He found that there was relatively little political discussion going on on Twitter. Instead, the space is dominated by entertainment. The twittersphere, he argued, is governed by celebrities, and the politicians who are prominent are those who are already established and who have lots of resources. Political agents that are critical of the status quo are much less visible and have fewer followers. Analysing a large number of tweets in relation to significant political events, Fuchs concluded that the critical public debate that Habermas imagined is simply not achieved on Twitter as it looks today. He then raised the question of whether the short-message format of Twitter and similar platforms really provide good opportunities for meaningful political debates at all. He worried that the brevity of the communication on the platform might lead to simplistic arguments. More generally, according to Fuchs' perspective, social media as public sphere risk falling into Habermas' (1989: 162) category of 'pseudo-public spheres', a form of public sphere that is hollowed out and rendered powerless by mass media and culture consumption. At the same time, we have seen in recent years how elections have been won, and lost, largely through social media, and also how large-scale hashtag movements (#BlackLivesMatter, #MeToo, and so on) have made strong impacts. We cannot be sure, however, in spite of these examples, that the social media platforms have been impactful through being democratic and equal. Their effects may still have followed the patterns of biased attention that Fuchs described.

Evaluating whether something is a public sphere or not, from the Habermasian perspective, can be distilled to two key criteria. First, that everyone has access, and second, that participants can confer in an unrestricted way. Obviously, however, not everyone has the same access to the internet (see the discussion about digital divides in Chapter 8). As of 2019, the internet penetration rate was at around 90 per cent in North America and Western Europe, and around 25 per cent in Africa and South Asia (International Telecommunication Union 2021). Furthermore, in the parts of the world where access to the internet and social media is at a high level, there is a hierarchy of different ways of reaping the participatory advantages. You will remember the discussion of internet competence and skills from the previous chapter. At one end of the spectrum, there is the highly active user who comments on and engages with content through whatever channels are available. This is a person who would probably be active in formal and informal networks of discussion and information-sharing even in a pre-digital society. At the other end of the spectrum is a passive, isolated, mass audience member who may indeed use the same platforms, but predominantly for the consumption of content rather than for engagement and contribution.

Communications researcher Allison Cavanagh (2007) states that the central question for evaluating whether the internet can function as a public sphere or not is to what extent the digital tools and platforms represent a break with traditional ways of relating to media. Television, for example, is not largely interactive, and is associated with being used for passive viewing, or even as background noise. Television is a mass medium built on the model of broadcast centres pumping out content to allegedly passive receivers, in a sort of master–slave architecture. By comparison, being on the internet at least means a minimum level of activity, as the user is to some degree forced to 'act' by clicking, making connections, and generally deciding what they want to do. This is in contrast to a passive television viewer. In the dystopia of the passive and dumbed-down mass audience, the internet, with its higher degree of interactivity, gives hope. Cavanagh (2007: 68) says:

> [The internet] appears as a redemptive force, offering the possibility of breaking through the walls which segment the audience from each other, and requiring participation above and beyond passive presence. However, this vision of the audience depends on ascriptions about the behaviour of people online which may or may not be warranted.

So, Cavanagh thinks that we can't be sure that just because the infrastructure is in place that people will start harnessing it for democratic ends. Furthermore, in line with Fuchs' concerns, Cavanagh states that even though there might be the possibility for new audience behaviours, the internet is largely colonised by mass media content. Even though people have the opportunity to take part in grassroots forums, and to engage with different forms of alternative media, much internet activity still looms towards traditional media content produced by newspapers, corporate television channels, and other well-established content providers.

There is a risk that the commercial centre of gravity of the internet draws inter-active and creative users in its periphery towards the less dynamic 'mass centre'. This is related to the 'rich-get-richer' mechanism, which exists in all networks (see the discussion of power law distributions in the previous chapter). Because of these factors, one must be careful in assuming that the internet has given birth to large num-bers of 'cybercitizens' who are all politically aware, civically involved, committed to progressive ideals, anti-authoritarianism, and who believe in rational debate. You will recognise from Chapter 3 how many cyberoptimist perspectives seem to rely on such assumptions.

When Habermas wrote about the structural transformation of the public sphere, he was referring to how the salons and coffee-houses of the 1700s were replaced by a public sphere, which was in turn replaced by the heavily mediatised public sphere around the beginning of the 1900s. He said that the coming of mass-circulated newspapers and radio removed the more direct forms of debate and deliberation from the public. But there have also been continued structural trans-formations since the 1960s when Habermas wrote his book. In most countries, there is no longer a total dominance of a small number of media organisations. Instead, there is a wide range of media forms and platforms. Most prominently of course, there has been a shift away from traditional broadcast and print towards online content. Axel Bruns and his internet researcher colleague Tim Highfield (2016: 57) argue that:

> News and public affairs reporting as it presents itself to the everyday user has thus transformed from a largely oligopolistic media environment, dominated by a few major public and commercial media organisations providing mass market news products for general consumption by a domestic audience, to a diverse, complex and even confusing media ecology.

So, while the public's attention might not have been as uniform as is sometimes assumed, even in the golden days of mass media, there is no doubt a vastly greater complexity today. Therefore, there is a need for updated concepts that can help account for an increased fragmentation of the public sphere, which now consists of a range of diverging publics. There is sometimes discussion, for example, of arenas such as the blogosphere, or the twittersphere, to indicate the existence of platform-specific sub-spheres. Furthermore, Bruns and Highfield point out that other researchers have suggested conceptual solutions for this. Some have envisaged that the public sphere is separated into different domain publics (a political public sphere, a cultural public sphere, an economic public sphere, and so on) (Hartley & Green 2006), while others have talked about a networked public sphere (Benkler 2006), or public sphericules, which are a form of mini-public spheres with small groups, following a similar logic to the Habermasian public sphere (Bruns & Highfield 2016). Habermas himself has also mentioned updating the original concept along similar lines. He wrote that:

> the Internet […] counterbalances the seeming deficits that stem from the impersonal and asymmetrical character of broadcasting by reintroducing deliberative elements in electronic communication. The Internet has certainly reactivated the grassroots of an egalitarian public of writers and readers. [But] the rise of millions of fragmented chat rooms across the world tend instead to lead to the fragmentation of large but politically focused mass audiences into a huge number of isolated issue publics. (Habermas 2006: 423)

In sum, the potential of the ever-evolving social media ecology for civil society will most likely continue to be debated, as it continues to challenge understandings of what a public sphere – whether in the singular or plural – may be. Calhoun (1998: 383) reminds us that:

> like other technologies, the Internet mainly makes it easier for us to do some things we were already doing and allows those with the resources to do some things they already wanted to do. […] The more a particular possible use of the Internet depends on social organization and the mobilization of significant resources, the more it will tend to be controlled by those who are already organized and well-off.

This echoes the more pessimist perspectives addressed in Chapter 3, but Calhoun (1998: 382) also remains optimistic that 'more radically novel uses will be found over time'.

CYBERSALONS AND PRIVATE SPHERES

Introducing the notion of *cybersalons*, Jodi Dean (2001) argues that the internet and social media might in fact – under good circumstances – function in ways that are similar to what Habermas imagined. She says that we must remember, however, that people come together in different ways online when compared to the salons and coffee-houses in the 1700s that Habermas described. This way of thinking is key to all research and theorising about digital society. On the one hand, we must remember to be careful with the extent of our cyberoptimism, but, on the other hand, we must also consider whether things might not be so bad after all, if we make the effort to actually also see the new things in new ways. Dean identifies how communication in cybersalons happens among people who are linked by their ability to use networked interaction, rather than by proximity or tradition. We need this new concept, Dean argues, because Habermas' notion of the public sphere is unable to deal adequately with the networked complexity in how people exchange information, communicate, and interact in digital society. She explains that this does not mean that networked interactions online can't possibly be good for democracy. The fact that social media fail to live up to Habermas' definition of the public sphere rather, she thinks, illustrates the limitations of his very concept.

As we saw, for example, in the discussions in Chapter 7 about digital culture phenomena such as trolling and cute cats, there are affective ambiguities and complex political potentials to the internet that are hard to grasp with concepts that were developed in a pre-digital world. Dean says, in line with this, that the internet resists being compiled into a normative vision of what politics and the public sphere is. So, if our definition of politics and the public sphere is too narrow, we will fail to identify any signs of emergent novel forms of politics or civic dialogue. Dean argues that if we rely on an understanding of democratic deliberation which is unitary and top-down, this will hinder identifying and conceptualising new terrains of contestation and debate. The disconnection between bodies and words in computer-mediated communication, as discussed in Chapter 4, is one of the factors that point to the inapplicability of the traditional notion of the public sphere in digital society. Online interaction draws on disembodiedness, plurality, and an uncertainty of identity. And as people on the internet and social media are not always certain what type of exchange they are engaged in, this changes the parameters for the type of public sphere that can emerge. For example, Habermas' ideal public sphere largely relies on being inclusive. This is a key part of his definition, signalling that without inclusivity there can be no public sphere. Dean (2001: 260), however, emphasises that in cybersalons there is no decisive or universal 'we'.

> Although some wide-eyed cyber enthusiasts celebrate the Net for its inclusiveness, this kind of naïveté has dwindled in the last few years as enthusiasts and critics alike have dealt with the issues of encryption, surveillance, modem speeds, incompatible protocols, the difficulty of finding useful information amid all the Net clutter, the problematic dominance of English, the comparatively fewer numbers of ethnic minorities online, and the basic economic inability of large numbers of people to take advantage of networked resources.

Because of such things, Dean says that we must pose the questions of inclusion in the public sphere anew, in a different way from how they were posed in the pre-digital age. While the social identities of those attending the salons and coffee-houses that Habermas talked about were stable and easy to verify, things are different online. As I have discussed in Chapter 4, the internet and social media enable more fluid and multifaceted identities. This is because there are more opportunities of presenting oneself in different ways in different contexts, for different audiences. So, while Habermas' view was premised on the notion that subjectivity was singular, Dean says that when theorising cybersalons we must account for a variety of confrontations between different kinds of subjectivity, rather than interactions between clear-cut individuals.

Rather than simply being included in a 'salon', digital society demands other things from individuals in order for them to take part in shaping politics and opinions in the public sphere. The technological possibilities produce societal pressures towards mobility, adaptability, and conformity. This means that different people will have very different social experiences, with increased freedom for some, while others will have their opportunities and liberties curtailed. Dean thinks that the issue must be raised as to whether one can convincingly conceive of any single universal subjectivity upon which the public sphere can rely. Furthermore, in digital society the space of interaction extends beyond the nation-state, as people meet in a variety of spaces. Therefore, Dean says, politics is by necessity about unequal exchanges among people who will have very different views and ways of reasoning.

Also drawing on Habermas' theory of the public sphere, Papacharissi (2010) argues that we must not forget about the role of its counterpart in the form of a *private sphere*, especially not in digital society. As you might remember, Habermas felt that it would diminish the power of the public sphere if it was too mixed up with the private sphere. Being in public means that at least parts of the private must be hidden away or kept out of view. Literary critic and social theorist Michael Warner (2002: 23) explains that, according to dominant understandings, 'being in public is a privilege that requires filtering or repressing something that is seen as private'. Topics that are unofficial and which belong to the personal domain did not, as Habermas saw it, belong in politically useful mainstream discussions. But in the face of this, many internet researchers have shown how the boundaries between the public and the private are eroded in digital society.

Papacharissi (2010) is eager to underline that from digital culture's increased focus on intimate and personal, or even seemingly ego-centric, things it does not automatically follow that there is a low level of civic engagement more generally. Rather, she argues, new ways of being active in society are emerging along with digitally networked tools and platforms. Today, people are doing highly political things in a variety of contexts, but just not in ways that we would have ever thought about before the internet and social media. Political engagement now happens in many different spheres, and not only the clearly political ones. Seemingly private acts that are digitally enabled and self-motivated can indeed have a public political effect. This hybrid dynamic is unique to digital society, as these private acts can be carried out in personal, familiar, and autonomous spaces but still have the same potential audience as a public act.

So, from the complex relationships between technology, social practices, and new types of social spaces, a private sphere is opening up as an arena for people to express entirely new forms of participation and citizenship. Under this new paradigm of civic engagement, Papacharissi contends, people discuss politics mixed up with other topics. So, things that in the Habermasian model belong to the public sphere (politics) are dealt with in new – potentially even more powerful – ways within a hybrid sphere, which encompasses both public and private aspects of an individual's social existence. Digital civil society therefore consists of a variety of atomised actions that happen in a range of different spaces which may be both public and private. This is similar to the point made by Warner (2002: 30) that:

> Because the contexts overlap, most things are private in one sense and public in another. Books can be published privately; a public theater can be a private enterprise; a private life can be discussed publicly, and so on.

And even though Warner makes this point more generally, this is especially the case on the internet. In the hybrid publicly private and privately public spaces online, people can link political issues to their own everyday concerns and actions. This changes the whole logic of civic engagement: people in digital society can do politically relevant things privately. You may recognise the idea that 'the personal is political' from the famous radical feminist slogan, so that line of thinking is not entirely new. But the internet offers a tangible infrastructure for mobilising private considerations politically. With the help of digital tools and platforms, political events, social issues, and news coverage can be aggregated and commented on by individuals on their various social – private – accounts. This, says Papacharissi (2010), can be interpreted in part as a boycott of mainstream discourse, from which many users might feel alienated. Making political comments in private spaces is not necessarily without value in comparison to committing political actions in public spaces.

This all sounds good and exciting, but it is still no guarantee that such a private sphere will be any more democratic than the public sphere. Late modern societies, as well as the internet, also abound with apathy, scepticism, disillusionment, and political disinterest. So why should people bother with politics? On the other hand, perhaps the comparably greater interest in social news sites, blogging, and online activism bears witness to the fact that people are not disinterested in politics, when seen from a wider perspective, but are simply fatigued by the mainstream conventions of politics and political debate. However, yet again, there appears to be a big risk that online spaces will be increasingly commercialised, marked by unequal access, and that there will not be enough communicative reciprocity. Papacharissi makes an important point: even though one may feel politically empowered while tweeting, TikToking, or blogging because of the potentially huge audience, the democratic character of the technology does not equal democratisation.

MONITORIAL CITIZENS

Another aspect of how civil society and public debate are changing in the age of the internet and social media relates to news reporting and journalism. First, the development of new platforms, and the emergence of new audience behaviours, have changed the context of news production and the conditions under which media companies and journalists operate. They increasingly have to adopt new editorial workflows, adapt to altered practices for news-gathering, and to a speeded-up production cycle. In digital society, one must see news production as a collective effort between journalists and members of the public. Today's participatory media culture has brought about a change of the relationship between news media and their audiences from being about one-way communication to being increasingly dialogical. People in digital society can be described as *monitorial citizens*. Journalism researcher Michael Schudson (1999: 310–311) has introduced this concept:

> Monitorial citizens scan (rather than read) the informational environment in a way so that they may be alerted on a very wide variety of issues for a very wide variety of ends and may be mobilized around those issues in a large variety of ways. [...] The monitorial citizen engages in environmental surveillance more than information-gathering. Picture parents watching small children at the community pool. They are not gathering information; they are keeping an eye on the scene. They look inactive, but they are poised for action if action is required. The monitorial citizen is not an absentee citizen but watchful, even while he or she is doing something else.

People today, in other words, are in constant connection with a number of streams of information. By way of a passive–active form of citizenship they can stay informed, networked, and ready for action. When needed, the public can burst into what Howard Rheingold (2002: 175) calls 'sudden epidemics of cooperation', which can be expressed in the form of 'peer-to-peer journalism'. In his 2002 book *Smart Mobs*, Rheingold envisions such a future. He asks the reader to imagine the impact of the 1991 Rodney King video, consisting of citizen witness footage of police brutality in Los Angeles, and to multiply the powerful impact of that video with 'the people power' of Napster (a file-sharing service popular at the time of writing). The result of such a calculation, we know now, is what has become known as *citizen journalism*.

Digital citizen journalism as a phenomenon goes back to the online posting of information in relation to the Clinton–Lewinsky sex scandal in 1998, to the breakthrough of web-based journalism during the war in Kosovo in 1999, and to people's sharing of eyewitness accounts, photographs, and video footage on 9/11 in 2001. The role of the online networked circulation of events of citizen witnessing in these cases proved the power of participatory storytelling in times of drama or trauma. On 9/12 in 2001, *The New York Times* quoted internet activist Rogers Cadenhead as saying that:

> This unfathomable tragedy reminds me of the original reason the Internet was invented in 1969 – to serve as a decentralized network that couldn't be brought down by a military attack. Amateur news reporters on weblogs are functioning as their own decentralized media today, and it's one of the only heartening things about this stomach-turning day. (Harmon 2001: n.p.)

Obviously, digitally networked communication and user-created content in times of crisis have contributed largely in shaping citizen journalism into what it is today. Journalism researcher Stuart Allan (2009: 18) cites the aftermath of the South Asian tsunami of December 2004 as a defining moment, as the first-person accounts documented with mobile and digital cameras – many of them posted online – became a unique addition to the coverage that mainstream journalism was able to provide. Citizen journalism is about the capacity, largely afforded by digital technology, of ordinary people to bear witness to and comment on things that happen in the world, big or small. It has developed from those occasions when 'ordinary people' find themselves in situations that urge them to temporarily enter the role of a journalist, communicating what goes on around them. And as digital technology and the internet has increasingly made it possible for people to act upon such impulses, citizen journalism as an emergent genre has contributed, in recent years, to a transformation of journalism from being seen as a domain exclusive to professional participants.

COMMUNICATION POWER

In the years around 2010, a wave of protest and revolutionary social action seemed to roll across the globe. This was, some said, a new wave of social movements that were different from the ones we knew from before, such as the workers' rights movement, the environmental movement, peace movements, and women's movements. The various movements that emerged around this time – including the uprisings during the so-called Arab Spring, the Indignados anti-austerity movement in Spain, together with similar movements in other countries, as well as the world-wide Occupy protests against social and economic inequality – are all examples of what Castells (2015) calls *networked social movements*. Recent years have seen the emergence of large-scale *hashtag movements* such as #BlackLivesMatter and #MeToo. Particularly,

Twitter hashtags have become increasingly important as a platform for various marginalised or disenfranchised groups to mobilise and make their voice heard. Jackson and colleagues (2020) argue that hashtags can be used to create diverse networks of resistance through which social change can be advocated. These movements have a common approach: they largely ignore political parties, circumvent the mainstream (news) media, do not recognise any traditional forms of leadership, and largely reject formal organisation. Importantly, many of them also started in social networks on the internet. Such networks, Castells says, are 'spaces of autonomy' where participants can coordinate, debate issues collectively, and come to different forms of agreements and decisions.

The networks that engage citizens and activists, formed by connection and interaction on the internet and in social media, are therefore autonomous, and potentially disruptive, spaces. This is because they are beyond the control of those governments and corporations that have monopolised most communication channels throughout history. Looking back once again at Chapter 3, we can see that Castells is an optimist in the sense that he thinks that the internet and social media will make the world a better place: these platforms offer a free public space for connecting with each other, and to envision projects in networks where people's other personal views or attachments are backgrounded. He concedes, however, that even though many present-day movements started on the internet, they then moved out into the streets. Social movements need to carve out public spaces, he says, that are not limited to the internet. This is why many of them occupy urban space through protests and manifestations. He describes the historical moment around 2010:

> From the safety of cyberspace, people from all ages and conditions moved towards occupying urban space, on a blind date with each other and with the destiny they wanted to forge, as they claimed their right to make history – their history. (Castells 2015: 2)

The potentially strong impact of these digitally networked social campaigns and movements can be explained with the help of Castells' (2009) theory of *communication power*. It suggests that power relationships are constitutive of society, because those who are in power will always construct social institutions according to their specific interests and worldviews. Power, in turn, can be partly exercised in a violent manner, by coercion and hands-on control. But power built on coercion alone will, by necessity, be short-lived. The fundamental struggle, Castells explains, is the struggle over the construction of meaning in people's minds, which happens through 'symbolic manipulation'. This is what Marxist theorist Antonio Gramsci (1971) meant when he wrote about the concept of hegemony, which refers to the process by which subordinated groups in society are made to accept the leadership, ideas, and values of the dominant group, without being forced. Gramsci (1971: 12) defined hegemony as being established through:

> The 'spontaneous' consent given by the great masses of the population to the general direction imposed on social life by the dominant fundamental group; this consent is 'historically' caused by the prestige (and consequent confidence) which the dominant group enjoys because of its position and function in the world of production.

According to this view, dominant groups in society maintain their dominant positions as a consequence of a consensus among both dominating and dominated groups that the unequal pattern of dominance is legitimate. Put simply, those in power stay dominant because everyone thinks that this is fine, even if they are being dominated themselves. Such consensus is built in the process by which humans create meaning through interaction with their social environment. This happens through communication – the practice by which people share meaning through exchanging information. Returning to Castells, he argues that the ongoing transformation of communication technology in the digital age has given rise to new ways of constructing meaning.

You will remember from Chapter 5 that Castells' name for the new mode of interaction in digital society is 'mass self-communication'. And now, because people are able to autonomously self-produce and self-select content, this mass self-communication has the potential to reach a huge multiplicity of receivers, as communication networks have become increasingly horizontal. Furthermore, as Castells points out, digital communication is multimodal – it is embedded in a complex system of networked text, images, video, and relationships that allows users to constantly reference a 'global hypertext' of content. Such digitally networked content can be reused and remixed by users according to many different specific needs and ends. In sum, mass self-communication offers a technological platform for the construction of autonomous social actors, both individual and collective. Castells (2015: 7) states that 'this is why governments are afraid of the Internet' and 'why corporations have a love–hate relationship with it and are trying to extract profits while limiting its potential for freedom'.

Historically speaking, social movements have always been dependent on the existence of different forms of communication mechanisms, such as rumours, sermons, pamphlets, and manifestos. These were spread by the movements involved, through whatever means of communication were available. And in digital society, the tools at hand are the multimodal, horizontal networks of communication that offer the possibility for largely unfettered deliberation and coordination of action.

CONNECTIVE ACTION

Bennett and Segerberg (2012) have explained the new modes of contentious action in examples such as the Arab Spring, Indignados, and Occupy in terms of the proliferation of what they call 'personal action frames'. They argue that all of these movements are unified by the fact that they use digital media in ways that go far beyond the mere sending and receiving of messages. The protests that they deployed operated with little to no involvement from conventional social movement organisations. Instead, they relied on digital peer-to-peer communication in densely layered networks. It was also striking, Bennett and Segerberg say, that even though these new movements appeared to be quite loose around the edges, and organised in highly informal ways, they were able to sustain themselves, even gaining some extra strength as time went on. Generally, these movements all communicated that they were leaderless, and that they wanted labour unions and political parties, as well as more radical groups, to stay at the margins.

The power of the movements was a result of them organising in quite invisible ways, but not affiliating or branding their actions with any particular organisations with conventional forms of memberships. Historically, social movements have largely shaped identities and actions by thinking in terms of a homogeneous collective 'we' – drawing on collective action frames. But these new movements were instead using more personal action frames. They function by casting a net of public engagement that is much broader, by drawing on easy-to-personalise action themes, even if those themes ultimately may be rooted in deep-reaching injustices based on collective identifications such as race and gender. Similar to Castells' concept of mass self-communication as an enabler for the wide circulation of personal ideas, Bennett and Segerberg argue that the new movements are characterised by people's digitally social sharing of very personalised accounts, as memes. One such example is the 'we are the 99 per cent' slogan that was widely used in the Occupy movement, and which was spread rapidly through online social networks of individuals; other examples are, of course, hashtags such as #JeSuisCharlie, #MeToo, or #BlackLivesMatter (Freelon et al. 2016; Rambukkana 2015).

At the same time, politics has increasingly become an expression of ideas, hopes, and grievances, which are highly personal. The issues dealt with by these new political formations may in many cases resemble older and well-known concerns of previous movements or parties, such as environmental issues, civil rights, trade fairness, gender equality, and so on. But in digital society, Bennett and Segerberg (2012) say, the mechanisms according to which action is organised are much more personalised. They are no longer based on strict group identities, formal membership, or shared full ideologies. People may indeed still join in large numbers – even larger than before – but the movement identity can be very heterogeneous and is the result of diverse forms of personal expression at a large scale, rather than of identification with a common group or ideology.

Digitally networked movements often spread their ideas in the form of easily personalised and meme-like (see Chapter 2) little pieces of activist raw material. An example of this is the wide and multifaceted adoption of the phrase 'Je suis Charlie' (I am Charlie) in the aftermath of the 2015 massacre at the offices of the French weekly magazine *Charlie Hebdo*. First used on Twitter, the slogan shortly became circulated in the form of placards, stickers, banners, and hashtags in many languages and contexts. Such personal action frames are inclusive, and enable a large variety of different individual reasons for people manifesting or contesting something. Digital society also offers a variety of personal communication technologies that make it possible to share such themes in the form of text, images, tweets, status updates, profiles, remixes, or mashups. Collective action frames, by contrast, demand that individuals share much more far-reaching common identifications and views in order to be able to act under the same banner.

Looking back at what was discussed in Chapter 5, this development in the field of political activism is related more broadly to the decline of social capital and traditional forms of community, and the emergence of networked individualism. Our present time is marked by individualisation as well as structural fragmentation, and the increased emphasis on personal action frames is certainly one aspect of this more general development. Fragmentation and individualisation may not sound like a good breeding-ground for collective action, but personal action frames have proven to be quite successful. Compared with conventional movements, in which traditional membership organisations have led the way, the more personalised and digitally mediated forms of collective action have often proven to scale up faster, and be more flexible in bridging different issues and tracking moving political targets.

The power of personal action frames can, at least in part, be explained by the fact that it is much more demanding to build and spread collective identifications than personalised ones. Producing commonly shared ideas and identities requires us to put more pressure on the socialisation of members and potential members. This, in turn, means that such forms of activism need to be formally organised, and cost more in terms of time, effort, and money. Conventional collective action also demands that people make more difficult choices. Joining traditional types of social movements entails the adoption of more self-changing social identities. Joining a movement such as Greenpeace may require a larger lifestyle change than engaging with more personal action frames on the internet and in social media. This illustrates the emergence of an alternative to the model of collective action, in the form of what Bennett and Segerberg (2012) call *connective action*.

189

Connective action is an increasingly common form of political engagement in digital society, where many formal organisations are losing their influence over individuals, and where conventional group ties are replaced by networked individualism. Connective action happens, Bennett and Segerberg explain, when communication becomes a dominant part of the organisational structure. Collective action relies on high levels of organisational resources that are devoted to forming collective identities, while connective action is based on people's personalised sharing of content across media networks. An important point here is that movements that are based on collective action can indeed use digital tools and platforms, but in such cases they do not transform the core dynamics of the action which is carried out. In movements based on connective action, however, they do. Here, the very logic of sociality in social media becomes the organising agent. As you may remember from Chapter 3, Yochai Benkler (2006) wrote about this logic in terms of peer production. As Benkler proposes, the parameters of collective action are altered as people participate and share things online with people who, in turn, recognise their efforts and therefore do the same thing – take part and share. This becomes a self-motivating participatory system.

Bennett and Segerberg (2012) conclude that when digital social platforms coordinate and scale the networks of action, something similar to collective action – but without formal organisation – can become the result. This is connective action – a mode for activism and contention, drawing on people's co-production and co-distribution of ideas.

When people take action, or contribute in other ways, within the logic of connective action, their acts of personal – but not necessarily self-centred – expression becomes part of a powerful aggregated whole. So, while a problem with collective action may be to get individuals to contribute, the contributions of individuals are the very starting building blocks of connective action. Conventional movements face the challenge of making supporters, and potential supporters, internalise and personalise the ideas, the imagery, and the essence of the movement. Movements built on connective action, to the contrary, come into their very being by connecting (yes!), via social media, personal – already internalised – ideas and resources with networks of others. Therefore, such movements are highly empowered from the start, because they already live in the hearts and minds of the participants, who now also connect in large-scale networks.

A DIGITAL REPERTOIRE OF CONTENTION

The perspectives that have been discussed in this chapter agree that digital tools and platforms, under the right circumstances, can enhance or transform activism, making it more powerful. But what factors decide such circumstances? What regulates whether the circumstances are right or wrong? Digital media researcher

Alex Galloway (2004) discussed such issues in his book *Protocol*, in which he asked how 'control exists after decentralisation'. If digital media can potentially enable mass self-communication and powerful forms of contention, how is it decided whether this potential is realised or not? Galloway approaches this by focusing on how the creation of a number of 'protocols' have been crucial for the creation, as well as for the continued development, of the internet and the web. He explains that internet communication demands the implementation of a whole package of different protocols – common languages for computers on the network. Digital society, according to Galloway (2004: 111), is a society in which 'protocol becomes the controlling force in social life'.

In other words, protocols are at the centre of all digital tools and platforms that use the internet. For example, protocols developed by the World Wide Web Consortium (WC3), such as Hypertext Markup Language (html) and Cascading Style Sheets (css), decide how much of the web's content works and how it is displayed. Other actors have created many other protocols, for a wide range of purposes. Referring to the relationship between the protocols of TCP/IP and DNS, Galloway (2004: 8) suggests that the internet rests on 'a contradiction between two opposing machines'. He explains how the former – the one assigning IP addresses to devices – distributes control among a huge number of autonomous agents. But the latter – the one translating IP addresses into URLs – organises control rigidly into a centralised and hierarchical database. The same reasoning can be extended into the domain of social media platforms, where the platforms, on the one hand, offer fairly open environments where people can express themselves. On the other hand, the owners are able to ban, censor, or 'deplatform' users as they wish (Rogers 2020). Also, governments can strike back against protesters and other activists by censoring, blocking, or shutting down internet services. In fact, anyone controlling a root server has the power to remove entire countries or continents from the web with the stroke of a delete key. This means that the internet can work in many different ways, as it is built on protocols which involve a complex set of forces, some reactionary, some progressive. Even though its distributed network structure marks an attempt at the level of code and technology to eliminate hierarchies, the internet is still structured around control and command. So, returning to the issue of contention and social movements, in order to successfully leverage the affordances of digital tools and platforms, activists must be able to deploy 'counter-protocological forces'. This is done through what Galloway (2004: 176) defines as *tactical media*:

> those phenomena that are able to exploit flaws in protocological and proprietary command and control [...] to sculpt protocol and make it better suited to people's real desires. [...] Tactical media propel protocol into a state of hypertrophy, pushing it further, in better and more interesting ways.

While Galloway's discussion relies heavily on the role of code in how machines interrelate, the argument can definitely be extended into the sphere of social action. He gives the example of how cyberfeminism, as a form of tactical media, has been a successful movement because it has been able to 'disturb' protocol. Much like computer 'bugs' are disturbances in code, cyberfeminism – or other forms of activism – can be seen as metaphorical bugs in the social system. Successful digital activism can be likened to the bugs, crashes, and viruses, which can disrupt protocol and can propel technology (or society) in new and interesting directions. In other words, successful activist tactics in digital society may be best performed by 'liminal agents' that are 'at once inside protocol and outside its reach' (Galloway 2004: 186).

Sociologist Charles Tilly (1977) wrote about the means through which social movements rely on different *repertoires of contention*, which means that these movements have different sets of tools and methods that are available to them, and through which they can create their actions. He wrote that 'every means of collective action [...] at a given point in history [...] belongs to a familiar repertoire of collective actions which are at the disposal of ordinary people' (Tilly 1977: 493). Tilly said that in the mid-19th century, a traditional repertoire that had shaped collective action up until then was replaced by a modern repertoire. A characteristic of the modern repertoire was that it enabled movements to be more enduring – lasting longer across space and time – for example, like the green movement, or the women's movement. But both repertoires demanded that members of a movement were co-present, and that the tactics that they used were seen as a coherent means to a clearly identifiable end. Both repertoires also assumed that movements were politically oriented and focused on what could be seen as 'important' issues in society.

In digital society, however, Earl and Kimport (2011) identify a rupture in this historically persistent pattern. A new *digital repertoire of contention* is emerging. The internet and social media have made collective action possible without participants being in the same place or time. Movements in digital society are mostly disconnected from larger, conventional social movements, and they can be short, sporadic, and episodic, just as easily as they may be of an enduring nature. Digital contention, furthermore, is not necessarily about politics in the narrow sense, or even about 'important' issues. The same tactics that are used for serious concerns can be used in a wide range of areas. As costs of activism are lower, perhaps the stakes can sometimes be lower too. Today we are seeing a completely new form of activism emerging, which is more based on swarms, seeming (or actual) randomness, or fragmentation, yet with a new sense of coordination.

CHAPTER SUMMARY

Continuing from Chapter 8's discussions about power and exploitation, this chapter has focused more on resistance 'from below' than dominance 'from above'.

I have introduced the various contributions to the academic debates over if and how the digital media can function as a public sphere where democratic deliberation among citizens can take place. In some ways, the internet may work as a public sphere in the historically established way, but in some respects in has some characteristics that demand us to update our conceptual framework. Furthermore, the chapter has addressed how digital media enable citizens to scrutinise those in power in new ways, for example through so-called citizen journalism. Documenting wrong-doings and making them visible to the world is a powerful way of exposing and critiquing the abuse of power. Digital media have become popular tools for social movement mobilisation, and while movements still sometimes work as they used to, but with digital platforms extending their reach, there is also a new digital repertoire of contention emerging. This includes natively digital forms, such as hashtag movements, connective (as opposed to collective) action, and other forms of activist disruption.

FURTHER READING

Habermas, Jürgen (1989). *The Structural Transformation of the Public Sphere*. Cambridge, UK: Polity Press.

Habermas' book is not about digital society, but his historical discussion as well as his ideas about what characterises an ideal public sphere are still useful to read. The book is a classic and anyone studying public debate or social deliberation won't get far without knowing its main points.

Calhoun, Craig (1998). Community without Propinquity Revisited. *Sociological Inquiry*, 68(3), 373–397.

Dean, Jodi (2001). Cybersalons and Civil Society. *Public Culture*, 13(2), 243–265.

These are two important papers about digital media, civil society, and the public sphere. Calhoun wrote about whether 'virtual community' has a capacity to enhance the power of citizens. He argued that digital media have ambiguous effects on democracy. For example, they can facilitate mobilisation, but can also foster categorical identities. Dean's paper is about the need to rethink the public sphere in the age of the internet. She says that 'cybersalons', computer-mediated discussion among people brought together by shared interests, provides a conceptual tool for thinking about democracy in digital society.

(Continued)

Enzensberger, Hans Magnus (1970). Constituents of a Theory of the Media. *New Left Review*, 64, 13–36.

Enzensberger's essay from 1970 about how citizens can use 'electronic media' not only for consumption but also for production is very commonly cited. It includes some amazingly apt insights that he made before the age of the widely available internet and social media. He wrote of the potential of new network-like communication models to reverse the ways in which media circulated: 'a mass newspaper, written and distributed by its readers, a video network of politically active groups'.

Bennett, W. Lance & Segerberg, Alexandra (2012). The Logic of Connective Action. *Information, Communication & Society*, 15(5), 739–768.

This article, published in 2012, really put its mark on the scholarly discussion about digital media and political activism. Bennett and Segerberg coin the notion of 'connective action' (as opposed to collective action) to refer to the organisational dynamics that emerge in organisations built on communication. Conventional collective movements will be less able than new connective ones to harness the power of digital media to enable personalised public engagement.

Earl, Jennifer & Kimport, Katrina (2011). *Digitally Enabled Social Change*. Cambridge, MA: The MIT Press.

This book by Earl and Kimport discusses the differences between online political activity and more traditional types of activism. The authors work through a number of empirical cases and discuss aspects of the new 'digital repertoire of contention'. They identify the two key affordances of digital media – that they reduce costs and bridge physical distance – and argue that the more these are leveraged the more transformative the activism will be.

Jackson, Sarah J., Bailey, Moya & Foucault Welles, Brooke (2020). *#HashtagActivism: Networks of Race and Gender Justice*. Cambridge, MA: The MIT Press.

The authors of this book present excellent work about hashtag campaigns and movements, such as #SayHerName, #MeToo, #BlackLivesMatter, and #GirlsLikeUs. Discussing the development from when hashtag activism had its breakthrough in 2011, up until today, they analyse the role of Twitter as a platform for resisting oppressive structures of power. A key focus of the book is on the diverse networks that have been mobilised, and on how hashtag activism has become a powerful tool for the historically disenfranchised.

10

DATAFICATION AND ALGORITHMS

DATAFICATION AND SURVEILLANCE CAPITALISM

Today's societies are not only digital – they are also datafied. The concept of datafication refers to the fact that different forms of data play an increasingly crucial role in society and culture, and that ever more aspects of the world – including those that were not previously quantified – are rendered into data. This includes the increased collection, by companies and governments, of demographic and profiling data, but also social media data drawing on what people do online, and behavioural data based on automatically registered timestamps and GPS-locations of, for example, smartphones (Kennedy et al. 2015).

A central buzzword in relation to society's datafication has been *big data*. This phenomenon has been defined in several different ways since the term was first used in the mid-1990s to refer to the handling and analysis of massively large datasets. According to a popular definition, big data conforms with three Vs: it has volume (enormous quantities of data), velocity (is generated in real-time), and variety (can be structured, semi-structured, or unstructured). To this, various writers and researchers have suggested a number of other criteria be added, such as exhaustivity, relationality, veracity, and value. During a review of a number of big data sets in order to find their common traits, Rob Kitchin and Gavin McArdle (2016) found that the two most important characteristics of big data are velocity and exhaustivity. This means that big data captures entire systems rather than samples (exhaustivity) and that it does so in real-time (velocity). Crawford and boyd (2012) think that 'big data' is in fact a poorly chosen term. This is because its alleged power is not mainly about its size, but about its capacity to compare, connect, aggregate, and cross-reference many different types of datasets (that also happen to be big). They define big data as:

a cultural, technological, and scholarly phenomenon that rests on the interplay of: (1) Technology: maximizing computation power and algorithmic accuracy to gather, analyze, link, and compare large data sets. (2) Analysis: drawing on large data sets to identify patterns in order to make economic, social, technical, and legal claims. (3) Mythology: the widespread belief that large data sets offer a higher form of intelligence and knowledge that can generate insights that were previously impossible, with the aura of truth, objectivity, and accuracy. (Crawford & boyd 2012: 664)

Datafication involves both the collection and analysis of data about users of the internet, and the process of feeding that data back to users through things such as search recommendations or targeted advertising. This means that there is reason to think critically about data in terms of surveillance and personal integrity. Shoshana Zuboff (2019) has claimed that we now live in the age of *surveillance capitalism*, where data on the lives of humans is increasingly used as free-for-all raw materials to be translated into actionable behavioural data. Zuboff wrote in 2014 about how the world was then standing on the threshold of the age of big data. Even though much of the hype around that buzzword, in the narrower sense where it had been assumed to pave the way for more profitable businesses and more correct prognoses, had waned, she pointed out that the history of its socio-political consequences had only just begun. Even though data are collected at breakneck speed in enormous volumes, there is much deliberation over what the data should be used for, and who should be allowed to decide. Applying a critical perspective on capitalism, Zuboff argues that the big digital businesses that dominate the markets where social media platforms are deployed and digital devices are bought and sold are driven by the goal of economic growth and free competition, and that they therefore want everyone to believe that this is what society 'objectively' needs. Data should be collected and used in ways that maximise profits. Paraphrasing the neoliberal theorist Friedrich Hayek, Zuboff (2014: n.p.) warns that this scenario can easily become like an unquestionable machinery – a self-determining order 'that individuals cannot understand but to which they must submit'. She describes the emerging big data age as a key historical moment in the history of technology.

In this moment, such as in other historical moments (e.g. that of industrialisation), it is important to remember that while the transformation may appear to be all about the technology, we must not forget that it is even more about people and relations of power. Zuboff states that life in 2050 will be decided by the choices we make now. Especially, she says, it is important to choose the political language that we use when we are talking about 'big data' and datafication. This is because, she argues, human civilisation – the future of our societies – is decided through how we create meaning around it. What Zuboff is saying, in other words, is that society and technology are mutually shaped, and that our social reality in general has no fixed meaning, aside from the meanings that we collectively ascribe to it. This is why it is so important to approach notions such as that of 'big data' from a critical perspective.

Datafication is the consequence of all of the information that is presently flowing, throughout our digital society, and that is generated largely by people's online behaviours (clicks, likes, shares, link follows, and so on), but also to a very large extent through things dispersed throughout places and spaces in the form of sensors, surveillance cameras, street view, satellites, and in databases of governments and of corporations in banking, telecommunications, credit ratings, and so on. These data, especially when they are all thrown into the same bucket, are unstructured. They have not been systematically collected by any single actor with any single agenda for any single purpose. Rather, they are data traces (see Chapter 12), or as Zuboff puts it: 'data exhaust'. The data which are 'harvested from the haphazard ephemera of everyday lives' (Zuboff 2014: n.p.) are user-generated and consist of the byproducts of our online and everyday lives. Our Google searches, Instagram likes, emails, texts, songs listened to, videos watched, our purchases, voice assistant commands, locations, movements, and so on, are being captured and datafied (as in them being translated into machine-readable data). Companies like Google and Facebook, and many others, offer their services to users for free, which increases the amount of 'data exhaust' that it can offer to its customers, that is advertisers and other buyers of data. Zuboff refers to what author George Orwell (1946: 265) once wrote about how political language 'is designed to make lies sound truthful and murder respectable, and to give an appearance of solidity to pure wind'. Just like other euphemisms, Zuboff writes, so can the words 'big data' distract us from an uglier truth that lies behind them. She goes on to explain that:

> The ugly truth here is that much of 'big data' is plucked from our lives without our knowledge or informed consent. It is the fruit of a rich array of surveillance practices designed to be invisible and undetectable as we make our way across the virtual and real worlds. The pace of these developments is accelerating. (Zuboff 2014: n.p.)

These practices are at the centre of surveillance capitalism, and as these operations are largely hidden, they can do significant harm, both material and political, social and psychological. What emerges is a new form of economic power where the likes, clicks, and movements of users becomes an asset that can attract investments. Zuboff calls these 'surveillance assets' and 'surveillance capital', respectively. Together, they make up the core of the variant of 'informational capitalism' (see Castells 2010), which she calls surveillance capitalism. By contrast to how Marx described industrial capitalism to be based on the extraction of value from the labour of people, in surveillance capitalism value is extracted from the 'leftover' data assets left behind by users. Because of this, Zuboff argues, we must realise that behind the neutral, or even positive, term 'big data' lies something more controversial and dangerous. As she puts it: 'one person's "big data" is another person's stolen good', so why not call it 'big contraband' instead? (Zuboff 2014: n.p.). In the wake of the revelations made by computer intelligence consultant Edward Snowden in 2013, when he disclosed information about a number of global surveillance programs that were run by the United States National Security Agency and others, an increased critical awareness of the reality and consequences of surveillance capitalism was raised among many. Similarly, as data consultant Christopher Wylie disclosed information about data misuse in relation to the much-publicised Facebook–Cambridge Analytica data scandal, even more voices have been raised calling for data justice.

From a more methodological standpoint, sociologist Deborah Lupton (2014: 101) argues that the hype that surrounds the new technological possibilities afforded by big data analyses contribute to the belief that such data are 'raw materials' for information – that they contain the untarnished truth about society and sociality. In reality, each step of the process in the generation of big data relies on a number of human decisions relating to selection, judgement, interpretation, and action. Therefore, the data that we will have at hand are always configured via beliefs, values, and choices that '"cook" the data from the very beginning so that they are never in a "raw" state'. So, there is no such thing as raw data, even though the orderliness of neatly harvested and stored big data sets can create a mirage to the contrary.

Lupton (2016) writes that the move towards tracking and monitoring users' movements within and across digitally networked tools and platforms has given rise to new ways of conceptualising people and what they do. Instead of conventional socially and culturally embedded identities, that can be either anonymous or not, we develop 'data selves' that are configured by the bits of information we generate and collect. As Lupton suggests, one might argue that rather than having a traditional sense of selfhood, people today may increasingly begin to understand themselves as an assemblage of data. As we are becoming data (Cheney-Lippold 2017), we must understand ourselves as such. This process is further extended with the development of our 'quantified selves' as a consequence of the increased use of techniques of 'lifelogging', personal informatics, and personal analytics, through apps and wearable technologies such as smart watches and exercise wristbands. These are parts of processes where we voluntarily track, monitor, and register ourselves with tools that push data to cloud servers, the right to which we probably signed away to someone else by accepting some lengthy and complicated user agreement that we probably did not read (cf. Maronick, 2014).

ALGORITHMS

One of the main uses of data is to feed it into the *algorithms* that increasingly are governing crucial parts of social, cultural, and political life. From a strictly computational point of view, algorithms are mathematical procedures that are performed in a controlled fashion on data in order to be able to present an output in the shape of other forms of data. Algorithms are the important procedural logics that undergird all computation. The storage and reading of data, the application of procedures to it, and the delivery of some form of output can be done by hand as well, but the way in which digital society relies on computational tools has turned automation and digital routines into a social key mechanism, which governs the flows of information on which we depend.

In the history of digital society, we have left concepts such as 'the computer age' or 'the internet age' behind. They refer to periods that are now passed, even though, of course, both computers and the internet live on. Similarly, we may even have left 'the social media age', even though social media live on deeply embedded in our everyday lives. Recently, there has been more talk about an 'age of datafication' or an 'age of algorithms'. Algorithms – the bits of computer code that are used to follow people around online, to manage political campaigns, to monitor health data, to suggest whom we should date, or to target us with advertising are often approached as a form of 'higher authority' (Louridas 2020: 2). Even though critical awareness of algorithms is on the rise in society, there is still often an air of mystery, of obscured agency, when we speak of algorithms. We refer to how things happen because of algorithms, but we seldom hold them accountable, or dig any deeper to find the human intentions behind them.

Computer scientist Pedro Domingos (2015: 1) writes of a 'machine-learning revolution' and states that:

> Today, algorithms are in every nook and cranny of civilization. They are woven into the fabric of everyday life. They're not just in your cell phone or your laptop but in your car, your house, your appliances, and your toys. Your bank is a gigantic tangle of algorithms, with humans turning the knobs here and there. Algorithms schedule flights and then fly the airplanes. Algorithms run factories, trade and route goods, cash the proceeds, and keep records. If every algorithm suddenly stopped working, it would be the end of the world as we know it.

Management and technology scholar Panos Louridas (2020) argues that it is important to realise that algorithms are by no means magical. Rather, they are often surprisingly basic. He explains that no matter how powerful an algorithm may be, its way of working can always be traced back to quite elementary operations. Indeed, algorithms may be very intelligently conceived and elegantly designed, but they are not mysterious. Algorithms, in essence, are simply a kind of mathematics. Louridas (2020: 3) explains that:

> They are tools that allow us to do certain things well; they are specific kinds of tools whose purpose is to allow us to solve problems. In this way they are cognitive tools; as such, they are not the only ones. Numbers and arithmetic are also cognitive tools. It took us thousands of years to evolve a number system that children can learn in school so that they can perform calculations that would be impossible without it. Now we take numeracy for granted, but a few generations back only a small minority of humans had any knowledge of it.

Such a view points forward to the fact that just as it is useful to know about addition, subtraction, and geometry, there will be an increased interest in the future for what has been called 'algorithmic literacy'. Critical data researcher Kelley Cotter (2020) argues that promoting critical algorithmic literacy is a means to strengthen people's involvement in various efforts and initiatives that can lead to algorithms being governed in more democratic ways, that promote the public interest rather than capitalist interests. At its core, algorithmic literacy is about understanding what algorithms do, and why they to it, but importantly also to understand what the consequences mean for society (Cotter 2020: 2). It is about resisting the social power of algorithms (Beer 2017).

Media and communications scholar Taina Bucher (2012: 1), writing about 'programmed sociality', argues that algorithms can 'establish certain forms of sociality' by way of how they 'produce the conditions for the sensible and intelligible'. We rely on search engines for the navigation of massive informational databases, or the entire web, and in this process, algorithms help us decide and select what information is important to us. For example, many online services and platforms have recommendation algorithms that suggest to us which book to buy, which Twitter users to follow, what TV series to watch next, who to 'friend', which content is 'hot' or 'trending', and so on. In doing their work, algorithms highlight some bits of the world, while hiding others. For Gillespie (2014: 168), the role of algorithms in society is important since where we may have previously relied on credentialled experts, scientists, 'common sense', or religious authority for correct knowledge about reality, we have now turned to algorithms. One of the risks with this development is the emergence of so-called *filter bubbles*. Activist and author Eli Pariser (2011) has argued that the evolution of Google and social media, with their underlying algorithms, has ushered people into a personalised and filtered world, where all search results and other information that they are served reinforces their pre-existing values as well as their view on the world. This compartmentalisation and customisation erodes the common ground that people need to share in order to build community and to engage in democratic politics. This development brings many problems; our beliefs are seldom challenged, which reduces our drive and desire to try to understand others and to incorporate alternative ways of thinking and seeing the world. An element of randomness is needed if we are to be open to discovery.

A consideration of exactly what algorithms might include or exclude is a vital area for research. In practice, algorithms and the databases upon which they are applied are seen as one and the same phenomenon. But, as Gillespie (2014) argues, from an analytic point of view, the two must be studied separately. Algorithms are meaningless without data, and before an algorithm can generate any type of output or result, some information must be collected as input. This process always includes a set of choices about what should be collected and how it should be ordered and 'readied for the algorithm'. The collected data must always be cleaned and ordered into some form of matrix or other readable structure. Furthermore, data – even before they are collected – can be trimmed, primed, and vetted by owners of sites and platforms. Content which is deemed to be 'problematic' can be removed altogether, but it can also be algorithmically demoted in subtler ways. YouTube, for example, withholds 'suggestive content' from lists of most watched videos, or in other recommendation systems. Generally, there is a process of tidying up data. Gillespie (2014: 172) says that: 'Indexes are culled of spam and viruses, patrolled for copyright infringement and pornography, and scrubbed of the obscene, the objectionable, or the politically contentious.'

Such tidying is of course necessary, and even helpful, to a certain degree. But it is still valuable to reflect upon this as a form of subtle censorship and to analyse what the choices mean, especially when algorithms have an aura of 'pure' automation and objectivity. It is also important to consider the social character of algorithms – after all, someone designed and devised them. Rather than thinking only about the effects of algorithms, it might be more fruitful to scrutinise them in terms of their entanglement with the lived world of their creators and users. The entanglement of algorithms with users leads to the rise of what Gillespie calls 'calculated publics'. He explains how algorithms create types of publics that don't really exist in the conventional sense:

> When Amazon recommends a book that 'customers like you' bought, it is invoking and claiming to know a public with which we are invited to feel an affinity – though the population on which it bases these recommendations is not transparent, and is certainly not coterminous with its entire customer base. When Facebook offers a privacy setting that a user's information be seen by 'friends, and friends of friends,' it transforms a discrete set of users into an audience – it is a group that did not exist until that moment, and only Facebook knows its precise membership. These algorithmically generated groups may overlap with, be an inexact approximation of, or have nothing whatsoever to do with the publics that the user sought out. (Gillespie 2014: 188–189)

Similarly, Twitter's algorithm that shows live 'trending' topics within a certain national or regional public also leads to the definition of a highly constructed public, shaped by criteria that are specific and unspecified at the same time. Gillespie defines the notion of *calculated publics* in relation to that of networked publics (see Chapter 2). His main point is that there is a friction in digital society between the – networked – publics that are forged by users through their social interaction with each other and the calculated, somewhat artificial, publics that are generated through algorithms.

Depending on how they are used, and by whom, algorithms may indeed be beneficial in some cases, but they may also be exploited to manipulate users. In February 2016, Twitter announced the launch of its 'algorithmic timeline', which was followed by a storm of protests from its users. The change meant that the service would depart from the presentation of tweets in reverse chronological order, in favour of the provision of algorithmically produced tweets, based on user activities. *Wired* magazine contributor Brian Barrett presented an analysis of the changes that indicated that new and uninitiated users might be aided by the new, more accessible method of presenting tweets – 'isolating the signal from the noise'. However, as Barrett wrote, power users who were comfortable with the platform, and had a longer history and familiarity with the original reverse chronological presentation became suspicious and launched hashtags such as #RIPTwitter. So, while some individuals, in some contexts, might be perfectly happy to have their content feeds 'refined' by algorithms, other individuals in other contexts may feel that the very same algorithms 'destroy' their feeds.

So once again, it is important to carry out critical social analyses of algorithms, because they have a certain unquestionable quality to them. Even if we know that an algorithm selectively puts our YouTube start page together, it is still somewhat natural to perceive it as being *the* YouTube start page. But, as Gillespie (2014: 169) argues, algorithms are socially constructed, rather than objective and precise:

> A sociological analysis must not conceive of algorithms as abstract, technical achievements, but must unpack the warm human and institutional choices that lie behind these cold mechanisms. I suspect that a more fruitful approach will turn as much to the sociology of knowledge as to the sociology of technology. [...] This might help reveal that the seemingly solid algorithm is in fact a fragile accomplishment.

Furthermore, Gillespie writes, the algorithms that underpin digital society, the internet, and social media platforms all contribute to the production and legitimisation of knowledge, according to a logic based on assumptions that are very specific. Hepp (2020) argues that in the age of deep mediatisation (see Chapter 1), the study of algorithms becomes vital, as the social world is now not only constructed by the people who inhabit it, but also through artificial intelligence and automated forms of data processing. Even though the algorithms are developed by humans, once implemented they can act as hidden infrastructures that underpin our lived realities. One out of many examples of this, shown in research, is that negative biases based on gender and race become embedded in algorithms in hidden ways (Noble 2018). When, in turn, the algorithms are implemented in, for example, search engines, recommendation systems, processes of automated decision-making, and policing, the social consequences can be far-reaching and devastating. This is why it is important to examine algorithms as a key feature of the media ecosystem of digital society. What are these specific assumptions in relation to given algorithms and contexts, and what are their social and political ramifications?

Algorithmic power derives from the fact that algorithms are active in monitoring us as citizens (cf. surveillance capitalism) and because algorithms have become unquestionable while we know nothing or too little about their inner workings. The development of algorithmic skills and literacy among people in general and in civil society appears to be the best way in which to respond to all of this. Studies in this area have shown that many people feel there is a problem that those who create the algorithms which increasingly govern social life are not scrutinised enough and held accountable (Rainie & Anderson 2017). There is a need to raise awareness about these issues, and to adopt a more critical approach so that people can develop and employ their critical skills more effectively when interacting with algorithms and their hidden logics. And there needs to be a higher degree of 'algorithm transparency' (Rainie &

Anderson 2017: 74). Just as people have had to develop critical skills in relation to previous historical technologies – media and others – and to understand their logics, so there is now a need to develop mechanisms that will give people more control and trust in the age of algorithms. A desirable way forward would be threefold: to teach people to understand how algorithms work and to be critical and aware; to pass legislation which is more apt to deal with the rapid technological and social changes; and to launch initiatives to ensure the tech giants are transparent about and accountable for the algorithms they use. Aside from this, academics and scholars also have a responsibility to carry out critical research on how algorithms function, and how they can be sometimes exposed and ousted, and sometimes evaluated and bettered.

Cotter (2020) argues that if we are able to develop critical algorithmic literacy, we will be able to involve citizens more in the development, deployment, and governance of algorithms. The problem persists, however, that most algorithms that have profound impacts on our lives are corporately owned, which means that those in control of them have no obligation to change them just because people point out their problems. But, Cotter (2020: 252) argues, the more knowledgeable the public becomes about algorithms, the stronger a foundation we will have for petitioning for changes and updates that can take the algorithms closer to serving their communities' interests and needs. Furthermore, she says, a high level of algorithmic literacy and awareness in society will also make it possible for people to more effectively urge elected officials to promote policies that put a check on platforms' power and accountability.

DISCUSSION

Algorithms are ubiquitous and pervasive. They are found everywhere, and they spread widely. As they are implemented in ways that we don't always think of, on our computers, smartphones, and other devices, as well as in the various digital services that we rely on, it is important to think critically about them. In 2018, Facebook announced that one of their main focus areas looking ahead would be to 'prioritise posts that spark conversations and meaningful interactions between people'. To achieve this, they would 'predict which posts you might want to interact with your friends about, and show these posts higher in [the] feed' (Mosseri 2018: n.p.). In light of the issues about algorithmic power and literacy, discussed above, think about what might be the potential negative consequences of the Facebook strategy to promote 'meaningful interactions' and to 'spark conversations'. Are there benefits, in terms of, for example, efficiency and convenience, of using algorithms in this way that may outweigh the potential downsides?

The proliferation of datafication and algorithms is also related to processes by which key aspects of social life become increasingly automated. Recent years have seen many examples of how these developments have affected democracy and participation in negative ways. These cases include instances and debates over 'fake news'/ post truth (Corner 2017; Flaxman et al. 2016), racism and sexism embedded in algorithms (Noble 2018), scandals surrounding data surveillance ('dataveillance') and psychometric profiling (Hu 2020; Orito 2011), and automated disinformation campaigns (Woolley & Howard 2016). In addition to these impacts on the public sphere, automation also affects society and democracy in more direct ways, such as through the increasing algorithmic governance of citizens, for example through systems for automated decision-making which are implemented in welfare administration and provision, and in police work through so-called predictive policing (Spielkamp 2019).

As mentioned in Chapter 3, a significant part of the debate over the relationship between digital technology and democracy in fact plays out today in relation to issues of datafication, algorithms, and automation. Key works in this area include Noble's *Algorithms of Oppression* (2018), as well as Cathy O'Neil's *Weapons of Math Destruction* (2016). The mark of truly critical research, such as that mentioned above, is that it doesn't simply say that we are all doomed, but instead offers critical analyses and suggests paths forward. More and more scholars now engage not in either/ or discussions, but let their critical analyses feed into suggestions for how to build better democracies in the face of potential risks. Such work is exemplified in Chris Bail's *Breaking the Social Media Prism: How to Make Our Platforms Less Polarizing* (2021) and Phil Howard's *Lie Machines: How to Save Democracy from Troll Armies, Deceitful Robots, Junk News Operations, and Political Operatives* (2020).

DATA JUSTICE

In the wake of the developments leading towards datafication and algorithmic power, there have been calls not only for promoting algorithmic literacy but for broader forms of *data justice*. The argument is that what we are facing as a society, as we are becoming datafied, is not primarily a technological question. Rather, it is about the social and political reasons and consequences of the transformation. The issues raised by datafication and algorithmic power are technologically new, but from a socio-historical standpoint they relate to political, economic, and cultural issues that are longstanding (Dencik et al. 2019). The issues are not only about people being fooled or nudged by algorithms, but about a potential reshaping of social relations that follows from the fact that new things become possible to know, which in turn enables new kinds of social actions.

Furthermore, the ways in which data are generated and collected, as well as the methods and agendas through which data are processed and used, are not void of social agency. Quite the contrary, advocates of the data justice perspective argue, a number of different social forces – actors and interests – contribute to the terms on which datafication happens. This once again actualises the issues about technological determinism that were addressed in Chapter 3. As argued by digital communication and society researcher Lina Dencik, who is also the co-founder and director of the Data Justice Lab in the UK, and colleagues (2019: 873):

> This shifts the focus of the data-society nexus away from simple binaries that frame the debate in terms of trade-offs or 'good' vs. 'bad' data in which data is an abstract technical artefact. Instead, data is seen as something that is situated and necessarily understood in relation to other social practices. By focusing on the concept of 'data justice', [we can address] questions of how our understanding of social justice is changing in the context of datafication, what concepts and practices are needed, and how social justice can be advanced in a datafied society.

In another publication, Dencik, Jansen, and Metcalfe (2018) outline some general ideas for how data justice should be approached by researchers. They suggest that it is important not to get stuck in conceptual discussions about what ideal justice is, but rather to look empirically at those social groups and communities that are affected by injustices rooted in datafication and to examine how this happens. This means being open to how notions of justice may change due to the technological development. At the same time, datafication must be situated historically in relation to longstanding and ongoing struggles and claims for justice. This contextualisation means looking beyond those issues that have been at the centre of early debates about datafication. For example, questions of data protection, integrity, surveillance, and privacy are very important, but a focus on those issues must not come at the cost of backgrounding the maybe even bigger impact that datafication may have more broadly through its impacts in areas of business, government, and civil society. They argue that a wider framework is needed for understanding fully what is at stake. What they propose is a '(re)framing of data as a social justice concern' in broad terms, while many previous perspectives have focused too narrowly on the technological aspects (Dencik et al. 2018: 5).

An all-encompassing perspective on data justice demands, for example, addressing how datafication contributes in far-reaching ways to the way people are seen and treated by states and businesses. This raises questions about a broader kind of data politics, while both datafication and the critiques of it have for some time been primarily technical. As expressed by inclusion and development researcher Linnet Taylor (2017: 1):

the power of data to sort, categorise and intervene has not yet been explicitly connected to a social justice agenda by the agencies and authorities involved. Meanwhile, although data-driven discrimination is advancing at a similar pace to data processing technologies, awareness and mechanisms for combating it are not.

Taylor argues that there must be some middle-ground between prevailing perspectives that emphasise only risk and harm and those that uncritically embrace datafication. An adequate perspective, however, must take into account issues of both technological engagement and non-engagement, and of datafied visibility and invisibility. Several different values must be reconciled as datafication changes the interfaces 'between the individual and the state, between the commercial and public sectors and between science and the public, and they mark out the uncomfortable territory where friction is taking place around privacy, responsibility and accountability' (Taylor 2017: 12).

The data justice perspective provides a way by which to approach the complex relationship between social justice and data, and to do it in a contextualised way that focuses both on socio-political continuities – injustices that prevail across decades or centuries – and on technologically-driven transformations – the new conditions created by datafication. At this intersection, there is the opportunity to understand how the expanding possibilities and practices for amassing large volumes of data, and to process them and let them guide social actions and interventions, may contribute to societal conditions that may both aggravate existing injustices and create new ones. This means moving past merely technological, ethical, or legal questions – however important they are in themselves – to look more sociologically at systemic injustices, and at people's lived experiences, as well as the conditions pertaining to marginalised and exploited groups and communities in society. Importantly, from a civil society perspective, as Dencik and co-authors (2018) argue, this means that data and datafication emerge as issues that should be dealt with not only by lawyers or privacy activists. Rather, they also become the concern of a wider spectrum of movements and groups working to promote social justice. Such initiatives can invite 'more voices to participate in articulating injustices and facilitates critical reflection of where and how governance and agency reside, questioning the boundaries of the investor, engineer, policy-maker, case-worker, and citizen' (Dencik et al. 2018: 6).

CHAPTER SUMMARY

This chapter has built further on some of the issues about the increased role of data in the evolving digital society (Chapters 1, 3 and 4), as well on the issues of exploitation (Chapter 8) and resistance (Chapter 9). We have looked more closely at the particular type of power that is exerted through the process of datafication, but also at how it can be challenged. I have introduced the notion that, following datafication, we live in an age of 'surveillance capitalism', and have thereby laid the foundation for critically analysing so-called big data. This chapter has also dug more deeply into the phenomenon of algorithms, trying to understand what they are and how these technological phenomena increasingly and sometimes covertly affect our social lives. There is a certain kind of algorithmic power being exerted, and we have looked at how some scholars have pointed out the need for increased algorithmic literacy. In the name of democracy, people must be skilled at deconstructing and criticising algorithms. In line with this, advocates of 'data justice' have argued that beyond the issues of transparency and literacy, we must understand these processes in broader terms. They are not primarily about technology, but are rather emerging as some of the key social justice issues in today's societies, meaning that we must contextualise them in terms of historical injustices along lines of class, gender, race, political geography, and so on.

FURTHER READING

Couldry, Nick & Mejias, Ulises (2019). *The Costs of Connection: How Data is Colonizing Human Life and Appropriating it for Capitalism*. Stanford, CA: Stanford University Press.

In this book, Couldry and Mejias critically analyse the age of datafication, focusing particularly on continuities between this present era and histories of capitalism and colonialism. Arguing that quantification is not a new phenomenon, they introduce the notion of 'data colonialism' as a name for the process by which data is extracted from human life for profit. Today, however, the machinery of quantification spins into entirely new levels driven by the big technology companies. This leads to an accelerated, rather than a new, form of capitalism through the maximisation of profit at the cost of individuals, and a concentration of wealth and power to a select minority.

Louridas, Panos (2017). *Real-World Algorithms: A Beginner's Guide*. Cambridge, MA: The MIT Press.

This book provides a fascinating introduction to algorithms, which is based on clarifying examples and real-world cases. While dealing with quite technical issues, the book still manages – through its pedagogical design – to provide a deep understanding of algorithms even for readers previously unfamiliar with its subject matter. Louridas defines algorithms as 'what we do in order not to have to do something', and goes on to show concretely how different forms of algorithms can be used to address problems in the real world.

DATAFICATION AND ALGORITHMS

Lupton, Deborah (2016). *The Quantified Self*. Cambridge, UK: Polity Press.

Lupton examines the emerging field of self-tracking through digital devices and software. She deals with a set of related issues from a social and cultural perspective. Lupton specifically pays attention to how the large amounts of data generated and collected via self-tracking tend to be collected and used for different purposes by businesses, governments, and researchers.

Pasquale, Frank (2015). *The Black Box Society: The Secret Algorithms That Control Money and Information*. Cambridge, MA: Harvard University Press.

Frank Pasquale's book is a critique of the role played by Silicon Valley and Wall Street in processes of datafication. Aligning with the surveillance capitalism perspective, Pasquale shows how such powerful interests are able to make a profit by abusing people's privacy through mapping our work habits and internet use. He argues that we must demand increased transparency, thus opening up the possibility of criticising datafication, with the aim of making it fairer and less discriminatory. In line with the data justice perspective, Pasquale argues that we all must be able to shape how the collected data is used.

11

SOFTWARE AND DEVICES

Key Questions

- What is the contribution of 'software studies' to other social and cultural perspectives on digital society?
- How can we tease out the sociologically interesting aspects of inherently digital things, such as links, likes, and search engine results?
- What is the internet of things, and how does it relate to digital devices?
- In what ways has mobile communication technology transformed social interaction?

Key Concepts

Software studies * the link economy * the like economy * digital devices * the internet of things * hyperconnectivity * approximeetings * perpetual contact

SOFTWARE STUDIES

As data, algorithms, and automation are becoming increasingly important phenomena in society and culture, researchers have become more and more interested in carrying out research in the area that has been labelled *software studies*. This broader academic interest in an area previously associated quite exclusively with developers and computer scientists has to do with the fact that software is becoming a force that structures and enables much of our contemporary world. Previously, 'software' was a word most commonly used to refer to computer programs and applications. Software, then, is the set of instructions (e.g. algorithms), the code, which instructs technological objects to function in the desired way, as opposed to hardware, which is the physical technological objects in the form of computers, telephones, televisions, or refrigerators. The first published use of the term 'software' in relation to computing was in an article from 1958 by statistician John Tukey (1958: 2):

> Today the 'software' comprising the carefully planned interpretive routines, compilers, and other aspects of automative programming are at least as important to the modern electronic calculator as its 'hardware' of tubes, transistors, wires, tapes and the like.

His point, then, was that not everyone who uses hardware devices has to learn all the details of what goes on 'under the hood', and of course, this is still the case. When we use a computer, smartphone, or a social media application, we generally do not think very much about the logic that governs these things. We just use the things without reflecting on the deeper details of how they were programmed or why. Even though those details and choices may have a huge effect on what we can do with the tools, and how we do it, it becomes impractical to consider their underlying logic.

New media theorist Lev Manovich (2013: 6) writes that software is 'the engine of contemporary societies'. Friedrich Kittler, a media theorist and literary scholar, said in an interview (in Griffin et al. 1996: 240) that software had become increasingly important for understanding culture. He said:

> I can't imagine that students today would learn only to read and write using the twenty-six letters of the alphabet. They should at least know some arithmetic, the integral function, the sine function – everything about signs and functions. They should also know at least two software languages. Then they'll be able to say something about what culture is at the moment.

Kittler underlined the importance of critical analysis of the 'essence' of computers as a complex phenomenon. First, he wrote that 'software does not exist as a machine-independent faculty'. This means that software can't be studied in separation from hardware. Second, he claimed 'there would be no software if computer systems were not surrounded any longer by an environment of everyday languages'. This means that software is not strictly confined to computers. Its logic and effects bleed out into the rest of society – and vice versa. But the social sciences and the humanities were for a long time largely ignoring the phenomenon of software – the underlying code of digital society – and instead focused more broadly on the social and cultural effects of digital media, as discussed elsewhere in this book. In the last decade or so, however, there has been an increased interest in the critical analysis of different aspects of how software enables and limits various social practices, and how software, defined as a general system of signs and functions, is shaped by, and shaping, social interaction. This covers a broad variety of objects of study, spanning how code, files, copies, visualisations, functions, glitches, interfaces, bugs, and so on 'leak out of the domain of logic and into everyday life' (Fuller 2008: 1). A substantial part of all of the applications and services that people interact with in their everyday lives run on remote servers, meaning that they can be invisibly – or secretly – updated anytime. This is often the case, as services that aspire to become the operating system of digital society – such as Google and Facebook – update their code, sometimes on a daily basis.

As cultural researcher Matthew Fuller (2008) explains, an important task of software studies is to show that software is a vital object of study, as well as an area of practice, for researchers and thinkers in fields that one would not conventionally associate with 'software', in the narrow sense. Lev Manovich (2013: 2) makes a convincing case, arguing that no matter what social and cultural things we do with digital devices – play, watch, listen, write, blog, tweet, call, talk, email, edit, take photos, film, and so on – we are all the time using software, and:

> Software has become our interface to the world, to others, to our memory and our imagination – a universal language through which the world speaks, and a universal engine on which the world runs. What electricity and the combustion engine were to the early twentieth century, software is to the early twenty-first century.

Software tends to become a transparent or invisible aspect of digital society, in spite of its crucial role for its functioning. In the same way that hegemonic power and ideologies are naturalised, uncriticised, and spontaneously consented to, software also has an 'ideological layer' (Fuller 2008: 3). Even though software is often extremely useful and even empowering, scholars in software studies remind us that much software – as a by-product or by design – also defines social relations in certain ways that become systematic and impossible to alter once they are set. For example, consider the worries, discussed in Chapter 3, of Jaron Lanier that abstract automated functions will remove humanity. The 'user-friendly' software of social networking will kill off the personal, varied, often nicely strange homepages from the days when 'the web had flavor' (Lanier 2010: 15). Software, in this case, leads to a form of self-reduction:

> The binary character at the core of software engineering tends to reappear at higher levels. It is far easier to tell a program to run or not to run, for instance, than it is to tell it to sort-of run. In the same way, it is easier to set up a rigid representation of human relationships on digital networks: on a typical social

networking site, either you are designated to be in a couple or you are single (or you are in one of a few other predetermined states of being) – and that reduction of life is what gets broadcast between friends all the time. What is communicated between people eventually becomes their truth. Relationships take on the troubles of software engineering. (Lanier 2010: 71)

Examples like this illustrate how software, something that is often defined as immaterial, actually has very material consequences in digital society. The design of software operates on many levels. It defines the characteristics of languages and interfaces; it enables certain kinds of use, and disables others.

DISCUSSION

Look with this new perspective at a website or app that you regularly use in your everyday life. Try to make it the subject of a rudimentary software analysis. Distance yourself from the position you are in now where the functions and resources that make up the site or app are very familiar – maybe nearly transparent – to you. Instead, pose critical questions about it: What is it actually designed to achieve? Which functions are offered, and how? What other things *could* it have been designed to achieve? What other functions *could* have been included? What does it seem to assume about, or expect from, its users in terms of interests, goals, skill level, gender (or any other dimension that will bring out interesting insights)? Which users are excluded? Is the site or app based on any particular values or convictions? Thinking in this way will make the software come into view so that it can be critically analysed.

ANALYSING THE NATIVELY DIGITAL

Scholars in the area of software studies are interested in natively digital things. These are things that would not exist if it was not for digital media and the internet. So, for example, while a conversation between two people, or a television broadcast can happen either through digital tools and platforms or without them, there are some phenomena that are distinctive to the digital. New media researcher Richard Rogers (2013: 25) argues for the importance of 'following the medium' and looking more closely at what is specific to the digital. Beyond analysing online culture, or what happens to society as it becomes digital, there is also a need for research to capture and analyse natively digital things such as 'hyperlinks, tags, search engine results, archived websites, social networking sites' profiles, Wikipedia edits', and so on (Rogers 2013: 19). Such an approach is about an analysis of what communications researcher Tarleton Gillespie (2010) names as 'the politics of platforms'.

New media researchers Carolin Gerlitz and Anne Helmond (2013) have explored how different types of 'web-native objects' have organised value production – economic and other – online. In the mid-1990s, in the days of web 1.0, the most important objects were the hit and the hyperlink. During this period, the number of *hits* on a website became widely used as the standard metric to measure user engagement and website traffic. Many websites had 'hit counters' that displayed how many visitors a page had attracted, based on the number of computerised requests to see the page. In the late 1990s, however, this standard was replaced as Google, which was then a new type of search engine, introduced a new way of measuring impact by combining hits and *links*. This was a watershed in the history of the internet as it gave rise to a new web economy with search engine rankings at the centre.

PageRank

Famously, Google introduced the analysis algorithm of PageRank, which was developed in 1996 by founders Larry Page and Sergey Brin as part of a research project at Stanford University. PageRank – the name playing off both the name of Page and the notion of a web page – calculates the relative importance of a page according to a rather intuitive logic:

> a page can have a high PageRank if there are many pages that point to it, or if there are some pages that point to it and have a high PageRank. [...] PageRank handles both these cases and everything in between by recursively propagating weights through the link structure of the Web. (Brin & Page 2012: 110)

The basic idea, in other words, is that a page A can have a higher PageRank than a page B, even if B has more links pointing to it. This is because A may be linked fewer times but by more important pages. The point with this was that by using PageRank in addition to conventional text indexing, one would be able to generate much more accurate search results. Google's algorithm brought in a focus on the relational value of sites and thereby shifted the way in which the value of web resources was determined away from the hit and towards the link as the main measure of relevance. This was done according to the logic of PageRank where links have different value depending on the authority of the source.

This made links into a commodity in a new form of web economy where search engine optimisation (SEO) emerged as a key practice for actors who wanted to capture people's attention online. SEO involves practices such as the careful choice of keywords for the site's meta-description, the creation of content that includes frequently searched words, frequent updates to lure the automated crawlers of the search engines to re-index the site, and so on. Many emerging SEO practices went beyond merely helping the search engines build appropriate indexes, instead bordering on spam – so-called spamdexing. One such practice to deliberately manipulate the indexing process is carried out through so-called 'link farms' – a group of websites that all link to each other in order to boost their PageRank. Links have a direct value in digital society, and they can therefore be seen as a 'pseudomonetary unit' (Rettberg 2005: 526). And it is not only the links themselves that have value, but the knowledge about the relationships between content that became a 'prime real estate' (2005: 525). Links were increasingly exchanged in strategically reciprocal ways. Jill Walker Rettberg (2005: 526) explains how the link economy functions:

> When I link to B, I give B a link. That link translates into a precise (though undisclosed) value in Google's PageRank and in other indexing systems […]. The link has a clearer value to B than the content of B's page has to me or to my readers. I pay B for B's content with my link. This instrumental view of links does not exclude its other qualities. Many people creating or following links on the Web link generously, carefully, or haphazardly but without thinking of the economy of links and their value.

Googlisation

Philosopher Michel Foucault wrote that knowledge is closely related to power. He said that the knowledge of the world that is established 'tends to exercise a sort of pressure, a power of constraint upon other forms of discourse' (Foucault 1972: 219). As Rettberg (2005) argues, this is also highly pertinent to the political economy of links. Links may be useful, functional, or provide us with happiness, for example, but links are also part of a power structure, which must not be ignored. Links define what can be found and so they define knowledge, which, once again, is power. Cultural historian Siva Vaidhyanathan (2011) thinks that there has been a googlisation of everything, and that in hindsight it might have been a better idea not to put the entire 'human knowledge project' in the hands of a single corporation. We must not assume, he argues, that Google will deliver to us what we 'actually need'. Even though Google might have grandly promised not to 'be evil', it is still big business. Vaidhyanathan (2011: 203) argues that:

About the same time that Google started, we could have coordinated a grand global project, funded by a group of concerned governments and facilitated by the best national libraries, to plan and execute a fifty-year project to connect everybody to everything.

DISCUSSION

Try to break out of the 'filter bubble' by experimenting with different search queries in different search engines with different settings. Choose a search query and enter it into the search field at google.com. Make note of the top search results. Enter the same query at, for example, google.jp, google.ru, google.tn, and google.co.uk. Make note of the respective search results. Try the same query at bing.com, duckduckgo.com, yandex.ru, or others. If you like, you can play around with settings for the different engines as well. Note your top search results throughout. When you have finished, analyse the differences, similarities, and overlaps in the search results. What conclusions can you draw from this?

As a consequence of the link economy, link bartering – loosely organised systems of linking someone and being linked in return – was made more formal through phenomena and functions such as webrings and blogrolls. Such practices subverted Google's 'objective' measurement of links, and when they became too overtly strategic, they were sometimes labelled as 'link slutting' or 'link incest' (Rettberg 2005: 528). It was frowned upon to shamelessly or inappropriately sell your integrity for links. But gradually, there was also an increasingly open exchange of links for real-world money. A black market for links emerged, where people could pay to be linked by link farms, circles, and other technological agents designed to do nothing but link to others. Consequently, Google developed different practices to police and ban such activities. Of course, it was in Google's interest to protect the integrity of its system, since the map of the web that they were, and are still, developing is priceless, not only for the generation of as 'good' search results as possible, but also for the ability to personalise searches and – by extension – ads. As more and more of our online activities are tied into our user profiles with corporations like Google, Facebook, or Apple, these actors will have even more data about us in their rapidly-expanding databases (see Chapter 10 on datafication).

After the arrival of the social web and, consequently, social media, there were further changes to the attribution of value to sites and content. Initially, the participatory features of web 2.0 made it possible for users who were increasingly engaged in the creation of their own content to be more active also in the creation of connections between sites, accounts, and platforms. The early renditions of the link economy had been predominantly based on expert recommendations and aggregation engines such as Technorati and Blogpulse. However, as Richard Rogers (2005: 27) explains, 'the blogsphere became a new kind of collective, aggregated source – one freed from the "tyranny of (old media) editors"'.

The emergence of 'social buttons' that could be placed on any website were a further development towards more participatory linking practices. These buttons enabled the submission of, or voting for, posts on platforms such as Digg and Reddit, which introduced sharing buttons in 2006 (Gerlitz & Helmond 2013: 1351). Many other platforms followed suit and offered different social buttons which allowed for a variety of predefined user activities: bookmarking, voting, recommending, sharing, and tweeting, and counters which showed how many times they had been clicked.

Buttons

Digital aesthetics scholar Søren Pold explains that buttons in web interfaces and apps have a certain social power, since buttons 'signify a potential for interaction' and because buttons feel very real and definite. Pold (2008: 32) writes:

> There is an analog connection between pressing the button and, by the force of one's finger transmitted through a lever, changing the state of the apparatus – as in old tape recorders, where one actually pushed the tape head into place with the button. The computer interface does away with the analog mechanical functionality, but the function of buttons here is to signify the same stable denotation, even though its material basis is gone. That is, interface buttons disguise the symbolic arbitrariness of the digital mediation as something solid and mechanical in order to make it appear as if the functionality were hardwired.

The major transformation came with Facebook's introduction of the like button in 2009. The now classic thumbs-up button was created in order to be a shortcut for comments, and to replace short affective statements such as 'Congrats!' or 'Awesome!'. Since 2009, there has been a longstanding debate on the absence of a 'dislike' button. Critics have argued that a button for positive sentiment only works to support commercial interests, such as building brands or promoting products and services. Mark Zuckerberg, head of Facebook, said in 2014:

> Some people have asked for a dislike button because they want to say, 'That thing isn't good.' And that's not something that we think is good for the world. So we're not going to build that. (Oremus 2014: n.p.)

However, in February of 2016, Facebook introduced a wider range of 'reaction' options: Like, Love, Haha, Wow, Sad, and Angry.

The social act of liking – or otherwise 'reacting' – can be performed on most things on Facebook, through actions such as status updates, shared photos, shared links, or comments. As with the social buttons that preceded it, from the very beginning, the like button had a counter, and also listed the names of those who had clicked it. A year later, in 2010, Facebook launched an external like button that could be used as a plugin by any site owner, 'potentially rendering all web content likeable' (Gerlitz & Helmond 2013: 1352).

This innovation made links – the main currency of the link economy – less interesting and instead put the focus on how 'liking', or performing other preset 'reactions', transforms user interactions into comparable and actionable forms of data. The emerging like economy facilitated a more social web experience, where being liked and seeing what others like enables new forms of engagement. But, Gerlitz and Helmond (2013: 1362) argue, it also creates 'an alternative fabric of the web in the back end'. In this obscured dimension, specific relationships are created 'between the social, the traceable and the marketable'. So, while the link economy bore traces of democratisation, as it was a system where anyone could link to anyone else, the like economy means a recentralisation. Many people are involved in the 'liking' part of the like economy, but most of them lack full access to the data they are part of producing. Instead of the patterns generated through mutual linking practices, the like economy presents an alternative fabric of the web, which is organised through data flows that emanate from social media platforms such as Facebook.

The like button, embedded both inside and outside Facebook, is an example of a 'tracking device', which establishes new markers of relationships online that go beyond the conventional hyperlink between websites. So, the fabric of the like economy is not organised through relationships between websites, but instead through third-party tracking devices, linked to data mining services. Fundamentally, the digital artefact of the Facebook like, or reaction, button sets up a particular relationship between the social and the economic dimensions of society. The widespread use of Facebook, the prominence of the like button, and the appearance of the embedded like button throughout the internet makes it possible to gather large amounts of valuable user data, and thereby enables such processes of datafication as were discussed in the previous chapter.

DISCUSSION

Try to reflect upon what a 'like' is to you. From the perspective described above, the like button is a tracking device for generating economic value. From another perspective, it can be a shorthand for conveying a positive sentiment. One could also imagine that the meaning of a like is very contextualised. In the cases when you 'like' something, do you ever think about how that click is going to be interpreted by others? Is 'liking' just something that we do, compulsively? Is the meaning of the like taken for granted? May the like even be an empty signifier, in the sense that its meaning is not fixed?

DIGITAL DEVICES

A vital factor for the progression towards a softwarised, datafied, and algorithmically governed society are the developments in the area of digital devices. Software runs on hardware. During the last decade or so, there have been increasing developments around the so-called *internet of things*, which refers to new applications of the internet where different identification and tracking technologies are used for self-tracking (exercise wristbands, smart watches, etc.), to provide better services (smart refrigerators, weather sensors, etc.), or for automated crowdsourcing (monitoring traffic, sensoring people's movements in urban space, and so on). The internet of things vision is about the integration of a wide range of technologies and platforms through the internet via largely wireless connections. As explained by Atzori, Iera, and Giacomo (2010: 2787), the internet of things is based on the idea of 'the pervasive presence around us of a variety of things or objects – such as Radio-Frequency Identification (RFID) tags, sensors, actuators, mobile phones, etc. – which, through unique addressing schemes, are able to interact with each other and cooperate with their neighbors to reach common goals'. As with datafication and algorithms, the internet of things can potentially have positive impacts in some areas, such as e-health, assisted living, logistics, and in so-called smart home technologies that makes life convenient for its users. At the same time, of course, implementing a vision of '"anytime, anywhere, anymedia, anything" communications' (Atzori et al. 2010: 2803), necessarily pose substantial challenges relating to privacy, security, trust, power, and exploitation.

The internet of things, then, relies strongly on *digital devices* being present in, and moving about, society in both the 'online' and 'offline' sense. On one end of the spectrum, these devices can be stationary objects, such as televisions and freezers keeping tabs on programmes watched and burgers eaten. At the other end of the spectrum, there are the *implantables* and *ingestibles* that are introduced into the biological human body (Pedersen & Iliadis 2020). In between there are the still more common devices, such as *wearables* – prominently including smart watches and wristbands, but also by definition smart rings, pendants, clip-ons, smart clothes and shoes, smart glasses and contact lenses, ear buds, and so on (Lupton 2020: 49) – and not least *portables*, such as tablets and smartphones.

While the actual device used by a given individual in a given setting may now vary, the massive change in the role played by digital devices in our everyday lives no doubt came with the smartphone revolution (Ahmad 2011; Hazlett 2017). Around the time that the first iPhone was launched, smartphones outsold laptops, at the same time paving the way for the emerging market for tablets. Today, our devices – still most often our smartphones – have become highly personal and can often be seen as extensions of our persons. The smartphone that one carries is 'a physical, technological embodiment' (Reid 2018: 13) that gives information cues to the social environment:

> [...] such as your preferred brand (Are you an iOS or an Android person?), your aversion to risk (Is your phone protected with a case? A plastic screen protector? Or is it naked?), your caretaking ability (Is your phone's screen broken?), even your propensity for technology adoption (Are you an early adopter? A laggard?). It takes only a split-second to make these assessments and use them to render our assumptions. (Reid 2018: 13–14)

Many people today could not imagine living without their smartphone, and we use our mobile devices for an ever-increasing number of different things: talking, texting, listening to music, taking photos, making video calls, accessing the web, getting directions and other location-based information, gaming, watching video, and so on. As we tend to carry our smartphone with us wherever we go, there is also often an emotional connection to it. The phone becomes an everyday companion: we take it for walks (listening to music or podcasts, tracking our steps), we cook with it (looking up recipes, watching video tutorials), we play with it (killing time with mobile games), it follows us to work, reminds us of things, we snuggle with it on the couch, and it puts us to sleep. Mobile phones, and especially smartphones, have altered the parameters of daily life for huge numbers of people globally, to such an extent that the mobile phone can be thought of as an 'agent of social change' (Nurullah 2009: 19). This is at least in the sense that a large number of the things we do to carry out everyday tasks and relate to others is done in very different ways in society after – as compared to before – mobile digital communication. And this development has happened fast. In the early 1990s, owning a mobile phone was something quite extraordinary or at least a bit odd. Ten years later, in the early 2000s, *not* having one made a person stand out.

While mobile phones, in their early incarnations in the 1980s and 1990s, made it possible to speak to – and also send text messages to – people in other places, their development did not stop there. Rainie and Wellman (2012) explain that this was due to a convergence of different technological advances in the mid- to late 2000s. Computer technology got better, data storage improved, and mobile connectivity became easier and cheaper due to new ways of managing the radio spectrum. These developments gradually led to the invention of the smartphone. Throughout this development, there have been a number of significant socio-cultural changes and, as a result, mobile communications as a specialised research field has rapidly emerged (Agar 2003; Aschoff 2020; Baron 2008; Goggin 2006, 2011; Goggin & Hjorth 2009, 2014; Ito et al. 2005; Ling 2012; Reid 2018). Lots of societal transformations have been mapped out and are said to be the consequence of mobile connectivity. Questions arise about privacy and norms for mobile phone use; the organisational structure of businesses are in flux; relationships between teens and parents – and among teens – are changing; new forms of distancing and intimacy take shape, and various struggles for status and power have shifted to a new ground.

A new situational geography

The greatest affordance of mobile connectivity is that humans are progressively able to communicate with each other without having to rely on devices that are fixed to certain physical places or geographical locations. This, in fact, was a realisation of sociologist Joshua Meyrowitz's work from 1985. He believed back then that electronic media would change the *situational geography* of social life and make physical location much less important. He wrote that:

> Electronic media have combined previously distinct social settings, moved the dividing line between private and public behavior toward the private, and weakened the relationship between social situations and physical places. (Meyrowitz 1985: 308)

While Meyrowitz referred particularly to the medium of television, mobile communications technology has a much stronger ability to 'break down the distinctions between here and there, live and mediated, and personal and public'. In digital society we get involved in – to use Meyrowitz's (1985: 308) words – 'issues we once thought were "not our business"', and 'physical barriers and passageways' are rendered 'relatively meaningless in terms of patterns of access to social information'. When it comes to the conditions for interaction, people can be in constant touch with each other, no matter where they happen to be located at a particular moment. Many of the social transformations following from this might appear to be quite everyday and undramatic at first glance, and related to how we book meetings, decide where to go for coffee, and when or whether to tell someone that we are running late, for example. But if one thinks about this apparent micro-change a little more, it is in fact quite revolutionary at a macro-level. Media researcher Santiago Lorente (2002: 10) writes that, being a 'child of Bell's telephone, for transmitting voice; child of the Morse telegraph, for transmitting text; child of Marconi's radio, for wireless transmitting of voice and texts. And, let us add, child of the first ENIAC computer', the mobile phone is possibly the most complex and transformative communicative artefact to date.

Around 2005, research exploring the extent to which mobile computing was changing society and social relations was in a similar stage to where research about the internet had been ten years earlier. Howard Rheingold's *The Virtual Community* was published in 1993 and brought on a wave of academic interest in social life on the internet. Similarly, his 2002 book *Smart Mobs* propelled research interest in mobile communications. Researchers started drawing connections between internet studies and mobile communications studies, and many researchers moved their operations from the former to the latter. It is important to realise, however, that one cannot simply use the established internet research tools and perspectives to achieve a full and adequate understanding of mobile communications in society. Researching how mobile phones and other portable gadgets, such as laptops and tablets, have changed how people relate to each other and to the world demands methodological and theoretical strategies that are quite different from those of internet research more generally. New interdisciplinary theoretical and methodological alliances have been formed, and the field of mobile communications studies is also much more connected across regional and national boundaries than that of internet research.

Mobile media has a certain kind of technological geopolitics to it, which is reflected in the associated intellectual thinking as well as the empirical research about the phenomenon. As Mimi Ito (2005) explains, mobile communications research has therefore foregrounded the socio-cultural diversity of uses and among users in a way that was not evident – especially not initially – in the field of internet research. One of the most obvious reasons for this is that while the USA had dominated both the technological development and the user adoption of the internet, the development and adoption of mobile phones was driven primarily by countries in Asia and Europe. This upset the geopolitics of the evolution of digital society. Ito (2005: 7) writes:

> Unlike the Internet, created by a relatively narrow and privileged social band (predominantly educated, white, male, North American), mobile technology owes not only its uptake but its actual form to people more on the social and cultural peripheries: Scandinavian texting teens, pager cultures of Japanese teenage girls, multitasking housewives, Filipino youth activists, mobile service workers.

In internet research, it was widely assumed from the beginning that the internet was a universal and cross-cultural solution that would be implemented and used in the same way everywhere. Only later came the realisation that its uses and effects might differ across the globe. But the early patterns of how infrastructures for mobile communications were implemented meant instead that wireless technology was seen, from the very start, as being located in specific socio-cultural and historical contexts. For example, mobile phones have had a revolutionary effect in many developing countries in the global south. The reason for this is that in many regions, mobile phones are actually the first telecommunications tool that people have ever known. Such insights also helped research on digital society more generally to recognise that the effects of technology are always dependent on the social and cultural setting where it is implemented and used. Rather than assuming that patterns should be universal, and then undertaking research in order to explain differences, one can instead take social, cultural, and technological diversity as a starting point.

As discussed elsewhere in this book, early observers of digital society were often quite preoccupied with defining and theorising the differences and demarcation lines between our online and offline lives and selves, and between the virtual space of flows and the physical space of places. Today, however, there is a rather widespread consensus that the online and the offline are intermingled in various types of intricate relations (Lindgren 2014). This transformation of research interests and perspectives is also a result of the emergence of mobile media studies. The first examples of internet research in the 1990s grew out of a theoretical interest in things like 'virtual reality' and 'cyberspace'. It was only later that this kind of research became interested in how the online world might relate to its offline counterpart. In the world of mobile phones, the process went in the opposite direction. Ito (2005: 8) explains:

> The extroverted, out-of-doors nature of mobile communication, as well as its low-profile origins in the pedestrian technology of telephony, has meant that

the online component of mobile communications has not been experienced as cut off from everyday reality, places, and social identities. Internet studies have been tracing the increasing colonization by real-life identity and politics of the hitherto 'free' domain of the Net; keitai [Japanese mobile culture] represent the opposite motion of the virtual colonizing more and more settings of everyday life.

So, even if mobile communications studies did not completely invent perspectives that account for context, locality, and place, they at least led to a (re-)vitalisation of those perspectives in internet studies. It is important to remember that any technology that is introduced in a social setting will both affect and be affected by the existing structures and practices. In the following section, we shall look at some of the everyday social transformations that mobile connectivity through digital devices have brought about.

ONLINE ALL THE TIME

An important social change following the development of mobile communications is that many people are now online all of the time. A majority of people throughout the world are constantly capable of looking up information, are available to others, and are able to create and distribute their own content. Many people take their phones to bed, and the small size of smartphones further enhances the sense of being easily accessible to one's social networks wherever one happens to be. It is as if we are carrying all of our social existence with us in our pocket. As mobile phones become ever more embedded and entangled in our lives, they change the dynamics of social situations. Even if we see it as quite natural today, it was not long ago that the arrival of calls at any time and place in front of any number of eavesdroppers and onlookers was a new phenomenon. This has meant that new social conventions and rules of etiquette for such situations have been developed. For example, people have had to develop methods to juggle the fact that one can be involved in two simultaneous situations – one on the phone and another in the physical place where the person happens to be. While some people aim for, and succeed, at keeping their interactions discreet, others choose the strategy of what Plant (2001: 49) calls 'stage-phoning'. She explains:

On a train, for example, a mobile can be used as a way of broadcasting a great deal of information to a pretty much captive audience. In some contexts, even the presence of the mobile can be used to inform the audience that this is a person with a life, a person of the mobile world. Calls can be invented for that purpose, in which case the mobile can communicate even when it is not in use.

The ability to handle such disturbances, both on the part of the recipient of the call and those within earshot, has become an important social skill. Furthermore, mobile use in various forms and degrees has come to be seen as inappropriate in certain places: when flying, driving, in hospitals, cinemas, and lecture theatres, for example. Trains have introduced 'quiet carriages' and some restaurants have introduced 'no-mobile' policies. Such negotiations reflect the process by which our socio-cultural environment is adapted to mobile media use, and vice versa. As Rainie and Wellman (2012: 95) suggest, this continuous access leads to people being nudged into 'an internet-first frame of mind'. If a question arises during a discussion, on- or offline, its answer can often be looked up through a quick search query. And if we have something that we want to publish, like a video, a photo, or a status update, the fast access to digitally networked tools and platforms via mobile devices will encourage us to share our content there. Furthermore, the internet-first thinking makes many people prefer to share stories with friends by texting, rather than phoning them up, or waiting until meeting in person. This *hyperconnectivity* brings about far-reaching changes in how individuals and groups in society relate to each other and to the world around them. Time and place, as well as the sense of being socially connected and present, assume new forms and meanings in digital society.

Language researcher Naomi Baron (2008) argues that one of the most important changes that result from the use of mobile communications is that we now have a growing ability to control when we interact with whom. She explains that even though we have always had options for 'controlling the volume' of our social interactions – crossing the street or pretending to look in shop windows to avoid unwanted interactions or offering a brief hello to then quickly dash off to made-up engagements – digital technology and, consequently, mobile communications technology have multiplied these possibilities. Indeed, people have always tried to find ways of controlling when and with whom they interact, but the mechanisms for taking control and the degree of control possible have shifted over time. The early landline telephones offered little opportunity to avoid interaction. The very first ones were always on, and the first phones that were actually ringing had to be picked up in order for the ringing to stop. The introduction of answering machines and, later on, caller ID and call-waiting features improved the technological possibilities for screening and choosing among potential interactions, and even blocking some of them. Yet another way of manipulating the context of interaction is to put people on speakerphone, and let others listen in, without the consent of the person at the other end.

Mobile phones, Baron explains, have introduced even more control mechanisms into the equation. In the case of text messaging, people can manipulate their settings so that they appear to be 'away' or offline even if they are not, or to make messages appear to be unread even though they have in fact read them. Text messaging also makes it possible to decide if, how, and when one should respond to an incoming call for interaction. Some messaging platforms enable getting knowledge about people's whereabouts and activities by just reading profiles or away messages instead of directly contacting them. Likewise, sending a text instead of having face-to-face or voice contact changes the parameters for what we say, and how we feel about it. It can be done to save time by eliminating small talk, but topics that feel embarrassing or otherwise sensitive can also be easier to deal with by texting. This type of connectivity transforms the nature of social encounters, sandwiching mobile texting with face-to-face encounters. People can be in touch before meeting up face-to-face in ways that lower the barriers to interaction when actually seeing each other, as there will exist something common and very recent to reference. And after the face-to-face meeting, mobile connectivity enables the interaction to linger on.

Mobile media have also introduced a new choreography of physical gatherings, in the sense that coordinating a date, party, meeting, or other form of rendezvous before the age of mobile phones was 'a formal negotiation yielding firm coordinates' (Rainie & Wellman 2012: 99). Previously, one was forced to decide beforehand more or less exactly when and where one was supposed to meet up. This state of affairs was a consequence of the industrialisation of society in the 19th century, when public clocks, wristwatches, 'big machines, cities, bureaucracies, stores, and railroad lines running on strict timetables' started to demand that people turn up at exact places and points in time – in contrast to what had been the case in pre-industrial times (2012: 99). Rainie and Wellman (2012: 99) write:

> This was a profound change from preindustrial village life, where people went to their farms, shops, or pubs according to their needs – not their clocks. To some extent, mobile phones allow us a slight return to this more casual negotiation of time. In the age of mobile connectivity, time is more fluid and people's expectations have changed.

This, in turn, changes the social rules and expectations regarding when and how one is supposed to be available to others, or when it is acceptable to contact others. As the networked individuals we are today, we rarely ever have to be completely alone, at least not in the social sense, as we can always stay in touch with family, friends, or connections near or far. Conversely, we sometimes use our devices to negotiate not being physically available or unavailable in social situations. People may pretend to be using their smartphone to avoid, for different reasons, being involved in interaction with people who are around them. More generally, Sadie Plant (2001) argues, mobile phones make certain physical and psychological demands that have caused people in society to develop new gestures, stances, and bodily movements, which did not exist before mobile media. Mobile phones have, for example, generated new ways in which the body, fingers, and thumbs are used while engaging in mobile interaction. Such actions and positions are part of a new body language, specific to digital society, which is now familiar to observers all over the world.

In digital society, some of our meetings – especially the ones that are informal and with a small number of participants – have become what Plant (2001) calls *approx-imeetings*. This is a name for the gradually fixed agreements that we make when deciding upon when and where to meet someone. If meeting someone for lunch, for example, we no longer have to rely on pre-made arrangements made face-to-face, in writing, or over landline telephones, as mobile telephones make it possible to first decide something roughly, and to decide more details through calling or texting as the event draws closer. While, at first glance, this appears to be a quite modest and practical improvement of how meetings are planned, this is in fact one of the more notable changes to the everyday social fabric brought on by digital technology. Plant (2001: 61) writes:

> Loose arrangements can be made in the knowledge that they can be firmed up at a later stage; people can be forewarned about late or early arrivals; arrangements to meet can be progressively refined. But this kind of flexibility – we can call it approximeeting – can also engender a new sense of insecurity. Everything is virtual until the parties, the places and the moments come together to make it real. In this context the person without a phone becomes something of a liability.

The transformation is part of a wider phenomenon that has been discussed by mobile media researchers Rich Ling and Birgitte Yttri (2002) in terms of a combination of *micro-coordination* and *hyper-coordination*. They describe micro-coordination as the activity where mobile phones are used for instrumentally logistical purposes to make things run smoothly. This is the type of coordination that Plant describes in the quote above: people can text or call to say that they are running late, trips that have already started can be modified and redirected, and meetings can be scheduled loosely to gradually become more definite. Hyper-coordination goes beyond the merely instrumental logistical uses and adds an expressive layer of chatting and gossiping – a cultural dimension of coordination by which social bonds and values are created, maintained, and expressed. So, while micro-coordination is about 'orchestrating each other's movements and positions in the space of flows to the point where they ultimately overlap and merge' (de Vries 2012: 144), hyper-coordination is more about maintaining intimate social bonds. It is about the constant confirmation of personal connections, and about sharing experiences, staying up to date about each other's lives, and exchanging various forms of symbolic gifts (images, jokes, emoji, and so on). Communication researchers James Katz and Mark Aakhus (2002: 11) argue that personal communication technology gives rise, at the nexus of 'the social person and the mobile machine', to a particular form of socio-technical spirit, or 'apparatgeist' – from the German words for machine (*Apparat*) and spirit (*Geist*). Digital society, Aakhus and Katz argue, is governed by a logic of *perpetual contact*. While industrial society was driven by an idea of perpetual motion – a steady enhancement of the means of production – today's society is driven by perpetual contact, as it has a focus on the means to communicate and interact socially.

CHAPTER SUMMARY

Moving on with a similar focus to that of Chapter 10 on data and algorithms, this chapter has focused on the emerging research area of software studies. This field, obviously connected to the issues of algorithmic critique that were dealt with in the previous chapter, has a focus on studying software not as delimited mere technological phenomena, but as extending into the social. In today's world, software runs everywhere and is embedded in our social life to the extent that just like researchers of society are interested in understanding how social structures and norms function, so are scholars of the digital society interested in deconstructing and critiquing the logic of software. I have discussed in this chapter how natively digital things, such as search engines and 'like' buttons, can be explored from a social studies perspective, where we approach them anthropologically and contextually rather than through their underlying lines of computer code. In line with this, we have explored how software-based things, such as 'links', 'likes', and 'buttons', gain a social significance. Stretching beyond the area of software to the hardware – the digital devices – on which the software runs, we have also explored in this chapter how the fact that software gets implanted throughout our material environment, following the emergence of the so-called internet of things, in refrigerators, televisions, lamps, and sensors, changes the fabric of society. In this respect, we have looked more closely at how the things we carry around with us all the time – increasingly wearables such as smart watches, but predominantly still the ubiquitous smartphone – have transformed social interaction. Echoing some of the points that were made in Chapter 4, I have discussed how mobile devices change social codes, the way we coordinate in physical space, as well as how we stay in constant touch.

FURTHER READING

Manovich, Lev (2013). *Software Takes Command.* London: Bloomsbury.
Manovich presciently called for 'software studies' in his 2001 book *The Language of New Media*. In this volume from 2013, he presented a further development of that idea. Focusing especially on 'media software' (such as Photoshop, After Effects, and Google Earth), Manovich discusses where such software comes from (historically), and how it shapes how media is created, viewed, and remixed.

Baron, Naomi S. (2008). *Always On.* Oxford: Oxford University Press.
In this book, language scholar Naomi Baron discusses how mobile technologies (but also social media platforms more generally) have a profound effect on our uses of language. She also discusses the variety of ways that people use their mobile devices to screen incoming communication as well as to camouflage themselves. As the title of the book suggests, she also engages with the issue of what kind of people we are becoming in a culture where more and more of us are 'always on'.

Aschoff, Nicole (2020). *The Smartphone Society: Technology, Power, and Resistance in the New Gilded Age.* Boston, MA: Beacon Press.
Aschoff's book discusses the ubiquity of smartphones in society, and how this means constant connectivity. It critically addresses how the smartphone society means radical transformations in love, family, work, politics, and economy, as well as how the changes are shaped by prevailing social structures of gender, class, and race. Aschoff also focuses on how smartphones are increasingly used by activists to resist power structures.

12

RESEARCHING DIGITAL SOCIETY

Key Questions

- What new types of data are available today that were unavailable to social researchers in pre-digital society?

- How can the divide between 'qualitative' and 'quantitative' methods be bridged through 'methodological bricolage'?

- What new opportunities and challenges for ethnography arise with the arrival of the internet and social media?

- How can the internet's functions – in apps, algorithms, and software – for collecting, sorting, and visualising data be harnessed as a new form of research instrument?

- What types of research questions can be answered through social network analysis and computational text analysis, and how can these methods be used in digital social research?

- What ethical principles should guide digital social research?

Key Concepts

Digital social research * the data environment * methodological bricolage * digital ethnography * digital anthropology * thick description * social network analysis * weak ties * small-world networks * computational text analysis * distant reading * digital research ethics

Much as the emergence and development of digitally networked tools and platforms has changed the parameters for social interaction, the digitalisation and datafication of society also changes how we think about research methods. In fact, because of its relative newness, social scientific research about the internet and digital media is a key area of methodological development. Routine research labour is rapidly transformed when one tries to capture the fast-evolving patterns of sociality online and through digital tools. In this chapter, I will give a general introduction to *digital social research*. First, I will address a number of challenges and general strategies when undertaking digital social research. Second, I will provide an overview of how an ethnographic approach, with its interpretative stance, provides a solid foundation to undertake research, with potential to generate sociologically relevant knowledge about the complexities of digital society. Sometimes ethnography alone can be more than enough as a research method, depending on what one wants to find out. But as I will argue in this chapter, the best strategy is often to combine ethnography with other methods. This is a consequence of the changing *data environment* and the increased social complexities which follow from the networked characteristics of digital society. Mixed-methods approaches entail, among other things, venturing beyond the longstanding and well-established divide between so-called qualitative and so-called quantitative methods, as well as crossing boundaries between conventional academic disciplines. I will therefore, third, discuss some more computational methods for exploring, mapping, and mining digital society that can be useful to expand on the ethnographic foundation. I pay particular attention to social network analysis, but also deal briefly with computational text analysis, which uses more or less automated techniques, developed in the fields of computer science and linguistics, for analysing large collections of documents. Finally, doing digital social research, still only a couple of decades into the 21st century, means entering new terrains and facing new challenges. I will address some of these challenges – for example those relating to *research ethics* – in this chapter.

THE DATA ENVIRONMENT

But first, let's think about what types of information we may be dealing with in digital social research. As you will remember from Chapter 10, 'big data' has become a buzzword that is repeatedly used to name and characterise some of the new types of data that have emerged in digital society. In reality, however, the emergence of big data is only one of many transformations in our data environment, which affects opportunities as well as challenges when doing digital social research. For example, Kingsley Purdam, an expert in research methods, and his data scientist colleague Mark Elliot (2015) aptly point out that what is commonly known as 'big' data is in fact data defined by several other things, rather than just its large size: it registers things as they happen in real time, it offers new possibilities to combine and compare datasets, and so on. Furthermore, Purdam and Elliot believe that even these characterisations are still not sufficient. This is because those definitions still seem to assume that data are 'something we have', when in fact 'the reality and scale of the data transformation is that data is now something we are becoming immersed and embedded in' (Purdam & Elliot 2015: 26).

The notion of a 'data environment' underlines that people today are at the same time generators of, but also generated by, this new environment. 'Instead of people being researched', Purdam and Elliot (2015: 26) say, 'they are the research'. Their point, more concretely, is that new data types have emerged – and are constantly emerging – that demand new, flexible approaches. Doing digital social research therefore often entails discovering and experimenting with challenges and possibilities of ever-new types and combinations of information.

Different types of data

In trying to describe the ever-changing data environment, Purdam and Elliot (2015: 28–29) outline an eight-point typology of different data types based on how the data in question have been generated:

1. **Orthodox intentional data**: Data collected and used with the respondent's explicit agreement. All so-called orthodox social science data (e.g. survey, focus group or interview data and also data collected via observation) would come into this category. New orthodox methods continue to be developed.

2. **Participative intentional data**: In this category data are collected through some interactive process. This includes some new data forms such as crowdsourced data [...].

3. **Consequential data**: Information that is collected as a necessary transaction that is secondary to some (other) interaction (e.g. administrative records, electronic health records, commercial transaction data and data from online game playing all come into this category).

4. **Self-published data**: Data deliberately self-recorded and published that can potentially be used for social science research either with or without explicit permission, given the information has been made public (e.g. long-form blogs, CVs and profiles).

(Continued)

5. **Social media data**: Data generated through some public, social process that can potentially be used for social science research either with or without permission (e.g. micro-blogging platforms such as Twitter and Facebook, and, perhaps, online game data).

6. **Data traces**: Data that is 'left' (possibly unknowingly) through digital encounters, such as online search histories and purchasing, which can be used for social science research either by default use agreements or with explicit permission.

7. **Found data**: Data that is available in the public domain, such as observations of public spaces, which can include covert research methods.

8. **Synthetic data**: Where data has been simulated, imputed or synthesized. This can be derived from, or combined with, other data types.

The most important point here is that while social research traditionally relies on orthodox intentional data (1), such as surveys and interviews, digital society has enabled much more far-reaching registration and collection of participative intentional data (2), consequential data (3), self-published data (4), and found data (7). These are types of data that indeed existed before digitally networked tools and platforms but which have been expanded and accentuated. The remaining types – social media data (5), data traces (6), and, at least chiefly, synthetic data (8) – are specific to digital society. Therefore, researchers who analyse this society face dramatically altered conditions for the generation and gathering of data about social processes and interactions. Researchers of digital society are often left to dealing with the data generated through the platforms to be analysed, rather than having the opportunity to elicit data in conventional ways controlled by the researcher. While choosing an approach – for instance, opting for a survey or for in-depth interviews – will have continued relevance in some contexts, scholars are now increasingly also facing the challenge of thinking up and constructing some of their 'methods' after the fact.

One of Purdam and Elliot's (2015) main points in the presentation of their typology is the argument that the complexity of today's data environment forces researchers to constantly think about the highly variable characteristics of data that they encounter or seek out. And one of the key challenges when entering this type of terrain is the need to constantly try out new methods for data gathering. In order to know that the data we elicit or download, as well as the strategies we choose to make sense of it, are appropriate, we may test our strategy to see whether it produces good research results.

However, the dilemma is that in order to know that the results are good, we must already have developed the appropriate method. Because of this constant – and potentially endless – need for experimentation and discovery, investigations drawing on new tools and approaches risk becoming stuck and intellectually unproductive very quickly.

For instance, you are researching some aspect of social interaction on a platform like YouTube, and have decided that an analysis of user comments on videos seems to be the data collection method of choice. Now, if this had been survey responses, or interview transcriptions, you could rely on an entire canon of literature on methods and well-established research practices in order to understand how to work with such data. Even though you might want to undertake new approaches or challenge the conventional ways of going about the research, you would at least have a sort of baseline or common practice to relate to and argue with. But in the case of YouTube comments, you would have to do a lot more groundwork. First, for example, you would have to find a way of collecting the comments. If the number of comments was large enough for it to be inconvenient to manually copy and paste them, which is often the case, you would have to find some tool or another to automatically capture and download them. This risks the use of trial and error as you work your way through a variety of browser plugins, scripts, or applications, none of which may eventually do what you want them to do. This process can be very time-consuming and it is not uncommon that the researcher becomes so engaged with this very quest for a tool that he or she – instead of doing the social research that was initially intended – starts to devote a lot of time searching for ever 'better' tools or learning how to code their own tools. And this is only the first step out of several subsequent ones where other challenges may throw you off track.

Once the comments are collected and ordered, there are a wide range of issues regarding how knowledge of the comments should be achieved as well as ethical issues to address. What are the comments actually? Are they individual comments or conversations? How should you, if at all, take the likes and dislikes of the comments into consideration? Do all of the comments relate to the YouTube video in question, or can the comment threads take on lives of their own, to become forums for the discussion of issues other than those instigated by the video? How can you, ethically, use these data for research? Do you need the informed consent of all the people who have posted in the thread? And so on. In sum, because of the inherent multidimensional complexity and unresolved questions, research on digital society must embrace research methods as a creative act. Instead of relying on previous work, copying and pasting run-of-the-mill methods sections into our papers, researchers must 'reveal the messy details of what they are actually doing, aiming toward mutual reflection, creativity, and learning that advances the state of the art' (Sandvig & Hargittai 2015: 5).

METHODOLOGICAL BRICOLAGE

More than twenty years ago, in the preface to a book about researching the internet, Steve Jones (1999: x) wrote that 'we are still coming to grips with the changes that we feel are brought about by networked communication of the type so prominently made visible by the Internet'. And this is still the case. Research on digital society has continued to be a trading zone between conventional academic disciplines – it is truly transdisciplinary. In their book about 'internet inquiry', Annette Markham and Nancy Baym (2009: xiv) explained that:

> While most disciplines have awakened to an understanding of the importance of the internet in their fields, most do not have a richly developed core of scholars who agree on methodological approaches or standards. This absence of disciplinary boundaries keeps internet studies both desirable and frustrating.

This frustration, they argued, makes researchers of digital society push the boundaries of 'disciplinary belonging' in ways that most academic research would benefit from doing more of. Furthermore, they write that as very few internet researchers have been specifically trained in how to do it well, one is by necessity forced to actively and critically navigate a landscape of old and new methods in order to seek out ways of engaging with data that suit one's particular project. It is seldom workable to just apply previously existing theories and methods when studying digital society. Some perspectives and approaches can most likely be, and have also to some extent been, repurposed for digital media research – for example, survey methods and interviews. But one must remember that the internet and its networked social tools and platforms are in many ways a different research context, possessing an 'essential changeability' that demands a conscious shift of focus and method (Jones 1998b: xi).

Because of this, researching digital society often demands that the person carrying out the data collection and analysis is even more critical, and more reflective, than what is already demanded by scholarship in general. The specific challenges of doing digital social research have, Markham and Baym (2009: vii–viii) argue, 'prompted its researchers to confront, head-on, numerous questions that lurk less visibly in traditional research contexts'. One such issue is the urgent need to address the longstanding dispute in social science between 'qualitative' and 'quantitative' methodological approaches, which has persisted, apparently unresolvable, for more than a century. Among researchers, there are still traces of a battle between case-oriented interpretative perspectives on the one hand, and variable-oriented approaches focused on testing hypotheses on the other. Scholars who prefer case-oriented methods will argue that in-depth understandings of a smaller set of observations are crucial for grasping the complexities of reality, and those who prefer variable-oriented approaches will argue that only the highly systematised analysis of larger numbers of cases will allow scholars to make reliable statements about the 'true' order of things.

Today, however, there is an increasingly widespread consensus that the employment of combinations of 'qualitative' and 'quantitative' methods is a valid and recommended strategy, which allows researchers to benefit from their various strengths and balance their respective weaknesses. The 'qualitative' tradition is seen as the more inductively oriented, interpretative study of a small number of observations, while the 'quantitative' tradition is characterised by the deductively oriented, statistical study of large numbers of cases. This has given rise to the common notion that 'qualitative' research produces detailed accounts through close readings of social processes, while 'quantitative' research renders more limited, but controllable and generalisable, information about causal relations and regularities of the social and cultural fabric.

I think that the best strategy is *methodological pragmatism*, focusing on the problem to be researched, and on what type of knowledge is sought. Instead of methodological positioning within the existing field of methods literature, one can instead, as methodologists Norman Denzin and Yvonna Lincoln (2000) have suggested, conceive one's research strategy as a form of *bricolage*. 'Bricolage' is a French term, popularised by cultural anthropologist Claude Lévi-Strauss (1966), which refers to the process of improvising and putting pre-existing things together in new and adaptive ways. From that perspective, our research method is not fully chosen beforehand, but rather emerges as a patchwork of solutions – old or new – to problems faced while carrying out the research. As critical pedagogy researcher Joe Kincheloe (2005: 324–325) observes: 'We actively construct our research methods from the tools at hand rather than passively receiving the "correct," universally applicable methodologies', and we 'steer clear of pre-existing guidelines and checklists developed outside the specific demands of the inquiry at hand'. So, developing your method as a bricolage means placing your specific research task at the centre of your considerations, and allowing your particular combination and application of methods to take shape in relation to the needs that characterise the given task.

So, while it is exciting to study the internet and digital society, it is also especially challenging. New platforms, concepts, and social practices emerge fast enough for making the 'internet' in itself into a compelling area of inquiry. The field, Markham and Baym (2009: xviii–xix) write, has a 'self-replenishing novelty [that] always holds out the promise for unique intellectual spaces'. But, as discussed above, new terrains of research bring with them new challenges and difficulties. First, there is a need for constant reflection about the role of the self in research. Processes of digital social research highlight that researchers are actually co-creators of the field of study. Our choices are made in contexts where there are no standard rules for research design and practice, and this makes such choices more meaningful. Furthermore, the often-disembodied character of digital social settings makes it important to think a little deeper about the relationship between the researcher and the researched:

> What decisions are we making to seek consent; what counts as an authentic self-representation? How are we conceptualizing the embodied persons we study? How are we framing our own embodied sensibilities? Do we approach what we are studying as traces left in public spaces or as embodied activities by people situated in rich offline contexts? We must consider how to interpret other people's selves and how to represent ourselves to the people we study, especially when we may not be meeting them in person. (Markham & Baym 2009: xviii–xix)

Researchers and their subjects, Purdam and Elliot (2015: 47) say, increasingly bleed into one another. This is because 'as the proportion of our lives spent online grows, so the boundary between data and subject becomes less distinct'. In the same sense that offline identities of people are partially coming together in the minds and memories of others, our online selves are partially constructed in our intentional or unintentional data footprints.

Second, Purdam and Elliot (2015: 47) argue, 'the activities of others also contribute to constructing these footprints, for example, a photograph of a person might be in the public domain as a result of being posted online by someone else'. Additionally, that photograph might also have been shared, tagged, liked, or remixed by somebody else, and it may contain 'meta-identity information' (2015: 47). So, if a 'researcher' analyses this photo, posted by a 'research subject', then who or what is actually being analysed? Things are further complicated in the movement from orthodox intentional datasets to various types of data streams or synthetisations, which blurs the distinction between data and analysis.

Third, and finally, it is important to think about the quality of the data used in research. Conventional social science has a set of established mechanisms for quality control, which assess things such as the reliability, validity, and generalisability of research results. The introduction of new types of data, and new modes of data gathering, demands that we ask ourselves questions about rigorous and robust methods of going about our research in order to avoid unnecessary errors or biases. When analysing different platforms, such as a discussion forum or Twitter, and making claims about society, we must remain critical to whose views – whose society – are being expressed on the platform in question, and in our particular sample. Generally, however, conventional and established ways for thinking about such things cannot be easily transferred to studies based on many of the new data types. The criterion of validity, for example, is about evaluating to what degree one is actually studying what one purports to study. Giving an example based on Twitter, Purdam and Elliot (2015: 48) posit:

For example, a tweet might be generated for fun, to provide information or to persuade or mislead; the motivation obviously affects the meaning of the tweet. With survey data and even, to some extent, administrative data, the impact of respondent motivations is, at least in principle, structured by (or perhaps mediated by) the data collection instrument itself. Thus, a well-designed social science research instrument can constrain motivational impact. But this is not so with Twitter data; here people's motivations are given full rein – a tweet might be designed to manipulate or obfuscate, to attract truth or to repel it. It might be designed to fantasize or 'try out an opinion', to provoke a response or simply to create controversy.

So, here we can choose different pathways: Do we want to find verification techniques with which to check the 'quality' of these data – for example, looking at a user's tweets over time to see whether a tweet is characteristic or not – or is it more feasible to argue that we are not studying the person, but something else? Society? Culture? The medium?

DIGITAL ETHNOGRAPHY

Ethnography is a pre-digital research strategy which is about creating detailed and in-depth descriptions and interpretations of people's everyday lives and social and cultural practices. This is most often done with the help of contextualised research data that have been collected through participant observation and in-depth interviews. Those data are then closely described, read, and interpreted to carefully map out patterns of thinking and acting. What one might call *digital ethnography*, then, is an approach aiming to generate such knowledge about lives and practices in digital society – both online and in settings where digital media intersect and entangle with our offline lives. Analysing digital society and sociality from an ethnographic point of view is about reading it as if it were a text, and trying to grasp the ways in which participants make meaning. An ethnographer must not simply report observed events and details, but must also render and explain those observations in ways that help decode the webs of meaning from an insider perspective. While each digital social researcher will, as was argued above, develop her or his own 'methodological bricolage' in different ways in relation to the different tasks that might be at hand, ethnographic exploration of some sort is often a very useful component.

In terms of data collection, ethnography does not rely on any single approach. Instead, ethnographic understanding is developed by exploring several different sources of data in close detail. The most common methods for collecting ethnographic data are observation studies – where the researcher may or may not be a participant in the analysed context of interaction – and interviews. Ethnographic researchers may also collect other sources of data, the character of which may differ depending on the specific nature of the research setting. The notion of ethnographic *fieldwork* is often used as an umbrella term for all of the different strategies that a researcher employs to gain an insight, as rich and detailed as possible, of the milieu under analysis. As linguistic anthropologists, Jan Blommaert and Dong Jie (2010: 7) note: 'Fieldwork is the moment when the researcher climbs down to everyday reality.' The underlying assumption of ethnography is that in order to develop an adequate understanding of what it is like to live in, or be part of, a setting, a balanced mix of immersion and detachment is needed on behalf of the ethnographer. Drawing on seminal work by Clifford Geertz (1973), the ultimate goal of ethnography is to provide a *thick description* of the patterns, modes, and functions of social life. The basic assumption on which this approach rests is that culture is 'semiotic' – it is made out of a complex set of symbols in the form of language, traits, customs, gestures, attitudes, actions, and so on, which are webbed together in systems 'within which they can be intelligibly – that is, thickly – described' (Geertz 1973: 14).

Similarly, anthropologist Bronislaw Malinowski (1922: 9) said that ethnography should lay bare unknown social and cultural principles that govern what previously seemed 'chaotic and freakish', 'sensational, wild and unaccountable'. As opposed to thin description, which merely provides an account of facts, without interpreting them, thick description is characterised by specifying many details, the laying bare of conceptual structures, and the revelation of meanings. According to Geertz, it is the task of the ethnographer not only to present facts, but to comment on and interpret them. The researcher must try to trace the ways in which meaning is ascribed. Against this background, it should be easy to see that ethnography is highly relevant in digital society, not least because now 'The Internet is the fabric of our lives' (Castells 2002: 1).

In her book *Virtual Ethnography*, Christine Hine (2000) argued that internet contexts deserve to be taken seriously as places in which to undertake ethnographic studies. Work such as that of Hine played an important part in the development of the internet as a serious setting for the social research of things other than cybercultural peculiarities. Her main idea was that as the internet had become a mainstream phenomenon, rather than a subcultural one, offering a significant and innovative resource for social science. No matter what social or cultural issues we research, it is becoming increasingly difficult to avoid dealing with online aspects of communication and interaction at some point. It is important to note Hine's argument that the internet and social media do not just provide researchers with an additional arena where social things occur. Rather, the analysis of online settings is helpful to research social issues that extend beyond the internet itself. This is because the internet can be understood not only as a cultural artefact – a thing in the world – but also as a culture – an important aspect of the world itself. As people are simply going about their everyday lives in their use of the internet, by necessity in the process they leave traces that researchers will be able to draw on. The internet makes it possible for researchers that use ethnography to observe a wide variety of social behaviours, patterns, and phenomena, which were not nearly as readily available to see before. It offers a mirror of people's everyday existence, and people often talk on the internet with a candour and frankness which is very rare in many other research settings, such as in interviews or surveys. Internet ethnography makes it possible to look at sociality and social interactions in their 'natural environment'. We can study discussions that arise for their own sake and which are not artificially topicalised by researchers' design. The internet also affords the possibility to search for social data in ways that were not at all possible before digital society.

In the years since writing *Virtual Ethnography*, Hine has increasingly questioned whether online settings should be used as ethnographic fieldsites in themselves. Is it enough to simply analyse online interactions in order to draw meaningful conclusions about social reality? Is it useful at all to adhere to the online–offline boundary when designing ethnographic studies? Hine (2012: 14) asks:

> Can the study actually be reliable if it is not rounded out by pursuing its concerns more deeply into the lives of participants? Would we be able to trust what participants said about themselves? Put bluntly, can a study that only looks at online phenomena be more than mere voyeurism?

And Hine does indeed think that 'online-only' studies can be justified. Sometimes a focus on online interactions alone may be enough, but sometimes such a focus will not be an appropriate choice. Obviously, no sociality between people can happen in total disconnection from any material reality, so it is to be expected that ethnographic projects in digital society will force the researcher to look for evidence in various places. Some of these places may be located online and others offline. Therefore, it is useful to think about the internet *in society* by moving beyond the idea that there is any clear distinction between what happens in and through digital mediation and what happens in other ways and places. Instead of the 'virtual ethnography' that may have been appropriate a few decades ago, Hine has suggested in more recent writings that researchers take a multimodal approach to doing ethnography in digital society. In this case, multimodality means that one should not see an online–offline boundary as important for delimiting ethnographic fieldsites. Instead, we must accept that the topics and issues we study will often cross that very boundary, or even be agnostic to its existence in a deeply mediatised world. The way in which people today experience the internet is characterised, Hine (2015) argues, by three Es, which refer to the internet being embedded, embodied, and everyday. This is what Hine calls 'the E^3 internet'. The internet is indeed best understood when it is contextualised and approached from an understanding of how it is embedded into people's material realities.

241

The view of the internet as embedded was also advocated by anthropologist Daniel Miller and sociologist Don Slater (2000: 1) in their ground-breaking study of 'the internet in Trinidad, and Trinidad on the internet'. They argued that, in spite of the views expressed in the first generation of scholarly literature about the internet, 'the Internet is not a monolithic or placeless "cyberspace"; rather, it is numerous new technologies, used by diverse people, in diverse real-world locations'. Their central idea is that ethnographies relating to the internet should investigate not 'the internet' in general, but 'how Internet technologies are being understood and assimilated somewhere in particular (though a very complex "somewhere")'. They write further that:

> Social thought has gained little by attempting to generalize about 'cyberspace', 'the Internet', 'virtuality'. It can gain hugely by producing material that will allow us to understand the very different universes of social and technical possibility that have developed around the Internet in, say, Trinidad versus Indonesia, or Britain versus India. (Miller & Slater 2000: 1)

They make the point that ethnography should focus not on 'the internet' as some sort of meta-entity, but on undertaking detailed studies of what people make of the internet, as such studies will tell us a great deal about both people and the internet. But the argument can be turned around once more, as it may not always be the case that checking what people do offline will reveal 'the truth' about what their specifically online existence means to them. Hine (2012: 27–28) writes:

> [T]he ethnographer needs to take the time to understand and reflect upon what that virtual-only knowledge of one another means for those concerned, rather than rushing off straight away to triangulate what they say online about their offline lives with face-to-face observation. We may, therefore, have to accept that not knowing all of the demographic details of informants, or not being able to pursue them into other aspects of their lives, is a part of the experience in which we are immersing ourselves rather than simply a lack for which the ethnographer has to apologize. [...] Face-to-face interactions, therefore, need not always be taken as the grounding context within which online interactions are framed.

However, that point is only valid if one agrees that a social sphere with its own distinctive characteristics actually exists online. A crucial point here is that, from an ethnographic point of view, it is the content rather than the platform that is of interest. For Miller and Slater (2000) there is, for example, nothing inherently 'virtual' about the internet. Rather, the internet is only virtual in those cases when it is used or perceived as a virtual space. 'Cyberspace' is not always present as soon as the internet is around. So, from the perspective of *digital anthropology*, it is more useful to study a platform such as Facebook by exploring it as being contextually embedded from the eyes of its users than to study what is posted online. An embedded approach to ethnography of the internet will lead the researcher to ask other questions beyond a cyberspatial approach. The aim is to embrace the multiplicity of the internet, and to pose questions about how it comes to mean different things in different settings among different people. Once again, this is because technology in itself does not have any pre-defined or given settings of use. Rather, different practices will generate different and divergent enactments of technology.

So, on the one hand then, there are 'online-only' studies that use milieus and platforms on the internet as fieldsites for ethnographic analysis, without going beyond what happens in those places. On the other hand, there are studies that focus on how the internet becomes meaningful, through an analysis of how the internet is embedded in material and physical settings. Still, in our deeply mediatised world it is imperative that the researcher moves 'between mediated and unmediated spaces' (boyd 2008: 45), as the distinction between the two is disappearing.

The ethnographic approach, as introduced above, offers a solid framework with which to embark on studies within the field of digital social research. As also noted earlier, sometimes ethnography alone can be a sufficient research method, depending on what one wants to find out. However, the changing data environment means that it is often a good idea to bring in other sources that are not conventionally associated with the ethnographic method. This is because the notions of what actually constitutes the 'field' or 'the data' of ethnographic analysis are altered in digital society. Kozinets (2015: 3) wrote about an approach that he calls 'netnography', and thinks that devising research methods for studying sociality online is about 'intelligent adaptation' and 'considering all options'. The root, he says, should be in the core principles of conventional ethnography, but digital social researchers must also seek to selectively and systematically seize 'the possibilities of incorporating and blending computational methods of data collection, analysis, word recognition, coding and visualization' (Kozinets 2015: 79).

In the following, I discuss two general approaches to exploring, mapping, and mining data that can extend our ethnographic understanding: *social network analysis* and *computational text analysis*. Depending on perspective, these approaches can either be seen as 'other' methods with which digital ethnography is combined, or – as in Kozinets' netnography – even as new forms of 'ethnographic' methods needed by the researcher in order to become fully immersed in that which is digitally social.

SOCIAL NETWORK ANALYSIS

As discussed, when we explored communities and networks in Chapter 5, social network analysis (SNA) is a method for looking at the structure of relations in social systems, and at the patterns of connections between and among those who take part in those systems. Even though SNA is a pre-digital method that can be used on datasets of any size, it is a method which is increasingly developed for, and used in, studies of 'big data' or other 'social data'. SNA is a set of theoretical perspectives and methodological tools that aim to give a better understanding of individuals and groups in the relational social systems of which they are part.

Many people may associate the concept of a social network to specific digital social network services such as Facebook and LinkedIn, and their predecessors, such as MySpace. However, the notion of 'social network' in SNA has to do with such networks and relations at the most basic level where we, as individuals and groups, are part of a number of different social networks, in the form of families, groups of friends, school classes, organisations, clubs, professional networks, and so on. In the context of this book, SNA is described as a method with which to obtain a better understanding of the social networks with which people engage online and offline in digital society. This often means that data on network relationships are collected through the internet, but that our analyses in many cases assume that the social patterns we identify stretch beyond what people do online. Some networks may take shape online only, others offline only, but, naturally, it is most often a bit of both.

SNA sees people as social beings and assumes that our interaction patterns affect what we believe, say, and do. It is also based on the idea that our positions in networks decide which other people we can influence, and how much. So, SNA argues that the behaviour of individuals and groups is, if not totally governed, at least deeply affected by the social networks – the sets of socially networked relationships – in which they are embedded. People will think and do the things they do largely as a consequence of their ties to others. As SNA can help to demonstrate, the interaction patterns among individuals and groups in society are far from random. For example, people have a tendency to interact with others who are similar to themselves, and repeated interaction can lead to the emergence of (among other things) norms of behaviour, symbols of group belonging, group solidarity, as well as a sense of identity. So, social networks enable and constrain what people do. They also help us make sense of the world around us and they influence the choices that we make.

With SNA, researchers can use different metrics and visualisation techniques to gain an understanding of how a certain network functions. When analysing digital society, one can think of any number of things and settings that we might want to analyse in terms of it being a social network, and it is also possible to do so on a number of analytical levels, ranging from the whole of the internet to text message exchanges among a small group of friends. Let's think of two concrete examples, simply in order to have something to draw upon in the following description of SNA. First, we envision that we have a very large dataset consisting of several millions of tweets, all of which have used the same hashtag while posting about a major global political event.

Second, let's imagine that we have copied and pasted around fifty posts to a thread in a discussion forum that deals with a topic relevant to our research. I will call these 'the Twitter example' and 'the forum example'.

The basis for being able to do SNA is what Simmel called the *dyad* – as discussed in Chapter 5. A dyad can be defined as a pair of social actors (a network of two) along with the status of the network tie connecting them. In other words, it is a connection between two people or groups, together with the information about how they are connected. A dyad is a group consisting of two people – a pair – and in order to be able to carry out SNA we need information about all such pairs that constitute the building blocks of the network that we want to analyse. As a result, it becomes crucial to decide what is seen, in the context at hand, to constitute a connection between two actors. Is it the fact that they exchange text messages, the fact that they are 'Friends' on Facebook, that they subscribe to each other's YouTube channels, that they have liked the same Instagram post, or that they have both commented on the same TikTok? In our Twitter example, with a dataset that consists of a large number of users who employ the same hashtag, one could decide, for example, that any one user directing a tweet to a specific user is also then part of a dyad with that user. We may also decide that the addressed user should also respond to the first one in order to constitute a dyad.

In the forum example, we could decide that all participants who have posted in the thread should be seen as being, theoretically, part of dyads with all others, as they have all somehow related to each other by being part of the forum thread. Another strategy could be to decide that any participant should be seen as having a dyadic relationship with only the participant who started the thread. Yet another strategy would be to say that all participants have entered into dyadic relationships with the participants who had posted the entry upon which their own entry followed in the thread. Or, one might decide that it is only in those cases when a participant explicitly mentions another participant in their post that they become related.

So, as you can see, this construction of pairs is driven by theoretical assumptions, and the choices we make will shape the patterns that we map out in the end. For example, in pre-digital versions of SNA, pairs could be identified by asking people in a workplace to suggest which of their colleagues they would be more likely to socialise with, then using the responses to analyse who was connected to whom. Another way would be to do an observation study of which persons were actually spending coffee-breaks together. Fundamentally, in order to do SNA, we must have information on pairs of actors. This does not mean that we assume that people understand their world on the basis of all of the different pair-wise connections they have with people, but for the sake of analysis, we must break it down to these paired connections because dyads are the fundamental unit of networks. If we take the Twitter example, we can draw on our dataset to create what is called an 'edge' list, like this:

User A mentions User B

User A mentions User C

User B mentions User C

User B mentions User C (again)

User D mentions User N

In most real-life analyses of social networks in digital society, the list would of course be much longer, and the graph much more complex. But we operate here with a small network for the sake of illustration. The most powerful analyses take place when we analyse networks that are complex enough for it to be hard to grasp how they function by just reading the edge list.

The list above gives us the information we need as a starting point for SNA. In reality, we can also register other data about both the users and their connections. For example, we may know that Users A and C are politicians, and that Users B, D, and N are journalists. And we may also want to add other types of relationships apart from mentions to the list, including, for example, follows and retweets. In some network analyses, attention is paid to the direction of connections (*directed networks*), and in others, not (*undirected networks*). Our mentions are directed because users are actively mentioning other users. The social act of mentioning is directed from the mentioner to the mentionee. As we imagined our example tweet dataset to consist of millions of tweets, the list would likely be very much longer as well. But let's keep it simple for now.

In SNA, networks are represented as mathematical objects called *graphs*. Graphs hold information about *nodes* (the Users in our example) and *edges* (the connections between them – the mentions in our example). So, if we were to input our edge list above into SNA software, it would know to create a graph which included the nodes A, B, C, D, and N. It would also know to create edges between A and B, A and C, B and C, and D and N. I would also assign the edge between B and C a weight of two, because B mentions C twice. All other edges would have a weight of one. The next step that many researchers take is to create a visualisation of (commonly) circular objects connected by lines or arrows (called 'arcs'). Such network maps are what SNA is famous for, and they are what most people who have heard of SNA imagine when they think of the method. The visualisations help explore the network data and assist in the interpretation of it. It is important to remember, however, that these network maps are not the same thing as the actual social networks that we analyse. The real-life network is not the same thing as the graph, as the graph is a simplification, which says nothing about many of the things that ethnography captures – such as people's thoughts, their driving forces, struggles, ambiguities, and so on.

Furthermore, the graph is not the same thing as the visualisation, because the visualisation is never automatic or 'standard'. Rather, it is the result of a process where the researcher thinks, from case to case, about the best way to abstract the observed social system as a network.

So, what types of patterns can be found through SNA? First, it is possible to identify *clusters*. As Rainie and Wellman (2012) explain, people in digital society (they call them 'networked individuals', as discussed in Chapter 5) have a tendency to have many of their connections in densely-knit groups where several people all have close and frequent connections with one another. Clusters, in other words, are parts of networks that are heavily interconnected internally. So, in our examples of the Twitter dataset and the forum posts, we may be interested to see whether some of the included actors form strong sub-networks that affect and are affected by the network as a whole. Networks can also be analysed in terms of *centrality*. One way of doing this is to calculate the 'degree' of nodes. This is a measure of how much of the activity in the network emanates from any particular node. The more connections a node has the higher its degree. *Path length* is another thing to consider when analysing social networks. Paths are the network roads along which information can travel from one node to another, even though the nodes in question are not directly connected. So, paths are a connected sequence of edges. If User A is connected by an edge to User B, and User B is connected by an edge to User C, there is a path (with the length of two) between User A and C. In a complex network, there can be more than one path between nodes. But the shortest path between any two nodes is called a 'geodesic' in SNA. While the above-mentioned centrality measure of degree gives information about which nodes are the most active, another centrality measure – that of 'betweenness' – measures how many of these shortest paths (geodesics) the node is on.

So, in other words, betweenness is a measure of how important a node is for the connection of other nodes with each other. Nodes with high betweenness are those that bridge social networks that are otherwise separated. Sociologist Mark Granovetter (1973) formulated a theory about the strength of such *weak ties*. The idea is that while the highly embedded 'strong ties' between close connections such as family and friends provide 'network closure' and align with the inclination of humans to operate in small groups, the 'weak ties' provide connectivity across a network. The weak ties function as bridges over 'structural holes' in the network. So, in spite of their name, weak ties can be very powerful and are more likely than strong ties to provide access to different social circles and to connect to more diverse networks.

Another social network theory is that of *small-world* network structures. The theory of such patterns of connection is also related to path length. You may have heard of the concept of 'six degrees of separation', which suggests that everyone in the world is connected to everyone else by roughly six steps in a chain of 'friend-of-a-friend' statements. According to the logic of 'it's a small world after all', social psychologist Stanley Milgram (1967: 67) wrote that 'we are all bound together in a tightly knit social fabric'. Having conducted experiments that involved mailing paper letters between acquaintances across the United States, he found that the average path length fell around five and a half or six. The experiment was repeated in the early 2000s, using email, by sociologist Duncan Watts and colleagues (2003). They gave more than 60,000 people from 166 different countries the task of reaching one out of 18 target persons by passing the message on to somebody they knew, and whom they thought was closer than themselves to the target person. The study showed that the typical chain length was five to seven steps, depending on the geographical distance between the source and the target. When it comes to social media, Rainie and Wellman (2012: 55) report that:

> The many bridges between Twitter clusters means that chains of information from one Twitter follower to a follower of that follower, and so on, encompass about 83 percent of all Twitter users within five steps of interconnection.

So, in sum, one can look at a number of different structural properties of the networks that are analysed through SNA. The method rests on the idea that social networks are not random. Rather, they are structures that affect and are affected by people. SNA as a method can help tease out the prominent patterns from networks by tracing the flow of different resources (such as information, ideas, money, social support, power, love, etc.). Through such analyses, one can start to explore and discover how flows in networks have effects on people and the other way around. In doing so, one can be interested both in individual persons or groups within the wider network, and in the network as a whole.

We may want to know more about a certain Twitter user in the Twitter example, or a specific forum participant in the forum example. What position does the actor have? What role does it play, and what are its resources? Which connections does it have, and what structural opportunities does it have to influence those it is connected to? We can also be interested in the entire Twitter dataset or the entire forum thread. What character does this social setting have as a whole? Is it tightly knit, with many actors being very active and connected to many others? Or is it sparsely knit, with just a small number of connections between a few key participants? Is it a centralised network, with most activity revolving around a key actor, or is it decentralised with some key actors sharing the role of holding the network together? Is it a distributed network instead, where everyone is connected to everyone else? Having the answers to such questions about the particular setting in digital society that we want to study can be very helpful, both as research results themselves but, even more powerfully, as a complement to the thick descriptions which are generated through ethnography.

COMPUTATIONAL TEXT ANALYSIS

Yet more digital methods can be brought in from the field of *computational text analysis* to complement ethnographic analyses. As digital society has expanded, and as the internet continues to make available vast sources of textual data, largely in the shape of user-created content (see Chapter 2), there have been rapid developments in computerised methods for text analysis. This is not in the least because new groups other than computational linguists and computer scientists – for example, social scientists – are now taking an increased interest in such methods. The massive amounts of text content that are generated on social media and through other forms of computer-mediated communication have prompted social scientists to think even more about how such data can be best used, and how the many technologies available to analyse it can be best harnessed.

The techniques that are then commonly used were originally developed by computer scientists and linguists who wanted to use computers to identify and extract useful information from large numbers of documents – generally, a number large enough for it to be hard to read and make sense of for any reasonable-sized group of human researchers. The large set of documents analysed in computational text analysis is called a *corpus*. When researching digital society, we may want to make sense of a corpus of blog posts, forum comments, YouTube video descriptions, Instagram posts, tweets, and so on. The computational methods are useful when we want to be able to see patterns in the corpus, which we would be unlikely to find by manually interacting with the documents one at a time. Computational text analysis, therefore, as opposed to close reading of the text, can be seen as a *distant reading*. Literary scholar Franco Moretti (2013: 48–49) coined this idea, arguing that there is an analytical point to not close-reading texts, since this removes focus from the more general patterns that he thinks research should be focused on:

> The trouble with close reading [...] is that it necessarily depends on an extremely small canon. [...] You invest so much in individual texts only if you think that very few of them really matter. Otherwise, it doesn't make sense. [...] What we really need is a little pact with the devil: we know how to read texts, now let's learn how not to read them. Distant reading: where distance [...] is a condition of knowledge: it allows you to focus on units that are much smaller or much larger than the text: devices, themes, tropes – or genres and systems. And if, between the very small and the very large, the text itself disappears, well, it is one of those cases when one can justifiably say, less is more. If we want to understand the system in its entirety, we must accept losing something. We always pay a price for theoretical knowledge: reality is infinitely rich; concepts are abstract, are poor. But it's precisely this 'poverty' that makes it possible to handle them, and therefore to know.

In relation to more interpretative – 'qualitative' – approaches, then, distant reading demands that the researcher is prepared to move away from conventional close reading in order to be able to grasp larger sets of data, and also to lose some degree of qualitative detail because of this. At its core, computational forms of text analysis are about making texts into numbers to be able to calculate things about the text. It is based on registering, ordering, or counting words or phrases in documents – for example, social media posts. Once the documents have been numericised, statistical or predictive modelling methods can be applied in order to gain information about patterns in them (Miner et al. 2012: 71). Typical applications of computational text analysis include analysing and structuring a text through strategies such as:

- 'Parsing' it to make it easier in later steps to extract information about specific parts of it.
- Finding the most relevant themes or *topics* (clusters of words and terms) that organise the analysed corpus.
- Automatically dividing documents into categories, which are defined beforehand or even computationally 'discovered'.
- Using dictionaries of positive and negative words to map *sentiments* in the text (for example, if things are mentioned in positive or negative ways).

These applications, which increasingly also leverage machine learning, are important to build things such as search engines, spam filters, and online recommendation systems. But of course, the same methods can also be useful in digital social research.

Some text analysis methods to start with

Corpus analysis is useful for 'distant reading' – seeing patterns in text from a holistic or large-scale perspective, which would be hard or impossible to see through close reading. Corpus analysis makes it possible to see how language is used more generally across a large number of documents (forum posts, tweets, comments, and the like). The method can respond to questions about which phrases are frequently occurring, about what types of expression would be more or less likely for a particular kind of document or author, and so on. You can start testing the method by playing around with the online resource voyant-tools.org.

Sentiment analysis – sometimes called 'opinion mining' – is a method for determining the attitude of a speaker or writer. This can be with respect to a particular topic or with the aim of assessing the overall tone of a larger or smaller chunk of text (see also Chapter 7, and O'Sullivan 2021).

Topic modelling is a form of text analysis that aims to identify 'topics' in a corpus. The method processes large bodies of text to find recurring patterns of co-occurring words (topics). An open-source tool for doing topic modelling is MALLET (McCallum 2002), for which accessible tutorials are also available (see, for example, Graham et al. 2012).

DIGITAL RESEARCH ETHICS

It has been argued throughout this chapter that research about digital society demands continuous critical reflection. This is true to an even larger degree than in many other types of research, since this is a field without, as yet, an established methodological tradition. The subject of digital research ethics is an especially urgent strand of this discussion. Here, too, there is an ongoing discussion about best practice. How the researcher navigates issues of research ethics will differ, depending on how the data in question have been generated and collected. Looking at the typology presented by Purdam and Elliot (2015), new ethical challenges arise especially in relation to self-published data, social media data, data traces, and synthetic data. New data types, and new ways of accessing and gathering data, demand that the researcher constantly navigates the data environment and makes choices in a critically reflective way.

Principles of research ethics, and how persons who are researched should be ethically treated, are codified in a number of documents and policies throughout the academic community. Most of these codifications work best in relation to what Purdam and Elliot (2015) call 'intentional data'. And although ethical principles about maximising the benefits and minimising the harm of research are a good starting point – as is the obvious need to respect fundamental rights of human autonomy, dignity, and safety – digital research demands consistent reflection, as discussed in the previous section, about what information one is really capturing. Like the other methodological considerations discussed in this chapter, issues that relate to how one should deal with the ethical treatment of data are highly context-sensitive. Markham and Baym (2009: xviii) emphasise that context-specific uses of the internet demand that the researcher continuously and carefully reconsiders notions such as privacy, consent, trust, and authenticity.

The emergent character of the field of digital social research, a field which is in a perpetual 'beta state', makes it impossible to escape questions about ethical decisions. Such questions must be posed and responded to iteratively. Even though one might wish there were clear rules, issues like these must always be navigated inductively. In light of these concerns, the Association of Internet Researchers (AoIR) has put together an Ethics Working Committee, composed of internet researchers from a variety of regions and countries (Buchanan & Markham 2012; franzke et al. 2020). The committee has argued that ethical issues are complex and that they can rarely be handled in any binary way. There is in fact 'much grey area' (Buchanan & Markham 2012: 5). The transdisciplinary character of digital social research means that researchers and institutions confront many contradictions and tensions that are impossible to resolve completely. Instead, 'many competing interests must be negotiated by researchers, ethics review boards, and institutions' (2012: 6). For the individual researcher, it is recommended, the committee writes, that ethical decision-making is approached as a process, dealing with the issues in a contextualised fashion throughout the research process. This is because different issues will be pertinent at different stages. This approach is in line with the perspective of research method as a bricolage.

In 2012, the AoIR Ethics Working Committee (Buchanan & Markham 2012: 4–5) presented the following key guiding principles:

> The greater the vulnerability of the community/author/participant, the greater the obligation of the researcher to protect the community/author/participant.

> Because 'harm' is defined contextually, ethical principles are more likely to be understood inductively rather than applied universally. That is, rather than one-size-fits-all pronouncements, ethical decision-making is best approached through the application of practical judgment attentive to the specific context [...]

> Because all digital information at some point involves individual persons, consideration of principles related to research on human subjects may be necessary even if it is not immediately apparent how and where persons are involved in the research data.

> When making ethical decisions, researchers must balance the rights of subjects (as authors, as research participants, as people) with the social benefits of research and researchers' rights to conduct research. In different contexts the rights of subjects may outweigh the benefits of research.

> Ethical issues may arise and need to be addressed during all steps of the research process, from planning, research conduct, publication, and dissemination.

> Ethical decision-making is a deliberative process, and researchers should consult as many people and resources as possible in this process, including fellow researchers, people participating in or familiar with contexts/sites being studied, research review boards, ethics guidelines, published scholarship (within one's discipline but also in other disciplines), and, where applicable, legal precedent.

Aligning with the open-ended and deliberative view of ethics, in 2020 the committee built further on the guiding principles by suggesting a continued pluralistic approach to internet research ethics, where greater attention was put on how to deal with ethical issues in various stages of the research process, and in relation to 'Big Data research approaches' (franzke et al. 2020). So, while discussions about the concept of the 'human subject' in digital social research, about definitions of public versus private, about data protection and ownership, and of several other pertinent dimensions must be continuously reviewed, the 2012 AoIR committee presented the above points as general principles for researchers to turn to as a starting point. The guidelines described in the quote above state that:

- The vulnerability of research subjects should decide how careful the researcher is.
- The rights of research subjects to be protected should be balanced against the importance of conducting the research.
- Research ethics must be continuously discussed among researchers and other relevant actors.

To this list, we can add some additional important things to keep in mind. Anthropologist Tom Boellstorff and colleagues (2012: 129–149) suggest the following:

- The principle of care. Taking good care of informants and making sure that they gain something from their participation.
- Informed consent. Make sure that informants know about the nature and purpose of the study.
- Mitigating legal risk. Being aware of relevant laws that govern one's research.
- Anonymity. Avoiding the inappropriate revelation of the identities of informants – or any sort of confidential details or otherwise – that might lead to their identification.
- Deception. Don't pretend to be something you are not, and don't use 'fly on the wall' practices to study sensitive topics.
- Empathy. Try to forge a 'sympathetic depiction of informants' lives, even when discussing aspects of informants' lives that some might find troubling'. This does not have to mean that the researcher 'agrees' with any actions or beliefs of the informants, but one must labour to 'grasp informants' own visions of their worlds'.

CHAPTER SUMMARY

In this final full chapter, before the book's epilogue, I have given an overview of the kinds of methods by which digital society can be studied. The methodological framework that I have proposed is one that draws on a combination of different methods. The complex data environment that scholars face today differs from the situation in pre-digital society where most social research data was collected intentionally, and for the purpose of being used as the empirical material for scholarly analyses. While this is still done, much of the data that are interesting to digital social researchers occur in the form of data traces of people's online behaviours. Most data are also largely unstructured and of varying quality. Therefore, drawing on the strengths of ethnographical approaches when it comes to providing so-called thick descriptions of social settings is a good starting point. Anthropologists and ethnographers have developed methods for analysing and collecting such trace data for centuries. At the same time, the data offered to scholars of the internet and of digital platforms are often in large volumes, where there may be an interest in overviews or otherwise abstracted research insights that cannot be achieved through the interpretative close readings of ethnography. Therefore, I have suggested that a complete toolkit for researching digital society will gain from also including computational analyses for studying social connections or patterns of expression in large datasets. In this chapter, I have provided some examples from the areas of social network analysis and computational text analysis. The new forms of data, alongside the new methodological combinations, actualise ethical issues, both old and new, and the chapter has also addressed some of the key ethical concerns to be aware of in digital social research.

FURTHER READING

Brady, Henry E. & Collier, David (Eds.) (2010). *Rethinking Social Inquiry*. Lanham, MD: Rowman & Littlefield.
With this edited volume, Brady and Collier engage in discussions about deficiencies of 'qualitative' versus 'quantitative' approaches, and focus on how to navigate and combine a variety of methodological strategies. The book makes the case for multi-method research and methodological pluralism in order to do as good social science as possible.

Hargittai, Eszter & Sandvig, Christian (Eds.) (2015). *Digital Research Confidential*. Cambridge, MA: The MIT Press.
This collection of texts, edited by Hargittai and Sandvig, aims to reveal 'the secrets of studying behavior online'. It addresses the constantly evolving character of the digital environment, and acknowledges that researchers must therefore often improvise, revise, and adapt when it comes to their methodological strategies. The book gives an insight into behind-the-scenes accounts of challenges in areas such as data collection, analysis, and ethics.

Hine, Christine (2015). *Ethnography for the Internet*. London: Bloomsbury Academic.

In this book, Hine specifically explores how one can adapt the complex process of doing ethnography, striving for thick descriptions, to the changing and challenging conditions of digital society. The internet becomes more and more embedded into our everyday lives, to the extent that it even becomes rather unremarkable. This poses methodological dilemmas for the ethnographer as regards whether one should look online, offline, or actually somehow in between.

Ignatow, Gabe & Mihalcea, Rada (2016). *Text Mining: A Guidebook for the Social Sciences*. London: Sage.

Ignatow and Mihalcea's book aims to make computational text analysis accessible to a wider group of researchers than before, particularly in the humanities and the social sciences. It addresses issues of how to deal with natural language data from the perspective of both sociology and computer science. The book covers areas such as web crawling and scraping, lexical resources, text processing, and text mining techniques from a variety of areas.

Lindgren, Simon (2020). *Data Theory: Interpretive Sociology and Computational Methods*. Cambridge, UK: Polity Press.

This book introduces a framework for how to do digital social research in the age of datafication, focusing particularly on how to move towards hybrid combinations of interpretative and computational methods. It gives several examples of how data science techniques (SNA and computational text analysis) can be incorporated in research that retains also a more 'qualitative' sensibility.

Markham, Annette & Baym, Nancy (Eds.) (2009). *Internet Inquiry*. Los Angeles, CA: Sage.

This textbook is built around a collection of dialogues between prominent internet researchers. The focus is on their experiences of working through and overcoming critical challenges. The addressed challenges are in areas such as defining the boundaries of a research project, combining online and offline data, dealing with issues of privacy and ethics, and how to assess the quality of the resulting research.

Miller, Daniel & Slater, Don (2000). *The Internet: An Ethnographic Approach*. Oxford: Berg.

This is Miller and Slater's seminal ethnography of 'the internet in Trinidad, and Trinidad on the internet', as introduced earlier in this chapter. The key contribution here is the notion that the internet, rather than being placeless, should be seen in terms of the variety of new

(Continued)

technologies that it encompasses, and more specifically of how such technologies are put to use and become socio-culturally decoded and translated in a variety of different 'offline' settings.

Robins, Garry (2015). *Doing Social Network Research: Network-Based Research Design for Social Scientists.* Los Angeles, CA: Sage.

This book offers hands-on guidance in how to design and carry out social network analysis research. Robins discusses topics ranging from data structures, data collection methods, and ethical issues, to techniques for analysis, visualisation, and interpretation.

13

EPILOGUE: DIGITAL MEDIA AND SOCIAL CHANGE

In this epilogue, I pull together some of the insights made throughout this book in an attempt to formulate a conceptual framework for how to think about digital media and social change more generally. Recalling Kranzberg's first law, from Chapter 1, that 'technology is neither good nor bad' but 'nor is it neutral', we must be aware that technology interacts continuously with the social ecology in ways where one and the same technology can have widely different effects on society, depending on the context and on the circumstances. This means that a mobile phone, a tweet, a YouTube video, a link, or a like mean different things in different settings.

Social change refers to transformations of social relations, symbolic meanings, value structures, and other things that make up the social fabric. Such changes can of course come from a number of sources – political, economic, demographic, technological, and so on. Some patterns of change may be cyclic, while others can be more or less one-directional. We are interested here in the type of social change that happens because people use digital technology. While social change was always multidimensional, we are faced today with ever-increasing complexities, irregularities, and unpredictable flows. This means that when we try to understand social change, we can never explain it in general and all-encompassing ways. Anthropologist Arjun Appadurai (1996: 33) has argued that there are five different cultural flows that must be taken into account:

- *Ethnoscapes*: flows of people.
- *Mediascapes*: flows of media.
- *Technoscapes*: flows of technology.
- *Financescapes*: flows of capital.
- *Ideoscapes*: flows of ideologies.

When we discuss social change and digital media, we deal with transformations that spring, on the whole, from flows of technology and media – from social actions and practices in the technoscapes and mediascapes.

CONTEXTUALISED OUTCOMES

Because different forms of mediated communication and interaction are so central to social life, it follows that different media throughout history have affected both how people relate to the world and the ways in which we have understood social transformations. Different media make it possible to carry out certain social actions, while disabling others. The media that we use will affect what we see, how we speak, and what we do. Therefore, it is impossible to talk about social and cultural change without taking into account the role of the ecologies (see Chapter 1) in which people and media are embedded.

There is no doubt that digital media have transformed society in several important ways but, as I have argued throughout this book, the actual outcomes in terms of social change are always contextualised. This means that the type and degree of social change differs depending on the specific situation. In the words of McLuhan (1964: 20), as cited in Chapter 1, 'the "message" of any medium or technology is the change of scale or pace or pattern that it introduces into human affairs'. So, 'the change of scale or pace or pattern' will differ from context to context. The transformational power that an act of digital media use exercises upon the social fabric is dependent upon situational factors.

Generally speaking, digital media can transform social behaviours and relationships completely, but they may also change them just a bit, and sometimes nearly not at all. Contextual factors are what decide which one of these scenarios – or what combinations of them – end up becoming realised. Throughout digital society, all of these three types of outcomes happen all of the time, everywhere, both at micro- and macro-levels, and anywhere in between. So, the effects of digital media on social change are ambiguous and complex. From an empirical and analytical perspective, however, we always have the possibility to look more closely at some settings or contexts to assess what types of social change – or what potential for social change – people's uses of digital media might contribute to in that specific case. Now let's have a look at the different potential outcomes of social uses of digital media.

DIGITALLY ANALOGUE

First, we can imagine a scenario where digital media are used in ways that result in what could be called 'conventional' outcomes. By this I mean situations when the digital media use in question imitates pre-digital media practices. It is analogous to the analogue. In some respects, and under some conditions, email, for example, is just mail. If we write a message in the style of an old-school letter to someone, who happens to deal with it a couple of days after we have sent it by returning a message in the same genre, then the socially transformative power of that digital message exchange is rather small. The digital tool of email in this case simply emulates the writing of regular letters of the pre-digital type that are stamped and dropped into an actual mailbox. Likewise, if a conventional media corporation makes content available on YouTube, and someone watches it via a streaming device on a TV in their living room, sitting on their sofa, it is very much like an imitation of television. Similarly, if the user of a mobile phone camera snaps pictures of birthdays, holidays, and Christmases, and uses an online service to have paper copies of the photos printed to show to friends and family, it is also pre-digital business as usual.

In all of these three cases, there are a number of differences in the digital versus the pre-digital scenario. The email does not have to be stamped, the YouTube programme can be paused by the viewer, and the mobile phone camera allows for the photographer to view the snapped photo immediately, without having to have film developed in a darkroom, and so on. But generally, these three scenarios are about sending letters, watching TV, and taking photos – things that people did in quite similar ways before the advent of digital media. In these cases, we are dealing with digitally analogue outcomes, because the digital tools and platforms are largely used in ways that emulate pre-digital social practices. If the uses are of the kind described in the examples above, the transformational effect upon social patterns and interaction is small. That is not to say people are doing things wrong, or that technology has failed. It is just that, from the sociological perspective, where we are interested in whether the technology has contributed to any change in social practices, there is really not much to be excited about in these scenarios.

At the level of hardware, one could argue, for example, that it is indeed very new and transformational that the letter-writing, the TV-watching, and the photography can now all be done with the help of one and the same handheld device. But at the level of social practice, however, the examples above describe situations where the potential of this is far from fully harnessed.

It is important to emphasise that no one person will engage in only one way with digital media. In practice, people will use YouTube, for example, in a number of different ways, sometimes harnessing its socially transformative potential, and sometimes using it in old media ways. The point is that sometimes, some parts of the social practices of some users align with the notion of the digitally analogue. Just because a tool or platform has transformative potential, it does not mean that all users always leverage that potential in all of their uses.

Drawing a parallel to the case of political activists who use digital media, Bennett and Segerberg (2012: 752) write that it is 'clear that the logic of the organization-centered brick and mortar world is often reproduced online, with little change in organizational logic'. They mean that just because the internet and social media make it possible to deploy new forms of 'connective' activism, this does not change the fact that many campaigns and initiatives still only use digital tools and platforms in ways that reproduce how things have worked in pre-digital settings. They make the point that social movement mobilisation does not automatically change at its core just because it goes digital, and this point can be transposed to account for the relationship between digital media and social change more generally. Just because society goes digital, it does not change at its core until people start using digital media in ways that produce transformative outcomes.

DIGITALLY ENHANCED

Second, we can imagine cases where digital media are employed in social practices that lead to novel outcomes. This refers to situations where somehow the new and alternative logics of how the internet and social media work are harnessed in ways that change social patterns and relations in significant, but not totally revolutionary, ways. Returning to my previous examples, email stops being just mail if an email exchange happens at a rapid pace or, for example, if an email list is used to reach a large number of people at exactly the same time, with the possibility that anyone can respond to the entire list. It also stops being just mail if a user blocks another user, if someone sets an auto-reply message, and so on. In such cases, the digital tool of email does not simply imitate the exchange of regular letters, because it is then used in ways that harness its digital affordances to a higher degree, thereby rendering the uses more novel.

Turning to the YouTube example, its uses cease to be just like watching TV the moment that someone posts a comment, registers a like or a dislike, links or embeds the video on the web, makes a playlist, and so on. Furthermore, if a conventionally organised media corporation does not produce the content – as it was in the previous example – the mere emulation of television has also been transcended.

The same goes if the mobile phone camera is used to take photos or videos in unconventional situations, and for sharing them through social media. In such cases, it is a question of digitally enhanced uses and outcomes. This is what happens when well-established social practices – such as sending each other messages, engaging with audio-visual material, or photographically documenting one's life and reality – persist, but do so in ways that are augmented or enhanced through the use of digital media.

The degree to which such digitally-enhanced outcomes are realised is related to how well the users – intentionally or unintentionally – leverage the affordances of the digital tools and platforms. As you will remember from Chapter 2, the concept of affordances refers to the action possibilities of technologies. Such action possibilities are realised – once again – depending on context, and on the aims and competencies of the user. As we have learnt throughout this book, digital media have the potential to enable a range of different social practices. To name a few key examples:

- Digital media have the potential to transform relationships between the production and consumption of content. Such potentials may be harnessed in democratising, just as well as in centralising, ways.
- Digital media provide infrastructures with features for creating communities and networks that enable users to communicate, collaborate, and connect rapidly in large networks and/or intimate groups over long distances.
- Digital media have a software dimension through which algorithms and monitoring can potentially be used for efficient forms of surveillance or consumer mapping.
- Digital media offer tools for self-presentation and the possibility to actively share creations, ideas, thoughts, and expressions within networked publics. This entails both opportunities and risks.
- Digital media potentially enable disembodied, invisible, and anonymous interaction between people. These features can lead to disinhibition, which may in turn have both positive and negative consequences.
- Digital media position the individual at the centre of her or his own unique social network, which overlaps with the social networks of others, potentially enabling fast coordination of behaviours and fast diffusion of information and ideas.
- Digital media are ubiquitous, and wirelessly connected in ways that can potentially alter the 'situational geography' of society by allowing for new types of coordination.

In those cases when users – individuals or groups, those already empowered or those who lack access to conventional power – make use of and leverage such potentials of digital media, they are able to enhance and augment social action and practices through the affordances of digital media. This changes the scale of the social action or practice as tapping into the technological capacities and networked structures of digital society enhances its impact.

What we see happening are what Earl and Kimport (2011) call 'scale changes', in the sense that things move faster, reach further, and grow larger. The augmentation of the social fabric achieved by the affordances of digitally networked media could mean, for example, that political mobilisation is scaled up as a message reaches larger, more globally interconnected publics in a shorter timeframe; that people looking for a partner may be able to find someone who matches their interests more effectively; that the process of peer-editing or consulting an encyclopaedia is enabled; that officials can crowdsource political decisions among citizens more efficiently; that aspiring writers or musicians can reach out with their creations to an audience in faster and more autonomous ways; that like-minded people with niche interests can find each other and connect in greater numbers, and so on.

These are examples of how the addition of 'digital', 'online', or 'e-' enhances previously existing social actions and practices. In the cases listed above, we are dealing with enhancements in the form of things like 'digital activism', 'online dating', 'online encyclopaedias', 'e-government', 'e-books', 'digital music distribution', 'online social support', 'online community', and so on. It can also be about less good 'enhancements', such as 'cyberbullying' or 'online hate'. If one were to remove the prefixes from all such concepts, however, we would still end up with social actions and practices that have a pre-digital existence: activism, dating, encyclopaedias, government, books, music distribution, social support, community, bullying, hate, and so on. This does not in any sense mean that the digital, the online, and the e- is a minor attribute. But it is an augmentation – a scale shift in terms of increased speed, impact, reach, and efficiency. The actions and practices, at their core, are not new and many of their key characteristics remain the same.

DIGITALLY TRANSFORMATIVE

There is a sliding scale, however, between scale changes and more substantial transformations. Consider, to take but one example, how online dating has changed beyond being a scale-shifted version of the older system with print personal ads. Today, some dating apps, such as Tinder, have GPS functionality, increasingly refined algorithms, and game-inspired interfaces for swiping potential partners in different directions on a touchscreen, depending on whether we prefer them or not. In this case, one could argue, we have moved beyond the level of digital augmentation and into the sphere of the digitally *transformative*. This is an example, then, not of scale change, but of model change, where not only the extent or degree of the practice is altered, but where the very practice itself comes to function in alternative ways, with other consequences, and new meanings (Earl & Kimport 2011: 27–29). And this is just an example from online dating. We can also look for similar developments in any number of areas of society and culture.

Digitally transformative outcomes – in the sense that digital media have changed the fabric of society – happen when the social actions and practices that are carried out rely so much on digitally-specific affordances that they would not be possible without them. So, when we look for traces of digital transformation, we must ask whether the social action or practice in question is uniquely digital. Consider memes as an example (see Chapter 2). They are images and text, so there is nothing new there. But the entire social practice around them – the handy image editing, the 'internet'-humour, and their sometimes-viral spread – could not have happened in, say, 1989. They are a product of digital society, and one – however small – piece of the puzzle we must consider when exploring how digital media transforms sociality. We could ask the same of hashtags, likes, blogging, vlogging, fanfiction, hacktivism, and so on. You will realise that all these phenomena have elements of the digitally analogue, enhanced, and transformative, all at the same time.

It is important to underline that the categories of digitally analogue, digitally enhanced, and digitally transformative are a set of abstract concepts, rather than an idea about a chronological historical development where one replaces the other. The digital media use of any society, group, or individual will simultaneously have elements of digitally analogue, digitally enhanced, as well as digitally transformative outcomes. This is not to say that transformation replaces enhancement replaces emulation. A person engaging in transformative practices – posting selfies, trolling, or using Tinder – will still sometimes use YouTube as television, and so on. Remember that people still rely on both the wheel and pen and paper for some social actions and practices. As art and technology scholars Robert Pepperell and Michael Punt (2000: 19) write: 'in the postdigital age we will still wear trousers, live in brick houses and eat from wooden tables as there is no compelling reason why these accessories to existence should change'. We simply keep much of the old, while bringing in new things alongside it. New and old technologies are layered on top of one another, and so are the different uses of digital media.

The taxonomy introduced here should therefore be seen as an analytical instrument that can be used to help make an assessment of the level of 'real' digitally-driven social change which is at work in relation to a given social action or practice. Selfies, for example, become distinctive not because they are photographic self-portraits, but in terms of how they are snapped in certain ways with mobile phone cameras, and how they are tagged and shared in digital social networks (see Chapter 6). Selfies could not have happened in '1989' either, even though self-portraits could. They are another small piece of the puzzle needed to understand how digital media contribute to the transformation of the fabric of society. Another example is trolling: satire, pranks, sarcasm, and irony are not new. But the social practice of trolling is born digital, and without the relative anonymity and invisibility of computer-mediated communication (see Chapter 7), and the development of a certain breed of 'internet humour', it would not be what it is.

It must also be emphasised that the taxonomy is not normative in the sense that the more transformative a digital social action or practice can be deemed, the more valuable it is to society. Indeed, there is nothing wrong with uses that are mostly digitally analogue. Nor is it to be seen as a partial failure that one is 'just' doing, for example, digital activism of the digitally enhanced, scale-change type. But if we are to focus on the question of digital media and social change from the overarching societal perspective, it is the digitally *transformative* phenomena that are the most uniquely digital, and that therefore are the most likely to hold clues as to what the future of society and sociality holds.

THE POWER OF THE SEEMINGLY NON-POLITICAL

It may appear odd that the most prominent examples of the digitally transformative are largely to be found among the cool, quirky, 'extreme', and seemingly random parts of digital society, such as memes, selfies, trolling, cute cats, and so on. It is not only about such things, however. There are also examples of digitally transformative types of social organisation and modes of operation, such as, for example, peer production (see Chapter 3), cybersalons (see Chapter 9), and the most decentralised and crowdsourced forms of citizen journalism.

But it is nonetheless also important to take the apparently random internet phenomena seriously, as pieces of the puzzle. Perhaps, in fact, such phenomena seem insignificant and random for the very reason that they are the most transformational. We simply don't have concepts yet that allow us to see them as anything other than oddities. This is in line with Earl and Kimport's (2011) view that model changes, as opposed to scale changes, are disruptions and alterations of which there is not yet a developed understanding. One might argue, then, that there can exist a politics of the seemingly non-political. Political scientist Jessica Beyer (2014) conducted a series of case studies of online groups and spaces – Anonymous, *The Pirate Bay*, *World of Warcraft*, and the IGN.com forum – from a mobilisation perspective. In these studies, she found that digital tools, platforms, and spaces that appear to be non-political are in fact crucial for gaining an understanding of civic engagement. Digital society has a certain nature, which tends to foster certain types of interaction. Beyer argues that environments where no individual owns the content, where there is high anonymity, and low levels of formal regulation give rise to creativity. Therefore, social interaction in online spaces that are 'non-political' is important for an understanding of how people conceive themselves in relation to political processes. This is because, no matter the aim or intended function of the tools and platforms in question, political conversations and negotiations over norms happen in unlikely places. In the online role-playing game *World of Warcraft*, for example, Beyer (2014: 128) found that:

> politically significant interactions permeated micro-interactions, such as the informal regulations players laid out for each other in one-on-one conversations in terms of acceptable speech, and macro-structures, such as the realm that

has become a widely known as a 'safe haven' for GLBTQ players and women because of the presence of large and powerful GLBTQ-focused guilds on the realm that discourage hateful speech and encourage inclusion.

Because of this, Beyer argues, movements and organisations have quite a lot to learn from spaces like these. There is a common normative assumption that for society to be healthy it should be characterised by 'high discourse', where highly educated people, who appear with their real names, interact with each other in a polite manner. Beyer argues, however, that in places such as 4chan or Reddit, the wide range of content – some of which can be deeply disturbing – and the wider range of conversation may create better possibilities and more opportunities for political action as well. For example, she describes how Christopher Poole, the creator of the 4chan board where Anonymous was born, said in a talk that he believed in 'content over creator'. Rather than having people 'bandwagon around certain individuals', the idea was that people should all be judged the same way, namely by their contribution.

Beyer (2014: 132) concludes that 'there is value not only in the places online that fit our expectations of civil society but also in the places online that make us cringe'. In such spaces, Beyer says, there are much better opportunities to foster activism than on privately-owned sites. And looking beyond the narrow scope of Beyer's empirical case of activism, unexpected and seemingly random spaces are also the ones likely to be disruptive in a broader sense, and to contribute more generally to digital social transformation. Whether this disruption is 'good' or 'bad', and if it brings about positive or negative transformation, is in the hands of the people who populate and use the platforms.

REFERENCES

ABC (2013). ABC Online's 'Selfie' Beats 'Twerk' as Word of the Year. *abc.net.au*. https://web.archive.org/web/2020*/www.abc.net.au/news/2013-11-19/selfie-beats-twerk-as-word-of-the-year/5102154

Abu-Salma, R., Krol, K., Parkin, S., Koh, V., Kwan, K., Mahboob, J., Traboulsi, Z. & Sasse, M. A. (2017). The Security Blanket of the Chat World: An Analytic Evaluation and a User Study of Telegram. In *Proceedings 2nd European Workshop on Usable Security*. Paris: Internet Society. www.ndss-symposium.org/wp-content/uploads/2018/03/eurousec2017_06_Abu-Salma_paper.pdf.

Adatto, K. (2008). *Picture Perfect*. Princeton, NJ: Princeton University Press.

Agar, J. (2003). *Constant Touch*. Cambridge, UK: Icon.

Ahmad, M. (2011). *Smartphone: Mobile Revolution at the Crossroads of Communications, Computing and Consumer Electronics*. North Charleston, SC: CreateSpace Independent Publishing Platform.

Ahmed, S. (2004). *The Cultural Politics of Emotion*. London: Routledge.

Allan, S. (2009). Histories of Citizen Journalism. In S. Allan & E. Thorsen (Eds.), *Citizen Journalism* (pp. 17–31). New York: Peter Lang.

Altheide, D. L. (1995). *An Ecology of Communication*. New York: Aldine de Gruyter.

Altheide, D. L. & Snow, R. P. (1979). *Media Logic*. London: Sage.

Amichai-Hamburger, Y. (2017). *Internet Psychology: The Basics*. London: Routledge.

Anderson, B. (1983). *Imagined Communities*. London: Verso.

Anderson, C. (2006). *The Long Tail*. New York: Random House.

Appadurai, A. (1996). *Modernity at Large*. Minneapolis, MN: University of Minnesota Press.

Aschoff, N. (2020). *The Smartphone Society: Technology, Power, and Resistance in the New Gilded Age*. Boston, MA: Beacon Press.

Atzori, L., Iera, A. & Giacomo M. (2010). The Internet of Things: A Survey. *Computer Networks*, *54*(15), 2787–2805. doi: 10.1016/j.comnet.2010.05.010

Auerbach, D. (2019). How Facebook Has Flattened Human Communication. *Medium*, August 28. https://onezero.medium.com/how-facebook-has-flattened-human-communication-c1525a15e9aa.

Bail, C. A. (2021). *Breaking the Social Media Prism: How to Make Our Platforms Less Polarizing*. Princeton, NJ: Princeton University Press.

Bakardjieva, M. (2003). Virtual Togetherness. *Media, Culture, and Society*, *25*(3), 291–313.

Barabási, A. L. (2003). *Linked*. New York: Plume.

Barbieri, F. & Camacho-Collados, J. (2018). How Gender and Skin Tone Modifiers Affect Emoji Semantics in Twitter. In *Proceedings of the Seventh Joint Conference on Lexical and Computational Semantics* (pp. 101–106). New Orleans, LA: Association for Computational Linguistics. http://aclweb.org/anthology/S18-2011. https://doi.org/10.18653/v1/S18-2011

Bargh, J. A. & McKenna, K. Y. (2004). The Internet and Social Life. *Annual Review of Psychology*, *55*, 573–590.

Baron, N. S. (2008). *Always On*. Oxford: Oxford University Press.

Barton, D. & Lee, C. (2013). *Language Online*. London: Routledge.

Bayer, J. B., Ellison, N. B., Schoenebeck, S. Y. & Falk, E. B. (2015). Sharing the Small Moments. *Information, Communication & Society*, *19*(7), 956–977.

Baym, N. (2010). *Personal Connections in the Digital Age*. Cambridge, UK: Polity Press.

Baym, N. (2011). Social Networks 2.0. In M. Consalvo & C. Ess (Eds.), *The Handbook of Internet Studies* (pp. 384–405). Chichester: Wiley-Blackwell.

Beer, D. (2017). The Social Power of Algorithms. *Information, Communication & Society*, *20*(1), 1–13.

Bell, D. (1973). *The Coming of Post-industrial Society*. New York: Basic Books.

Ben-Ze'ev, A. (2004). *Love Online*. New York: Cambridge University Press.

Beniger, J. (1986). *The Control Revolution*. Cambridge, MA: Harvard University Press.

Beniger, J. R. (1987). Personalization of Mass Media and the Growth of Pseudo-Community. *Communication Research*, *14*(3), 352–371.

Benkler, Y. (2006). *The Wealth of Networks*. New Haven, CT: Yale University Press.

Benkler, Y., Faris, R. & Roberts, H. (2018). *Network Propaganda: Manipulation, Disinformation, and Radicalization in American Politics*. New York: Oxford University Press.

Bennett, W. L. & Livingston, S. (Eds.) (2020). *The Disinformation Age: Politics, Technology, and Disruptive Communication in the United States*. Cambridge, UK: Cambridge University Press.

Bennett, W. L. & Segerberg, A. (2012). The Logic of Connective Action. *Information, Communication & Society*, *15*(5), 739–768.

Benski, T. & Fisher, E. (2014). Introduction. In T. Benski & E. Fisher (Eds.), *Internet and Emotions* (pp. 1–14). New York: Routledge.

Berners-Lee, T. (1996). WWW: Past, Present, and Future. *Computer*, *29*(10), 69–77.

Betts, Lucy R. (2016). *Cyberbullying*. London: Palgrave Macmillan.

Beyer, J. L. (2014). *Expect Us*. Oxford: Oxford University Press.

Bimber, B. (1994). Three Faces of Technological Determinism. In M. R. Smith & L. Marx (Eds.), *Does Technology Drive History? The Dilemma of Technological Determinism* (pp. 79–100). Cambridge, MA: The MIT Press.

Blommaert, J. & Jie, D. (2010). *Ethnographic Fieldwork*. Bristol: Multilingual Matters.

Boellstorff, T., Nardi, B., Pearce, C. & Taylor, T. L. (2012). *Ethnography and Virtual Worlds*. Princeton, NJ: Princeton University Press.

Bolter, J. D. & Grusin, R. (1999). *Remediation*. Cambridge, MA: The MIT Press.

Borgmann, A. (1999). *Holding on to Reality*. Chicago, IL: University of Chicago Press.

Bourdieu, P. (1990). *The Logic of Practice*. Stanford, CA: Stanford University Press.

boyd, d. (2008). *Taken Out of Context*. Berkeley, CA: University of California.

boyd, d. (2014). *It's Complicated*. New Haven, CT: Yale University Press.

Brady, H. E. & Collier, D. (Eds.) (2010). *Rethinking Social Inquiry*. Lanham, MD: Rowman & Littlefield.

Brandtzæg, P. B. (2012). Social Networking Sites: Their Users and Social Implications – A Longitudinal Study. *Journal of Computer-Mediated Communication*, *17*(4), 467–488.

Brin, S. & Page, L. (2012). The Anatomy of a Large-Scale Hypertextual Web Search Engine. *Computer Networks*, *56*(18), 3825–3833.

Bruns, A. (2008). *Blogs, Wikipedia, Second Life, and Beyond*. New York: Peter Lang.

Bruns, A. & Burgess, J. (2011). The Use of Twitter Hashtags in the Formation of Ad Hoc Publics. http://mappingonlinepublics.net/

Bruns, A. & Highfield, T. (2016). Is Habermas on Twitter? In A. Bruns, G. Enli, E. Skogerbø, A. O. Larsson & C. Christensen (Eds.), *The Routledge Companion to Social Media and Politics* (pp. 56–73). London: Routledge.

Bryce, M. (2006). Cuteness Needed. *International Journal of the Humanities*, *2*(3), 2265–2275.

Buchanan, E. & Markham, A. (2012). *Ethical Decision-Making and Internet Research*. AoIR. Retrieved from https://aoir.org/reports/ethics2.pdf.

Bucher, T. (2012). *Programmed Sociality: A Software Studies Perspective on Social Networking Sites*. Oslo: University of Oslo.

Burge, J. (2019). Correcting the Record on the First Emoji Set. *Emojipedia*. https://web.archive.org/web/2020*/https://blog.emojipedia.org/correcting-the-record-on-the-first-emoji-set/

Burns, A. (2015). Self(ie)-Discipline. *International Journal of Communication*, *9*(2015), 1716–1733.

Butler, J. (1990). *Gender Trouble*. New York: Routledge.

Calhoun, C. (1998). Community without Propinquity Revisited. *Sociological Inquiry*, *68*(3), 373–397.

Carr, N. G. (2010). *The Shallows*. New York: W. W. Norton.

Castells, M. (1996). *The Rise of the Network Society*. Malden, MA: Blackwell.

Castells, M. (2002). *The Internet Galaxy*. Oxford: Oxford University Press.

Castells, M. (2004). Informationalism, Networks, and the Network Society: A Theoretical Blueprint. In M. Castells (Ed.), *The Network Society: A Cross-Cultural Perspective* (pp. 3–45). Northampton, MA: Edward Elgar.

Castells, M. (2009). *Communication Power*. Oxford: Oxford University Press.

Castells, M. (2010). *End of Millennium* (2nd ed., with new preface). Oxford: Blackwell.

Castells, M. (2015). *Networks of Outrage and Hope*. Cambridge, UK: Polity Press.

Cavanagh, A. (2007). *Sociology in the Age of the Internet*. Maidenhead: Open University Press.

Ceruzzi, P. E. (2003). *A History of Modern Computing*. Cambridge, MA: The MIT Press.

Chan, J. & Pun, N. (2010). Suicide as Protest for the New Generation of Chinese Migrant Workers. *The Asia-Pacific Journal*, *37*(2), 1–50.

Chang, W. (2020). The Monstrous-Feminine in the Incel Imagination: Investigating the Representation of Women as 'Femoids' on /r/Braincels. *Feminist Media Studies*. Online first August 5. https://doi.org/10.1080/14680777.2020.1804976

Cheney-Lippold, J. (2017). *We Are Data: Algorithms and the Making of Our Digital Selves*. New York: New York University Press.

Citron, D. K. (2009). Cyber Civil Rights. *Boston University Law Review*, *89*, 61–125.

Citron, D. K. (2014). *Hate Crimes in Cyberspace*. Cambridge, MA: Harvard University Press.

Clough, P. T. & Halley, J. O. (2007). *The Affective Turn*. Durham, NC: Duke University Press.

CNN (2011). CNN: Egyptian Activist, Wael Ghonim 'Facebook to Thank for Freedom'. *YouTube*. www.youtube.com/watch?v=JS4-d_Edius

Cohen, G. A. (1978). *Karl Marx's Theory of History: A Defence*. Princeton, NJ: Princeton University Press.

Cohen, S. (1972). *Folk Devils and Moral Panics*. Oxford: Basil Blackwell.

Comolli, J. L. (1980). Machines of the Visible. In T. de Lauretis & S. Heath (Eds.), *The Cinematic Apparatus* (pp. 121–142). London: Macmillan.

Cormode, G. & Krishnamurthy, B. (2008). Key Differences between Web 1.0 and Web 2.0. *First Monday*, *13*(6).

Corner, J. (2017). Fake News, Post-Truth and Media-Political Change. *Media, Culture & Society*, *39*(7), 1100–1107. doi: 10.1177/0163443717726743

Cotter, K. (2019). Playing the Visibility Game: How Digital Influencers and Algorithms Negotiate Influence on Instagram. *New Media & Society*, *21*(4), 895–913.

Cotter, K. (2020). Critical Algorithmic Literacy: Power, Epistemology, and Platforms. *ProQuest Dissertations and Theses*. Ann Arbor, MI: Michigan State University (Thesis).

Couldry, N. & Hepp, A. (2017). *The Mediated Construction of Reality*. Cambridge, UK: Polity Press.

Couldry, N. & Mejias, U. (2019). *The Costs of Connection: How Data is Colonizing Human Life and Appropriating it for Capitalism*. Stanford, CA: Stanford University Press.

Crawford, K. & boyd, d. (2012). Critical Questions for Big Data. *Information, Communication & Society*, *15*(5), 662–679.

Culnan, M. J. & Markus, M. L. (1987). Information Technologies. In L. Putnam & D. Mumby (Eds.), *Handbook of Organizational Communication* (pp. 420–443). Beverly Hills, CA: Sage.

Curran, J. (2012a). Reinterpreting the Internet. In J. Curran et al., *Misunderstanding the Internet* (pp. 3–33). London: Routledge.

Curran, J. (2012b). Rethinking Internet History. In J. Curran et al., *Misunderstanding the Internet* (pp. 34–65). London: Routledge.

Danesi, M. (2017). *The Semiotics of Emoji: The Rise of Visual Language in the Age of the Internet*. London: Bloomsbury Academic.

Dawkins, R. (2006). *The Selfish Gene* (30th Anniversary Edition). Oxford: Oxford University Press. (Originally published 1976.)

de Vries, I. O. (2012). *Tantalisingly Close*. Amsterdam: Amsterdam University Press.

Dean, Jodi (2001). Cybersalons and Civil Society. *Public Culture*, *13*(2), 243–265.

Dean, Jodi (2010). *Blog Theory*. Cambridge, UK: Polity Press.

Dean, Jonathan (2019). Sorted for Memes and Gifs: Visual Media and Everyday Digital Politics. *Political Studies Review*, *17*(3), 255–66. https://doi.org/10.1177/1478929918807483

Debray, R. (1996). *Media Manifestos*. London: Verso.

Dencik, L., Hintz, A., Redden, J. & Treré, E. (2019). Exploring Data Justice: Conceptions, Applications and Directions. *Information, Communication & Society*, *22*(7), 873–881.

Dencik, L., Jansen, F. & Metcalfe, P. (2018). A Conceptual Framework for Approaching Social Justice in an Age of Datafication. Working Paper, DATAJUSTICE. https://datajusticeproject.net/2018/08/30/a-conceptual-framework-for-approaching-social-justice-in-an-age-of-datafication/

Denzin, N. K. & Lincoln, Y. S. (2000). *Handbook of Qualitative Research*. Thousand Oaks, CA: Sage.

Dery, M. (1993). *Flame Wars*. Durham, NC: Duke University Press.

DiMaggio, P. & Hargittai, E. (2001). *From the 'Digital Divide' to 'Digital Inequality'*. Princeton, NJ: Center for Arts and Cultural Policy Studies.

Domingos, P. (2015). *The Master Algorithm: How the Quest for the Ultimate Learning Machine Will Remake Our World*. New York: Basic Books.

271

Dooley, E. (2014). Selfies are Turning Politicians into Teenagers. *ABC News*. https://web.archive.org/web/2020*/https://abcnews.go.com/blogs/politics/2014/04/are-selfies-are-turning-politicians-into-teenagers/

Drotner, K. (1999). Dangerous Media? *Paedagogica Historica*, *35*(3), 593–619.

Drucker, P. F. (1959). *Landmarks of Tomorrow*. New York: Harper.

Durkheim, É. (1912). *The Elementary Forms of Religious Life*. New York: Free Press.

Durkheim, É. (1895/1982). *The Rules of Sociological Method*. New York: Free Press.

Dyer-Witheford, N. (2015). *Cyber-Proletariat*. London: Pluto Press.

Earl, J. & Kimport, K. (2011). *Digitally Enabled Social Change*. Cambridge, MA: The MIT Press.

Ehlin, L. (2015). *Becoming Image*. Stockholm: Fashion Studies, Stockholm University.

Ellison, N. B. & boyd, d. (2007). Social Network Sites: Definition, History, and Scholarship. *Journal of Computer-Mediated Communication*, *13*(1), 210–230.

Enzensberger, H. M. (1970). Constituents of a Theory of the Media. *New Left Review*, (64), 13–36.

Etzioni, A. & Etzioni, O. (1999). Face-to-Face and Computer-Mediated Communities. *The Information Society*, *15*(4), 241–248.

Eubanks, V. (2011). *Digital Dead End*. Cambridge, MA: The MIT Press.

Evans, V. (2017). *The Emoji Code: The Linguistics Behind Smiley Faces and Scaredy Cats*. New York: Picador.

Fahlman, S. (1982). Original Bboard Thread in Which:-) was Proposed. https://web.archive.org/web/*/www.cs.cmu.edu/~sef/Orig-Smiley.htm.

Felbo, B., Mislove, A., Søgaard, A., Rahwan, I. & Lehmann, S. (2017). Using Millions of Emoji Occurrences to Learn Any-Domain Representations for Detecting Sentiment, Emotion and Sarcasm. In *Proceedings of the 2017 Conference on Empirical Methods in Natural Language Processing* (pp. 1615–1625). September. Copenhagen, Denmark: Association for Computational Linguistics. https://doi.org/10.18653/v1/D17-1169

Fernandez, M., Asif, M. & Alani, H. (2018). Understanding the Roots of Radicalisation on Twitter. In *Proceedings of the 10th ACM Conference on Web Science* (pp. 1–10). Amsterdam, Netherlands: ACM. https://doi.org/10.1145/3201064.3201082

Ferrada Stoehrel, R. & Lindgren, S. (2014). For the Lulz: Anonymous, Aesthetics and Affect. *tripleC (cognition, communication, co-operation): Journal for a Global Sustainable Information Society*, *12*(1), 238–264.

Flaxman, S., Goel, S. & Rao, J. M. (2016). Filter Bubbles, Echo Chambers, and Online News Consumption. *Public Opinion Quarterly*, *80*(S1), 298–320. doi: 10.1093/poq/nfw006

Foucault, M. (1972). *The Archaeology of Knowledge and the Discourse on Language*. New York: Pantheon Books.

Foucault, M. (1988). *Technologies of the Self* (L. H. Martin, H. Gutman & P. H. Hutton, Eds.). Amherst, MA: University of Massachusetts Press.

franzke, a. s., Bechmann, A., Zimmer, M. & Ess, C. (2020). *Internet Research: Ethical Guidelines 3.0*. AoIR. https://aoir.org/reports/ethics3.pdf

Freelon, D., McIlwain, C. D. & Clark, M. (2016). *Beyond the Hashtags: #Ferguson, #Blacklivesmatter, and the Online Struggle for Offline Justice*. Washington, DC: Center for Media & Social Impact.

Friedman, U. (2016). Boaty McBoatface and the False Promise of British Democracy. *The Atlantic*. https://web.archive.org/web/20210416031808/www.theatlantic.com/international/archive/2016/04/boaty-mcboatface-britain-democracy/479088/

Fuchs, C. (2017). *Social Media: A Critical Introduction* (2nd ed.). London: Sage.

Fuchs, C. (2018). *Digital Demagogue: Authoritarian Capitalism in the Age of Trump and Twitter*. London: Pluto Press.

Fuchs, C. & Mosco, V. (Eds.) (2016). *Marx and the Political Economy of the Media*. Leiden: Brill.

Fuller, M. (2008). Introduction: The Stuff of Software. In M. Fuller (Ed.), *Software Studies: A Lexicon* (pp. 1–13). Cambridge, MA: The MIT Press.

Galloway, A. R. (2004). *Protocol*. Cambridge, MA: The MIT Press.

Gardiner, B. (2018). 'It's a Terrible Way to Go to Work': What 70 Million Readers' Comments on the Guardian Revealed about Hostility to Women and Minorities Online. *Feminist Media Studies*, *18*(4), 592–608. https://doi.org/10.1080/1468077.2018.1447334

Gauntlett, D. (2018). *Making is Connecting: The Social Power of Creativity, from Craft and Knitting to Digital Everything* (2nd ed.). Cambridge, UK: Polity Press.

Gee, J. P. (2005). Semiotic Social Spaces and Affinity Spaces: From the Age of Mythology to Today's Schools. In D. Barton & K. Tusting (Eds.), *Beyond Communities of Practice: Language, Power and Social Context* (pp. 214–232). New York: Cambridge University Press.

Geertz, C. (1973). *The Interpretation of Cultures*. New York: Basic Books.

Gergen, K. J., Gergen, M. M. & Barton, W. H. (1973). Deviance in the Dark. *Psychology Today*, *7*(5), 129–130.

Gerlitz, C. & Helmond, A. (2013). The Like Economy. *New Media & Society*, *15*(8), 1348–1365.

Giannoulis, E. & Wilde, L. R. A. (Eds.) (2019). *Emoticons, Kaomoji, and Emoji: The Transformation of Communication in the Digital Age*. New York: Routledge.

Gibson, J. (1977). The Theory of Affordances. In R. Shaw & J. Bransford (Eds.), *Perceiving, Acting, and Knowing*. Hillsdale, NJ: Erlbaum.

Gibson, W. (1984). *Neuromancer*. New York: Ace Books.

Giddens, A. (1984). *The Constitution of Society*. Cambridge, UK: Polity Press.

Gillespie, T. (2010). The Politics of 'Platforms'. *New Media & Society*, *12*(3), 347–364.

Gillespie, T. (2014). The Relevance of Algorithms. In T. Gillespie, P. Boczkowski & K. Foot (Eds.), *Media Technologies: Essays on Communication, Materiality, and Society* (pp. 167–193). Cambridge, MA: The MIT Press.

Ging, D. (2019). Alphas, Betas, and Incels: Theorizing the Masculinities of the Manosphere. *Men and Masculinities, 22*(4), 638–657. doi: 10.1177/1097184X17706401

Ging, D. & Siapera, E. (Eds.) (2019). *Gender Hate Online: Understanding the New Anti-Feminism*. Cham, Switzerland: Springer International.

Goffman, E. (1959). *The Presentation of Self in Everyday Life*. New York: Doubleday.

Goggin, G. (2006). *Cell Phone Culture*. London: Routledge.

Goggin, G. (2011). *Global Mobile Media*. Abingdon, Oxon: Routledge.

Goggin, G. & Hjorth, L. (2009). *Mobile Technologies*. New York: Routledge.

Goggin, G. & Hjorth, L. (Eds.) (2014). *The Routledge Companion to Mobile Media*. London: Routledge.

Graham, S., Weingart, S. & Milligan, I. (2012). Getting Started with Topic Modeling and MALLET. *Programming Historian*. https://doi.org/10.46430/phen0017

Gramsci, A. (1971). *Selections from the Prison Notebooks* (Q. Hoare & G. Nowell-Smith, Eds.). London: Lawrence & Wishart.

Gran, A., Booth, P. & Bucher, T. (2020). To Be or Not to Be Algorithm Aware: A Question of a New Digital Divide? *Information, Communication & Society*. Online first March 9. https://doi.org/10.1080/1369118X.2020.1736124

Granovetter, M. S. (1973). The Strength of Weak Ties. *American Journal of Sociology, 78*(6), 1360–1380.

Green, E. & Singleton, C. (2013). Gendering the Digital. In K. Orton-Johnson & N. Prior (Eds.), *Digital Sociology* (pp. 34–50). London: Palgrave Macmillan.

Griffin, M., Herrmann, S. & Kittler, F. A. (1996). Technologies of Writing: Interview with Friedrich A. Kittler. *New Literary History, 27*(4), 731–742.

Grusin, R. A. (2010). *Premediation*. Basingstoke: Palgrave Macmillan.

Habermas, J. (1971). *Toward a Rational Society: Student Protest, Science, and Politics*. London: Heinemann.

Habermas, J. (1989). *The Structural Transformation of the Public Sphere*. Cambridge, UK: Polity Press.

Habermas, J. (2006). Political Communication in Media Society. *Communication Theory, 16*(4), 411–426.

Hall, S. (1972). Encoding/decoding. In *Culture, Media, Language: Working Papers in Cultural Studies* (pp. 128–138). Birmingham: CCCS.

Halupka, M. (2014). Clicktivism: A Systematic Heuristic. *Policy & Internet, 6*(2), 115–132.

Hannan, J. (2018). Trolling Ourselves to Death? Social Media and Post-Truth Politics. *European Journal of Communication, 33*(2), 214–226.

Haraway, D. (1991). *Simians, Cyborgs, and Women*. New York: Routledge.

Hardey, M. (2002). Life beyond the Screen. *The Sociological Review*, *50*(4), 570–585.

Hargittai, E. (2002). Second-Level Digital Divide. *First Monday*, *7*(4).

Hargittai, E. (2012). Open Doors, Closed Spaces. In L. Nakamura & P. A. Chow-White (Eds.), *Race after the Internet* (pp. 223–245). New York: Routledge.

Hargittai, E. & Sandvig, C. (Eds.) (2015). *Digital Research Confidential: The Secrets of Studying Behavior Online*. Cambridge, MA: The MIT Press.

Harmon, A. (2001). A Day of Terror: The Talk Online – Web Offers Both News and Comfort. *The New York Times*, September 12. www.nytimes.com/2001/09/12/us/a-day-of-terror-the-talk-online-web-offers-both-news-and-comfort.html

Harsin, J. (2015). Regimes of Posttruth, Postpolitics, and Attention Economies. *Communication, Culture and Critique*, *8*(2), 327–333. https://doi.org/10.1111/cccr.12097

Hartley, J. & Green, J. (2006). The Public Sphere on the Beach. *European Journal of Cultural Studies*, *9*(3), 341–362.

Hawley, G. (2017). *Making Sense of the Alt-Right*. New York: Columbia University Press.

Hazlett, T. W. (2017). *The Political Spectrum: The Tumultuous Liberation of Wireless Technology, From Herbert Hoover to the Smartphone*. New Haven, CT: Yale University Press.

Hebdige, D. (1979). *Subculture*. London: Routledge.

Henderson, S. & Gilding, M. (2004). 'I've Never Clicked This Much with Anyone in My Life': Trust and Hyperpersonal Communication in Online Friendships. *New Media & Society*, *6*(4), 487–506.

Hepp, A. (2020). *Deep Mediatization*. London: Routledge.

Hillis, K., Paasonen, S. & Petit, M. (Eds.) (2015). *Networked Affect*. Cambridge, MA: The MIT Press.

Hine, C. (2000). *Virtual Ethnography*. London: Sage.

Hine, C. (2012). *The Internet: Understanding Qualitative Research*. Oxford: Oxford University Press.

Hine, C. (2015). *Ethnography for the Internet*. London: Bloomsbury Academic.

Hjarvard, S. (2013). *The Mediatization of Culture and Society*. London: Routledge.

Howard, P. N. (2020). *Lie Machines: How to Save Democracy from Troll Armies, Deceitful Robots, Junk News Operations, and Political Operatives*. New Haven, CT: Yale University Press.

Hsieh, C. (2016). 'Dicks Out for Harambe': How 2 Average Guys Started the Year's Most Controversial Meme. *Cosmopolitan*. https://web.archive.org/web/2020*/www.cosmopolitan.com/politics/a8354653/dicks-out-for-harambe-internets-most-fascinating/

Hu, M. (2020). Cambridge Analytica's Black Box. *Big Data & Society*, *7*(2), doi: 10.1177/2053951720938091

Hutto, C. J. & Gilbert, E. (2014). VADER: A Parsimonious Rule-Based Model for Sentiment Analysis of Social Media Text. In *Eighth International AAAI Conference on Weblogs and Social Media*, May 16. www.aaai.org/ocs/index.php/ICWSM/ICWSM14/paper/view/8109

Ignatow, G. & Mihalcea, R. (2016). *Text Mining: A Guidebook for the Social Sciences*. London: Sage.

International Telecommunication Union (2021). Data and Analytics: Taking the Pulse of the Information Society. *itu.int*. www.itu.int/itu-d/sites/statistics/

Ito, M. (2005). Introduction. In M. Ito, D. Okabe & M. Matsuda (Eds.), *Personal, Portable, Pedestrian*. Cambridge, MA: The MIT Press.

Ito, M. (2008). Introduction. In K. Varnelis (Ed.), *Networked Publics* (pp. 1–14). Cambridge, MA: The MIT Press.

Ito, M., Matsuda, M. & Okabe, D. (Eds.) (2005). *Personal, Portable, Pedestrian*. Cambridge, MA: The MIT Press.

Jackson, S. J., Bailey, M. & Foucault Welles, B. (2020). *#HashtagActivism: Networks of Race and Gender Justice*. Cambridge, MA: The MIT Press.

Jakobson, R. (1990). The Speech Event and the Functions of Language. In L. R. Waugh & M. Monville-Burston (Eds.), *On Language* (pp. 69–79). Cambridge, MA: Harvard University Press.

Jenkins, H. (2006). *Convergence Culture*. New York: New York University Press.

Joinson, A. N. (2001). Self-Disclosure in Computer-Mediated Communication. *European Journal of Social Psychology*, *31*(2), 177–192.

Jones, S. (1998a). Information, Internet, and Community. In S. Jones (Ed.), *CyberSociety 2.0* (pp. 1–34). Thousand Oaks, CA: Sage.

Jones, S. (1998b). Introduction. In S. Jones (Ed.), *CyberSociety 2.0* (pp. xi–xvii). Thousand Oaks, CA: Sage.

Jones, S. (1999). Preface. In S. Jones (Ed.), *Doing Internet Research* (pp. ix–xiv). Thousand Oaks, CA: Sage.

Jordan, T. (2013). *Internet, Society and Culture*. London: Bloomsbury.

Juris, J. S. (2012). Reflections on #Occupy Everywhere. *American Ethnologist*, *39*(2), 259–279.

Katz, J. E. & Aakhus, M. A. (2002). *Perpetual Contact*. Cambridge: Cambridge University Press.

Katz, J. E. & Crocker, E. T. (2015). Selfies and Photo Messaging as Visual Conversation. *International Journal of Communication*, *9*, 1861–1872.

Kayany, J. M. (1998). Contexts of Uninhibited Online Behavior. *Journal of the American Society for Information Science*, *49*(12), 1135–1141.

Keen, A. (2007). *The Cult of the Amateur*. New York: Doubleday.

Keen, A. (2012). *Digital Vertigo*. London: Constable.

Keen, A. (2015). *The Internet is Not the Answer*. New York: Atlantic Monthly Press.

Kendall, L. (2011). Community and the Internet. In M. Consalvo & C. Ess (Eds.), *The Handbook of Internet Studies* (pp. 309–325). Chichester: Wiley-Blackwell.

Kennedy, H., Poell, T. & van Dijck, J. (2015). Data and Agency. *Big Data & Society*, *2*(2), 1–7. doi: 10.1177/2053951715621569

Kincheloe, J. L. (2005). On to the Next Level. *Qualitative Inquiry*, *11*(3), 323–350.

Kitchin, R. & McArdle, G. (2016). What Makes Big Data, Big Data? *Big Data & Society*, *3*(1), 1–10.

Knuttila, L. (2011). User Unknown: 4chan, Anonymity and Contingency. *First Monday*, *16*(10), October 3.

Kozinets, R. V. (2015). *Netnography: Redefined*. Thousand Oaks, CA: Sage.

Kranzberg, M. (1986). Technology and History. *Technology and Culture*, *27*(3), 544–560.

Kumar, K. (2009). *From Post-Industrial to Post-Modern Society*. New York: John Wiley & Sons.

Lange, P. G. (2007). Publicly Private and Privately Public. *Journal of Computer-Mediated Communication*, *13*(1), 361–380.

Lange, P. G. (2009). Videos of Affinity on YouTube. In P. Snickars & P. Vonderau (Eds.), *The YouTube Reader* (pp. 70–88). Stockholm: National Library of Sweden.

Lanier, J. (2010). *You are Not a Gadget*. New York: Alfred A. Knopf.

Lanier, J. (2018). *Ten Arguments for Deleting Your Social Media Accounts Right Now*. London: The Bodley Head.

Latour, B. (2005). *Reassembling the Social*. Oxford: Oxford University Press.

Lennings, C. J., Amon, K. L., Brummert, H. & Lennings, N. J. (2010). Grooming for Terror: The Internet and Young People. *Psychiatry, Psychology and Law*, *17*(3), 424–437.

Lessig, L. (2006). *Code*. New York: Basic Books.

Lévi-Strauss, C. (1966). *The Savage Mind*. Chicago, IL: University of Chicago Press.

Lévy, P. (1997). *Collective Intelligence*. New York: Plenum Trade.

Lexico (2021). Definition of CYBERSPACE by Oxford Dictionary. *Lexico Dictionaries*. www.lexico.com/definition/cyberspace

Lindgren, S. (2012). 'It Took Me about Half an Hour, but I Did It!' Media Circuits and Affinity Spaces around How-to Videos on YouTube. *European Journal of Communication*, *27*(2), 152–170. https://doi.org/10.1177/0267323112443461

Lindgren, S. (2013). *New Noise*. New York: Peter Lang.

Lindgren, S. (Ed.) (2014). *Hybrid Media Culture*. London: Routledge.

Lindgren, S. (2019). Movement Mobilization in the Age of Hashtag Activism: Examining the Challenge of Noise, Hate, and Disengagement in the #MeToo Campaign. *Policy & Internet*. Online first July 29. https://doi.org/10.1002/poi3.212

Lindgren, S. (2020). *Data Theory: Interpretive Sociology and Computational Methods*. Cambridge, UK: Polity Press.

Ling, R. (2012). *Taken for Grantedness*. Cambridge, MA: The MIT Press.

Ling, R. & Yttri, B. (2002). Hyper-coordination via mobile phones in Norway. In J. E. Katz & M. A. Aakhus (Eds.), *Perpetual Contact* (pp. 139–169). Cambridge: Cambridge University Press.

Lipietz, A. (1987). *Mirages and Miracles*. London: Verso Books.

Lister, M., Dovey, J., Giddings, S., Kelly, K. & Grant, I. (2009). *New Media: A Critical Introduction*. London: Routledge.

Livingstone, S. (2019). Audiences in an Age of Datafication: Critical Questions for Media Research. *Television & New Media*, *20*(2), 170–183. doi: 10.1177/1527476 418811118

Lobato, R. & Meese, J. (2014). Kittens All the Way Down. *M/C Journal*, *17*(2).

Lobinger, K. & Brantner, C. (2015). In the Eye of the Beholder. *International Journal of Communication*, *9*, 1848–1860.

Lorente, S. (2002). Youth and Mobile Telephones. *Revista De Estudios De Juventud*, *57*, 9–24.

Losh, E. (2015). Feminism Reads Big Data. *International Journal of Communication*, *9*, 1647–1659.

Louridas, P. (2017). *Real-World Algorithms: A Beginner's Guide*. Cambridge, MA: The MIT Press.

Louridas, P. (2020). *Algorithms*. Cambridge, MA: The MIT Press.

Lovink, G. (2008). *Zero Comments*. New York: Routledge.

Lovink, G. (2011). *Networks without a Cause*. Cambridge, UK: Polity Press.

Lovink, G. & Rossiter, N. (2005). Dawn of the Organised Networks. *Fibreculture Journal*, 5.

Lovink, G. & Tuters, M. (2018). Memes and the Reactionary Totemism of the Theft of Joy. *non.copyriot.com*, https://non.copyriot.com/memes-and-the-reactionary-totemism-of-the-theft-of-joy/

Lüders, M. (2008). Conceptualizing Personal Media. *New Media & Society*, *10*(5), 683–702.

Lupton, D. (2014). *Digital Sociology*. London: Routledge.

Lupton, D. (2016). *The Quantified Self*. Cambridge, UK: Polity Press.

Lupton, D. (2020). Wearable Devices: Sociotechnical Imaginaries and Agential Capacities. In I. Pedersen & A. Iliadis (Eds.), *Embodied Computing: Wearables, Implantables, Embeddables, Ingestibles* (pp. 49–70). Cambridge, MA: The MIT Press.

Lyotard, J. F. (1984). *The Postmodern Condition*. Manchester: Manchester University Press.

Machimbarrena, J. M., Calvete, E., Fernández-González, L., Alvarez-Bardón, A., Álvarez-Fernández, L. & González-Cabrera, J. (2018). Internet Risks: An Overview of Victimization in Cyberbullying, Cyber Dating Abuse, Sexting, Online

Grooming and Problematic Internet Use. *International Journal of Environmental Research and Public Health, 15*(11), 2471.

MacKinnon, R. (2012). *Consent of the Networked*. New York: Basic Books.

Malinowski, B. (1922). *Argonauts of the Western Pacific*. London: Routledge & Kegan Paul.

Malkin, Nathan, Wijesekera, P., Egelman, S. & Wagner, D. (2018). Use Case: Passively Listening Personal Assistants. *Symposium on Applications of Contextual Integrity*. https://privaci.info/symposium/passive_listening_ci.pdf.

Manovich, L. (2013). *Software Takes Command*. London: Bloomsbury.

Mäntylä, M. V., Graziotin, D. & Kuutila, M. (2018). The Evolution of Sentiment Analysis: A Review of Research Topics, Venues, and Top Cited Papers. *Computer Science Review, 27*, 16–32. https://doi.org/10.1016/j.cosrev.2017.10.002

Markham, A. & Baym, N. (2009). Introduction. In A. Markham & N. Baym (Eds.), *Internet Inquiry* (pp. vii–xix). Los Angeles, CA: Sage.

Maronick, T. J. (2014). Do Consumers Read Terms of Service Agreements when Installing Software? A Two-Study Empirical Analysis. *International Journal of Business and Social Research, 4*(6), 137–145.

Marwick, A. (2013). Donglegate: Why the Tech Community Hates Feminists. *Wired*, March. www.wired.com/2013/03/richards-affair-and-misogyny-in-tech/.

Marx, K. & Engels, F. (1932/1998). *The German Ideology*. Amherst, MA: Prometheus Books.

Massanari, A. (2017). #Gamergate and the Fappening: How Reddit's Algorithm, Governance, and Culture Support Toxic Technocultures. *New Media & Society, 19*(3), 329–346. https://doi.org/10.1177/1461444815608807

McCallum, A. K. (2002). *MALLET: A Machine Learning for Language Toolkit*. http://mallet.cs.umass.edu

McChesney, R. W. (2013). *Digital Disconnect*. New York: The New Press.

McKay, T. (2014). A Psychiatric Study Reveals Selfies are Far More Dangerous than You Think. *Mic*. https://web.archive.org/web/2020*/http://mic.com:80/articles/86287/a-psychiatric-study-reveals-selfies-are-far-more-dangerous-than-you-think (May 11, 2021).

McKenna, K. Y. A. & Bargh, J. A. (2000). Plan 9 from Cyberspace: The Implications of the Internet for Personality and Social Psychology. *Personality and Social Psychology Review, 4*(1), 57–75.

McLuhan, M. (1962). *The Gutenberg Galaxy*. London: Routledge & Kegan Paul.

McLuhan, M. (1964). *Understanding Media*. Berkeley, CA: Gingko Press.

McLuhan, M. & Nevitt, B. (1972). *Take Today*. New York: Harcourt Brace Jovanovich.

McNeill, J. R. & McNeill, W. H. (2003). *The Human Web*. New York: W. W. Norton.

Mead, G. H. (1934). *Mind, Self and Society*. Chicago, IL: University of Chicago Press.

Merica, D. (2016). Hillary Clinton Laments 'Tyranny of the Selfie'. *CNN*, January 7. www.cnn.com/2016/01/07/politics/hillary-clinton-selfie-esquire/index.html (May 11, 2021).

Merrin, W. (2019). President Troll: Trump, 4Chan and Memetic Warfare. In C. Happer, A. Hoskins & W. Merrin (Eds.), *Trump's Media War* (pp. 201–226). Cham, Switzerland: Springer International.

Merton, R. K. (1968). The Matthew Effect in Science. *Science, 159*(3810), 56–63.

Meyrowitz, J. (1985). *No Sense of Place*. Oxford: Oxford University Press.

Milgram, S. (1967). The Small World Problem. *Psychology Today, 2*(1), 60–67.

Miller, D. & Slater, D. (2000). *The Internet: An Ethnographic Approach*. Oxford: Berg.

Miltner, K. (2011). SRSLY Phenomenal. MSc Dissertation, London School of Economics and Political Science.

Miltner, K. & Baym, N. (2015). The Selfie of the Year of the Selfie. *International Journal of Communication, 9*, 1701–1715.

Miner, G., Dursun, D., Fast, A., Hill, T., Elder, J. & Nisbet, B. (2012). *Practical Text Mining and Statistical Analysis for Non-Structured Text Data Applications*. Waltham, MA: Academic Press.

Mirzoeff, N. (2013). *The Visual Culture Reader*. London: Routledge.

Mondal, M., Correa, D. & Benevenuto, F. (2020). Anonymity Effects: A Large-Scale Dataset from an Anonymous Social Media Platform. In *Proceedings of the 31st ACM Conference on Hypertext and Social Media* (pp. 69–74). Virtual Event USA: ACM. https://doi.org/10.1145/3372923.3404792

Moor, P. J. (2007). *Conforming to the Flaming Norm in the Online Commenting Situation*. Retrieved from http://purl.utwente.nl/essays/58838.

Moretti, F. (2013). *Distant Reading*. London: Verso.

Morozov, E. (2011). *The Net Delusion*. New York: Public Affairs.

Morozov, E. (2013). *To Save Everything, Click Here*. New York: Public Affairs.

Mossberger, K. (2009). Toward Digital Citizenship: Addressing Inequality in the Information Age. In A. Chadwick & P. N. Howard (Eds.), *The Routledge Handbook of Internet Politics* (pp. 173–185). London: Routledge.

Mosseri, A. (2018). News Feed FYI: Bringing People Closer Together. *Facebook for Business*. https://en-gb.facebook.com/business/news/news-feed-fyi-bringing-people-closer-together

Mullaney, T., Peters, B., Hicks, M. & Philip, K. (Eds.) (2021). *Your Computer is on Fire*. Cambridge, MA: The MIT Press.

Murray, J. H. (1997). *Hamlet on the Holodeck*. Cambridge, MA: The MIT Press.

Nakamura, L. (2002). *Cybertypes*. New York: Routledge.

Nardi, B. (2005). Beyond Bandwidth. *Computer Supported Cooperative Work (CSCW), 14*(2), 91–130.

Naughton, J. (1999). *A Brief History of the Future: The Origins of the Internet*. London: Weidenfeld & Nicolson.

Negroponte, N. (1995). *Being Digital*. New York: Knopf.

Nielsen, M. A. (2012). *Reinventing Discovery*. Princeton, NJ: Princeton University Press.

Noble, S. U. (2018). *Algorithms of Oppression: How Search Engines Reinforce Racism*. New York: New York University Press.

Nurullah, A. S. (2009). The Cell Phone as an Agent of Social Change. *Rocky Mountain Communication Review*, *6*(1), 19–25.

O'Neil, M. (2009). *Cyberchiefs*. London: Pluto Press.

O'Neil, C. (2016). *Weapons of Math Destruction: How Big Data Increases Inequality and Threatens Democracy*. New York: Crown.

O'Reilly, T. (2007). What is Web 2.0? *Communications & Strategies*, *65*, 17–37.

O'Sullivan, C. (2021). Introduction to Sentiment Analysis. *Medium: Towards Data Science*. https://towardsdatascience.com/introduction-to-sentiment-analysis-f623f7d40bfa

Oldenburg, R. & Brissett, D. (1982). The Third Place. *Qualitative Sociology*, *5*(4), 265–284.

Oremus, W. (2014). You Can't Dislike This Article: Facebook's Inability to Handle Criticism is Bad for Democracy. *Slate Magazine*, December. https://slate.com/technology/2014/12/facebook-dislike-button-why-mark-zuckerberg-wont-allow-it.html.

Orito, Y. (2011). The Counter-Control Revolution: 'Silent Control' of Individuals through Dataveillance Systems. *Journal of Information, Communication and Ethics in Society*, *9*(1), 5–19. doi: 10.1108/14779961111123197

Orwell, G. (1946). Politics and the English Language. *Horizon*, *13*(76), 252–265.

Oxford Dictionaries (2013). Word of the Year 2013. https://web.archive.org/web/20180307053057/https://en.oxforddictionaries.com/word-of-the-year/word-of-the-year-2013

Paasonen, S. (2011). *Carnal Resonance*. Cambridge, MA: The MIT Press.

Paasonen, S. (2015). A Midsummer's Bonfire. In K. Hillis, S. Paasonen & M. Petit (Eds.), *Networked Affect* (pp. 27–42). Cambridge, MA: The MIT Press.

Paasonen, S., Hillis, K. & Petit, M. (2015). Introduction: Networks of Transmission. In K. Hillis, S. Paasonen & M. Petit (Eds.), *Networked Affect* (pp. 1–24). Cambridge, MA: The MIT Press.

Papacharissi, Z. (2010). *A Private Sphere*. Cambridge, UK: Polity Press.

Papacharissi, Z. (2015). *Affective Publics*. Oxford: Oxford University Press.

Pariser, E. (2011). *The Filter Bubble*. London: Viking.

Pasquale, F. (2015). *The Black Box Society: The Secret Algorithms That Control Money and Information*. Cambridge, MA: Harvard University Press.

Pedersen, I. & Iliadis, A. (Eds.) (2020). *Embodied Computing: Wearables, Implantables, Embeddables, Ingestibles*. Cambridge, MA: The MIT Press.

Penny, L. (2013). *Cybersexism*. London: Bloomsbury.

Pepperell, R. & Punt, M. (2000). *The Postdigital Membrane*. Bristol: Intellect.

Phillips, W. (2015). *This is Why We Can't Have Nice Things*. Cambridge, MA: The MIT Press.

Piore, M. J. & Sabel, C. F. (1984). *The Second Industrial Divide*. New York: Basic Books.

Plant, S. (1997). *Zeroes + ones*. New York: Doubleday.

Plant, S. (2001). *On the Mobile*. Schaumburg, IL: Motorola.

Pold, S. (2008). Button. In M. Fuller (Ed.), *Software Studies* (pp. 31–26). Cambridge, MA: The MIT Press.

Porter, C. E. (2015). Virtual Communities and Social Networks. In L. Cantoni & J. A. Danowski (Eds.), *Communication and Technology* (pp. 161–179). Berlin: De Gruyter Mouton.

Post, D. (2013). The History of the Internet, Typography Division, Cont'd. *The Volokh Conspiracy*. https://web.archive.org/web/20210414114401/http://volokh.com/2013/11/12/history-internet-typography-division-contd/

Postill, J. (2008). Localizing the Internet beyond Communities and Networks. *New Media & Society*, *10*(3), 413–431.

Postman, N. (1970). The Reformed English Curriculum. In A. C. Eurich (Ed.), *High School 1980* (pp. 160–168). New York: Pitman Publishing.

Postman, N. (1992). *Technopoly: The Surrender of Culture to Technology*. New York: Knopf.

Purdam, K. & Elliot, M. (2015). The Changing Social Science Data Landscape. In P. Halfpenny & R. Procter (Eds.), *Innovations in Digital Research Methods* (pp. 25–58). London: Sage.

Putnam, R. D. (2000). *Bowling Alone*. New York: Simon & Schuster.

Qian, H. & Scott, C. R. (2007). Anonymity and Self-Disclosure on Weblogs. *Journal of Computer-Mediated Communication*, *12*(4), 1428–1451.

r/aww (2021). r/aww: A Subreddit for Cute and Cuddly Pictures. *Reddit*. www.reddit.com/r/aww/wiki/index

Rainie, H. & Wellman, B. (2012). *Networked*. Cambridge, MA: The MIT Press.

Rainie, L. & Anderson, J. (2017). *Code-Dependent: Pros and Cons of the Algorithm Age*. Washington, DC: Pew Research Center. www.pewinternet.org/2017/02/08/code-dependent-pros-and-cons-of-the-algorithm-age.

Rambukkana, N. (Ed.) (2015). *Hashtag Publics: The Power and Politics of Discursive Networks*. New York: Peter Lang.

Ramsetty, A. & Adams, C. (2020). Impact of the Digital Divide in the Age of COVID-19. *Journal of the American Medical Informatics Association*, *27*(7), 1147–1148. doi: 10.1093/jamia/ocaa078

Reid, A. J. (2018). *The Smartphone Paradox: Our Ruinous Dependency in the Device Age*. Cham, Switzerland: Springer International.

Rényi, A. & Erdős, P. (1961). On the Evolution of Random Graphs. *Bulletin De l'Institut International de Statistique*, *38*(4), 343–347.

Rettberg, J. W. (2005). Links and Power: The Political Economy of Linking on the Web. *Library Trends*, *53*(4), 524–529.

Rettberg, J. W. (2014). *Seeing Ourselves Through Technology*. Basingstoke: Palgrave Macmillan.

Rheingold, H. (1993). *The Virtual Community*. Reading, MA: Addison-Wesley.

Rheingold, H. (2000). *The Virtual Community* (2nd ed.). Cambridge, MA: The MIT Press.

Rheingold, H. (2002). *Smart Mobs*. Cambridge, MA: Perseus.

Rizzo, C. (2015). More People Have Died from Selfies than Shark Attacks This Year. *Mashable*, September 21. https://web.archive.org/web/2020*/http://mashable.com/2015/09/21/selfie-deaths/#jUUIabtqgkq8

Robins, G. (2015). *Doing Social Network Research: Network-Based Research Design for Social Scientists*. Los Angeles, CA: Sage.

Roden, L. (2017). 'I Can Guarantee with My Life That the Train Will Be Called Trainy McTrainface'. *The Local: Sweden*. https://web.archive.org/web/2020*/www.thelocal.se/20170720/i-can-guarantee-with-my-life-that-the-train-will-be-called-trainy-mctrainface/

Rogers, R. (2005). Old and New Media. *Theory & Event*, *8*(2).

Rogers, R. (2013). *Digital Methods*. Cambridge, MA: The MIT Press.

Rogers, R. (2020). Deplatforming: Following Extreme Internet Celebrities to Telegram and Alternative Social Media. *European Journal of Communication*, *35*(3), 213–229.

Rutledge, P. (2013a). #Selfies: Narcissism or Self-Exploration? *Psychology Today*, April. www.psychologytoday.com/intl/blog/positively-media/201304/selfies-narcissism-or-self-exploration

Rutledge, P. (2013b). Making Sense of Selfies. *Psychology Today*, July. www.psychologytoday.com/intl/blog/positively-media/201307/making-sense-selfies

Sampson, T. (2012). *Virality: Contagion Theory in the Age of Networks*. Minneapolis, MN: University of Minnesota Press.

Sandvig, C. & Hargittai, E. (2015). How to Think about Digital Research. In E. Hargittai & C. Sandvig (Eds.), *Digital Research Confidential* (pp. 1–28). Cambridge, MA: The MIT Press.

Schiffer, Z. (2021). Timnit Gebru was Fired from Google – Then the Harassers Arrived. *The Verge*, March 5. www.theverge.com/22309962/timnit-gebru-google-harassment-campaign-jeff-dean

Scholz, T. (Ed.) (2013). *Digital Labor*. New York: Routledge.

Schudson, M. (1999). *The Good Citizen*. Cambridge, MA: Harvard University Press.

Senft, T. (2008). *Camgirls*. New York: Peter Lang.

Senft, T. M. & Baym, N. (2015). What Does the Selfie Say? *International Journal of Communication*, *9*, 1588–1606.

Shafer, L. (2012). I Can Haz an Internet Aesthetic?!? Presentation at the Northeast Popular/American Culture Association Conference.

Shifman, L. (2014). *Memes in Digital Culture*. Cambridge, MA: The MIT Press.

Shirky, C. (2008). *Here Comes Everybody: The Power of Organizing without Organizations*. London: Allen Lane.

Shirky, C. (2009). How Social Media Can Make History. *ted.com*. www.ted.com/talks/clay_shirky_how_social_media_can_make_history

Shirky, C. (2010). *Cognitive Surplus*. London: Allen Lane.

Short, J., Williams, E. & Christie, B. (1976). *The Social Psychology of Telecommunications*. London: John Wiley.

Simmel, G. (1910). How is Society Possible? *American Journal of Sociology*, *16*(3), 372–391.

Simmel, G. (1950). *The Sociology of Georg Simmel*. (K. H. Wolff, Ed.). Glencoe, IL: The Free Press.

Simmel, G. (1971). *On Individuality and Social Forms*. (D. N. Levine, Ed.). Chicago, IL: University of Chicago Press.

Skog, D. (2005). Social Interaction in Virtual Communities: The Significance of Technology. *International Journal of Web Based Communities*, *1*(4), 464. https://doi.org/10.1504/IJWBC.2005.008111

Slevin, J. (2002). The Internet and Forms of Human Association. In D. McQuail (Ed.), *McQuail's Reader in Mass Communication Theory* (pp. 146–156). London: Sage.

Smythe, D. W. (1977). Communications: Blindspot of Western Marxism. *Ctheory*, *1*(3), 1–27.

Spielkamp, M. (Ed.) (2019). *Automating Society: Taking Stock of Automated Decision-Making in the EU*. Berlin: AlgorithmWatch.

Standing, G. (2011). *The Precariat*. London: Bloomsbury Academic.

Stark, L. & Crawford, K. (2015). The Conservatism of Emoji: Work, Affect, and Communication. *Social Media + Society*, *1*(2), 2056305115604853.

Steinkuehler, C. A. & Williams, D. (2006). Where Everybody Knows Your (Screen) Name. *Journal of Computer-Mediated Communication*, *11*(4), 885–909.

Stoehrel, R. F. & Lindgren, S. (2014). For the Lulz: Anonymous, Aesthetics and Affect. *tripleC: Communication, Capitalism & Critique. Open Access Journal for a Global Sustainable Information Society*, *12*(1), 238–264.

Stoll, C. (1999). *High-Tech Heretic*. New York: Doubleday.

Strickland, L. H., Guild, P. D., Barefoot, J. C. & Paterson, S. A. (1978). Teleconferencing and Leadership Emergence. *Human Relations*, *31*(7), 583–596.

Suler, J. (2004). The Online Disinhibition Effect. *CyberPsychology & Behavior*, *7*(3), 321–326.

Sunstein, C. R. (2006). *Infotopia*. Oxford: Oxford University Press.

Sunstein, C. R. (2017). *#Republic: Divided Democracy in the Age of Social Media*. Princeton, NJ: Princeton University Press.

Surowiecki, J. (2004). *The Wisdom of Crowds*. London: Little, Brown.

Sweeney, M. E. & Whaley, K. (2019). Technically White: Emoji Skin-Tone Modifiers as American Technoculture. *First Monday*. https://journals.uic.edu/ojs/index.php/fm/article/view/10060

Syvertsen, T. & Enli, G. (2020). Digital Detox: Media Resistance and the Promise of Authenticity. *Convergence: The International Journal of Research into New Media Technologies*, *26*(5–6), 1269–1283. https://doi.org/10.1177/1354856519847325

Tapscott, D. & Williams, A. D. (2006). *Wikinomics*. New York: Portfolio.

Tarde, G. (1903). *The Laws of Imitation*. New York: Henry, Holt and Co.

Taylor, Linnet (2017). What is Data Justice? The Case for Connecting Digital Rights and Freedoms Globally. *Big Data & Society*, *4*(2), 2053951717736335.

Thierer, A. (2010). The Case for Internet Optimism. In B. Szoka & A. Marcus (Eds.), *The Next Digital Decade*. Washington, DC: TechFreedom.

Thompsen, P. A. (1996). What's Fueling the Flames in Cyberspace. In L. Strate, R. Jacobson & S. Gibson (Eds.), *Communication and Cyberspace* (pp. 297–315). Cresskill, NJ: Hampton.

Tilly, C. (1977). Getting It Together in Burgundy, 1675–1975. *Theory and Society*, *4*(4), 479–504.

Tinworth, A. (2012). What is Post Digital? Retrieved June 4, 2016, from http://nextconf.eu/2012/01/what-is-post-digital/

Toffler, A. (1970). *Future Shock*. New York: Bantam Books.

Toffler, A. (1980). *The Third Wave*. London: Collins.

Tolbert, C. J. & McNeal, R. S. (2003). Unraveling the Effects of the Internet on Political Participation? *Political Research Quarterly*, *56*(2), 175–185.

Tolins, J. & Samermit, P. (2016). GIFs as Embodied Enactments in Text-Mediated Conversation. *Research on Language and Social Interaction*, *49*(2), 75–91. https://doi.org/10.1080/08351813.2016.1164391

Tönnies, F. (1887/1974). *Community and Association*. London: Routledge & Kegan Paul.

Toole, B. A. (1992). *Ada: The Enchantress of Numbers*. Mill Valley, CA: Strawberry Press.

Tukey, J. W. (1958). The Teaching of Concrete Mathematics. *The American Mathematical Monthly*, *65*(1), 1–9.

Turkle, S. (1995). *Life on the Screen*. New York: Simon & Schuster.

Turkle, S. (2011). *Alone Together*. New York: Basic Books.

Tyler, I. (2008). Methodological Fatigue and the Politics of the Affective Turn. *Feminist Media Studies*, *8*(1), 85–90.

Unicode Consortium (2021). Full Emoji List, V13.1. *unicode.org*. https://unicode.org/emoji/charts/full-emoji-list.html

Vaidhyanathan, S. (2011). *The Googlization of Everything (and Why We Should Worry)*. Berkeley, CA: University of California Press.

van Dijck, J. & Poell, T. (2013). Understanding Social Media Logic. *Media and Communication*, *1*(1), 2–14.

van Dijck, J., Poell, T. & de Waal, M. (2018) *The Platform Society: Public Values in a Connective World*. Oxford: Oxford University Press.

van Dijk, J. (2006). *The Network Society*. London: Sage.

van Dijk, J. (2020). *The Digital Divide*. Cambridge, UK: Polity Press.

von Behr, I., Reding, A., Edwards, C. & Gribbon, L. (2013). *Radicalisation in the Digital Era: The Use of the Internet in 15 Cases of Terrorism and Extremism*. RAND Corporation. www.rand.org/pubs/research_reports/RR453.html.

Wajcman, J. (2004). *TechnoFeminism*. Cambridge, UK: Polity Press.

Walther, J. B. (1996). Computer-Mediated Communication: Impersonal, Interpersonal, and Hyperpersonal Interaction. *Communication Research*, *23*(1), 3–43.

Warner, M. (2002). *Publics and Counterpublics*. New York: Zone Books.

Watts, D. J., Dodds, P. S. & Muhamad, R. (2003). An Experimental Study of Search in Global Social Networks. *Science*, *301*(5634), 827–829.

Watts, D. J. & Strogatz, S. H. (1998). Collective Dynamics of 'Small-World' Networks. *Nature*, *393*(6684), 440–442.

Weber, M. (1922/1978). *Economy and Society*. Berkeley, CA: University of California Press.

Webster, F. (2006). *Theories of the Information Society*. London: Routledge.

Wendling, M. (2018). *Alt-Right: From 4chan to the White House*. London: Pluto Press.

Wendt, B. (2014). *The Allure of the Selfie*. Amsterdam: Institute of Network Cultures.

Wiberg, M. (2004). *The Interaction Society*. Hershey, PA: Information Science Publishing.

Wikipedia (2021a). On the Internet, Nobody Knows You're a Dog. https://en.wikipedia.org/wiki/On_the_Internet,_nobody_knows_you%27re_a_dog

Wikipedia (2021b). Facebook Real-Name Policy Controversy. https://en.wikipedia.org/wiki/Facebook_real-name_policy_controversy

Williams, A. A. & Marquez, B. A. (2015). The Lonely Selfie King. *International Journal of Communication*, *9*, 1775–1787.

Williams, R. (1985). *Keywords*. New York: Oxford University Press.

Williams, R. & Edge, D. (1996). The Social Shaping of Technology. *Research Policy*, *25*(6), 865–899.

Winner, L. (1978). *Autonomous Technology: Technics-Out-of-Control as a Theme in Political Thought*. Cambridge, MA: The MIT Press.

Wittkower, D. (2012). On the Origins of the Cute as a Dominant Aesthetic Category in Digital Culture. In T. W. Luke & J. Hunsinger (Eds.), *Putting Knowledge to Work & Letting Information Play* (pp. 167–175). Rotterdam: Sense Publishers.

Woodcock, J. & Graham, M. (2020). *The Gig Economy: A Critical Introduction*. Cambridge, UK: Polity Press.

Woolley, S. C. & Howard, P. N. (2016). Automation, Algorithms, and Politics| Political Communication, Computational Propaganda, and Autonomous Agents: Introduction. *International Journal of Communication, 10*, 9.

Wu, T. (2010). *The Master Switch*. New York: Alfred A. Knopf.

Zimbardo, P. G. (2007). *The Lucifer Effect*. New York: Random House.

Zittrain, J. (2008). *The Future of the Internet and How to Stop It*. New Haven, CT: Yale University Press.

Zuboff, S. (2014). A Digital Declaration. *Frankfurter Allgemeine Zeitung*, faz.net.

Zuboff, S. (2019). *The Age of Surveillance Capitalism: The Fight for a Human Future at the New Frontier of Power*. New York: PublicAffairs.

Zuckerman, E. (2015). Cute Cats to the Rescue? In D. Allen & J. S. Light (Eds.), *From Voice to Influence* (pp. 131–154). Chicago, IL: University of Chicago Press.

INDEX